LSD
THE WONDER CHILD

"An original synthesis of rare information, precious anecdotes, and scientific adventure stories. A masterful storyteller, Thomas Hatsis is our knowledgeable guide on this insightfully written history of pharmacology's most notorious chemical agent. From hopeful research into LSD's therapeutic potential and the hidden potential of the human mind to its sacramental use and the dark mind-control experiments of the CIA, Hatsis provides a page-turning historical perspective on the origins of psychedelic culture and how we got to where we are today in the psychedelic renaissance. Highly recommended!"

DAVID JAY BROWN, AUTHOR OF *THE NEW SCIENCE OF PSYCHEDELICS* AND *DREAMING WIDE AWAKE*

"A highly readable history of how psychedelics filtered through the wards of hospitals and prisons; the U.S. military and the MKUltra program; Huautla de Jiménez and Hollywood; university laboratories and the fields of parapsychology, mysticism, and literature; and into the clinics of psychiatrists, setting the stage for psychedelics spilling onto the streets of America in the 1960s."

MICHAEL JAMES WINKELMAN, PH.D., M.P.H., COEDITOR OF *ADVANCES IN PSYCHEDELIC MEDICINE*

"Tom Hatsis brings this story to life with vivid characters, mystical and scientific intrigue, and exciting exploits in this colorful history of psychedelic adventures. His passion for the topic comes to life in this page-turner of a book."

ERIKA DYCK, PH.D., AUTHOR OF *PSYCHEDELIC PSYCHIATRY: LSD FROM CLINIC TO CAMPUS*

"This wonderful book by Thomas Hastis is the most beautifully written, detailed, candid, personal, and informative text on the subject of Albert Hofmann's serendipitous stumbling. Get on the bus. Take that bike ride. Whatever. But make sure Tom's book is in your backpack. You'll be hard pressed to find a better guide for your trip."

BEN SESSA, MBBS (M.D.), MRCPSYCH, PSYCHEDELIC THERAPIST AND CHIEF MEDICAL OFFICER AT AWAKN LIFE SCIENCES

LSD

THE WONDER CHILD

The Golden Age of
Psychedelic Research in the 1950s

Thomas Hatsis

Park Street Press
Rochester, Vermont

Park Street Press
One Park Street
Rochester, Vermont 05767
www.ParkStPress.com

Text stock is SFI certified

Park Street Press is a division of Inner Traditions International

Cataloging-in-Publication Data for this title is available from the Library of Congress

ISBN 978-1-64411-256-4 (print)
ISBN 978-1-64411-257-1 (ebook)

Printed and bound in the United States by Lake Book Manufacturing, Inc.
The text stock is SFI certified. The Sustainable Forestry Initiative® program
promotes sustainable forest management.

10   9   8   7   6   5   4   3   2   1

Text design and layout by Virginia Scott Bowman
This book was typeset in Garamond Premier Pro and Futura with George and Grota
Sans used as display typefaces

To send correspondence to the author of this book, mail a first-class letter to the
author c/o Inner Traditions • Bear & Company, One Park Street, Rochester, VT
05767, and we will forward the communication, or contact the author directly at
https://psychedelichistorian.com.

Contents

Foreword

Martin A. Lee

If you think the psychedelic sixties were something special, check out the phantastic fifties. There's no better place to start than this book by Tom Hatsis. It is the definitive romp through the hidden paisley underbelly of the Eisenhower years, an era otherwise known for its pre-dayglo blandness.

A full decade before counterculture figure and novelist Ken Kesey and psychologist Timothy Leary turned on, lysergic acid diethylamide (LSD) and mescaline emerged as hot topics that catalyzed the nascent field of neuroscience. In the early 1950s, researchers drew attention to the similar molecular structures of LSD and serotonin, on the one hand, and mescaline and adrenaline, on the other, giving rise to novel theories about the biochemical basis of mental illness and the (supposed) madness-mimicking properties of these mind-altering compounds.

While brain scientists sleuthed for clues to unravel the riddle of schizophrenia, the Central Intelligence Agency (CIA) and the U.S. military secretly embraced hallucinogens as weapons that could revolutionize the cloak-and-dagger game to give America a strategic edge over its Cold War enemies. Odorless, colorless, tasteless, and super powerful, yet nonlethal, LSD, in particular, stoked the lurid imagination of U.S. spymasters, who employed the drug to disorient unwitting individuals and extract information from tightlipped targets. Army brass, for their part, were high on the possibility of disseminating a huge cloud of aerosol LSD ("madness gas") as a battlefield tactic to incapacitate a large population without killing anyone.

Curiously, around the same time, a growing number of psychiatrists began touting LSD as a wonder drug for psychotherapy, an expeditious healing aid with an uncanny ability to quickly surface long-held sources of stress by dredging up whatever might have gotten stuck in the mental depths; thus, the word *psychedelic,* which literally translates as "mind manifesting."

The psychedelic saga took an unexpected turn when the therapeutic potential of LSD was projected onto a broad social landscape. Leary and others trumpeted LSD as a cure-all for a sick society, a species-booster capable of propelling humankind to the next evolutionary level. The phrase "stranger than fiction" doesn't do justice to the real-world trajectory of LSD as it shapeshifted into a potent counterculture catalyst that dazzled the minds of artists, inventors, health professionals, and many more.

But how is it possible that the same compound could be used as both a mind-control weapon and a mind-expanding entheogen? How could it be both a psychochemical warfare agent and a profound healing modality?

With the benefit of hindsight, we can look back and see that every group that got involved with LSD during the phantastic fifties became very enthusiastic about the grandiose possibilities conjured by the drug. The brain scientists, the doctors, the spooks, and the generals—each had their own ideas about LSD and how it could be used to advance their specific agendas. But they also shared something in common: they all viewed it as the key to the big breakthrough. In each case, their encounter with psychedelics triggered an envisioning of new possibilities. Whether or not these different possibilities would ever be actualized is another matter, but the opening, the awakened sense of potential, was real and exciting.

In essence, LSD and other psychedelic drugs are best understood as potentiators of possibility—for good or ill. Much depends on the context in which these compounds are consumed. The CIA ended up defining LSD as an "anxiety-producing agent"—as if anxiety were embedded in the molecular structure of LSD—because that's what Cold War espionage stiffs often experienced when they tripped on acid. The CIA projected its own paranoia and obsessions onto LSD and mistook those attributes as if they were inherent properties of the drug itself. That's an example of what British philosopher Alfred North Whitehead referred to as "the fallacy of misplaced concreteness." Many LSD enthusiasts succumbed to this fallacy when they assumed that the same beatific vision would be shared by all if everyone took the sacrament (dose the president and the war will end!). For those with messianic dreams, LSD was tantamount to the Second Coming, a pill with world-changing implications.

But taking LSD does not guarantee that a person's consciousness will automatically be "expanded" or that one will necessarily have a religious epiphany or live a spiritual life thereafter. Under the right circumstances, however, the astonishing immediacy and experiential density of LSD can be conducive to deep insight and healing. Albert Hofmann, the Swiss chemist who discovered LSD, described it as "medicine for the soul."

Today we are in the midst of a psychedelic revival. Psilocybin, the magic mushroom extract, has supplanted LSD as the go-to psychedelic among researchers. Fast-tracked by health authorities as a cure for treatment-resistant depression, psilocybin is not burdened by associations with sixties excess and social strife, which continue to stigmatize LSD. Hopefully, as efforts to decriminalize psychedelics gain momentum, we can move forward unencumbered by the misplaced fallacies of the past.

Martin A. Lee has written several books, including *Acid Dreams: The Complete Social History of LSD, the CIA, the Sixties and Beyond* and *Smoke Signals: A Social History of Marijuana—Medical, Recreational, and Scientific*. He is cofounder and director of ProjectCBD.org, an educational platform that focuses on cannabis science and therapeutics.

For Eden
Leaena meus
Regina fungorum meus
Cor meus

Before I Forget . . . Again

People [under the influence of LSD or mescaline] will think they are going mad, when in fact they are beginning, when they take it, to go sane—or at least to understand what going sane must be like.

ALDOUS HUXLEY

~ 2006 ~

Against the very good advice of my thesis advisor, Peter Conolly-Smith, I decided to write *The Witches' Ointment*. I had just graduated from Queens College and Peter had suggested I turn my thesis into a book—the book you're now holding.

I'll never forget the day I met Peter. I was in my penultimate year of my master's degree at Queens College and I had to find a professor to work with on my thesis. The best candidate for me, I was told, was Peter—who, I was also told, rarely worked with students on their theses. What did I have to lose? If he said "no," then I was just another student he rejected. I walked into his office, introduced myself, and awaited the dressing-down. It didn't happen. Instead, he asked me if I had read *Acid Dreams*.

"By Martin Lee!" I quickly piped up.

I wanted him to know that I knew, ya know?

I had digested *Acid Dreams* during my undergraduate years. It was where I first learned that psychedelia existed before the 1960s. It was my favorite book. I knew it cover to cover. So did he.

What I had intended to be a ten-minute conversation that ended in dismissal of my request for thesis mentorship turned into a three-hour conversation about LSD in mid-twentieth century Western culture. By that time in my life, I had eaten mushrooms, dropped LSD, felt the warm pleasantries of ecstasy, and had spent my undergraduate years reading every book on psychedelics on which I could get my hungry paws. I knew my shit. So did Peter.

~ *Summer 2007* ~

I worked my ass off—waiting tables, delivering pizzas, tutoring SATs, and slinging mushrooms and cannabis—so I could afford to live in Italy while I finished writing my master's thesis, which dealt with the LSD revolution of the 1950s. While we often associate LSD with the more colorful "psychedelic sixties" I felt that I had stumbled upon a whole decade of overlooked medicine investigation. I filled two large suiter suitcases with books and research materials, crammed a small gym bag with enough clothing to last half a week, and flew to Malpensa Airport, an hour outside Milano, Italy.

I'll never forget my very first culture shock—the language. My future roommate had assured me that my background in Spanish would ensure an easy transition to following Italian directions. *Not. At. All.* The two languages, I quickly learned, while seemingly similar at a distance, are worlds apart up close. Perhaps I should have asked my friend, who did not speak a lick of Spanish, how he arrived at such a conclusion. Somehow, I managed to get on the right train, which (in retrospect, *vaguely,* but at the time, *specifically*) said "Milano."* I then walked around the city for a few hours trying to find where I lived. I stopped in a metal/punk bar—my first metal/punk bar in Italy!—for a drink

---

*The train number was actually "666." I pulled out my camera and snapped a photo of it—the first picture I took in Italy. The Dark Lord was pleased.

and to ask directions. Turned out, I lived right around the block—right around the block from a metal/punk bar!

Score!

For months, I worked on my thesis in my apartment on Villa Fumagalli, a street that overlooked the Da Vinci Canal. My thesis detailed LSD's journey from its perception as a "psychosis causing" research chemical in the early 1950s to being considered a mystical sacrament by the late 1950s—what I refer to as the "wonder child" decade of LSD. When I needed company, I went to the metal/punk bar and failed miserably trying to talk to Italian riot girls. When I needed inspiration, I walked down the road to the *vineria,* paid a few euro for a bottle of freshly produced wine, returned to my apartment, sat on my porch, and played my guitar. Once sufficiently inspired, I would return to the computer and write. For extra money, I tutored two Italian kids in English. Other times, I played cover songs (Sublime, Nirvana, and Weezer always went over well) on the corner of Villa Fumagalli for spare change. When I could, I also continued my research into my two other loves, the witches' ointment* and the holy mushroom hypothesis.[†] Living in Italy gave me access to ideas and perspectives about medieval witchcraft that, at the time, I knew nothing about.[‡] I also visited medieval *duomi,* camera in hand, and experienced the intoxicating joy

---

*The "witches' ointment" was an early modern way for religious authorities to demonize women's spirituality. Briefly, before the overblown, truly laughable "devil's weed" campaigns launched by Harry Anslinger during the 1930s, there was the "witches' ointment" campaign launched by religious authorities during the 1500s. For my full thoughts, see *The Witches' Ointment* (Rochester, Vt.: Park Street Press, 2015).

[†]The "holy mushroom" is a bogus conspiracy theory, which holds that medieval Christians secretly painted mushrooms in their art as a way of carrying on an ancient secret: namely, that Jesus Christ was a metaphor for an entheogenic experience. I will outline my full thoughts on the "sacred mushroom" in my forthcoming book, which I hope to title something along the lines of *The Mushroom Heretic* and hope to publish sometime in 2022.

[‡]Europe also gave my first real contact with someone in psychedelic research. I spent a weekend in the U.K. and checked out Andy Letcher's band *Telling the Bees* at Wenlock Arms, London.

of fooling myself into thinking the pictures I took of trees and other objects in medieval art represented secret "holy mushroom" insertions.

Oh, the indiscretion of youth.

Still other times, I'd get high and chill with this three-piece blues band (my cannabis suppliers while in Italy). They rolled spliffs, but since I don't smoke tobacco, I always had to buy my own grass. One night, before the band was going to open up some gig, I rolled an American joint—all cannabis, no tobacco. We smoked it. Halfway through, the band decided that they were all too high to play. The singer/guitar player, Matteo, pushed the joint back on me. "*'Mericano pazzo! 'Mericano pazzo!*" "Crazy American," he said over and over. All three musicians sat on the curb and buried their heads in their arms. They had to postpone the show.

I rolled a joint that held up a blues show.

In Italy.

Life was good.

After being stranded at Malpensa Airport for twenty-four hours, I flew to Pittsburg, and then to New York. Not too long after, I submitted the final version of my thesis. When I graduated that May, I learned that my thesis had won the Frank Merli prize, an honor that was annually available, but seldom awarded.

It was then that Peter suggested I write this book. In those days, very little had been written about the phantastic fifties—save maybe a chapter or two in a few books. But even those works that mentioned the phantastic fifties tended to use that decade as a springboard into the more popular psychedelic sixties.

But my heart had been taken by another. The allure of the witches' ointment—encouraged by my language studies while in Italy—held too much sway over my attention and I decided to focus all my efforts there. Further still, I had fallen in love with a sport, roller derby. I decided to mix and match: I drove around the country as a derby coach (or a mascot) and visited archives at places like Yale, Stanford, Tulane, UCLA, Washington University, and others—places I needed to visit in pursuit of the witches' ointment. I mostly lived in my car, although I did meet some tender folks along the way who took me in here or there. By now I had realized that the majority of crucial documents about early modern witchcraft were all in Latin, so I could either give up my quest for the witches' ointment or teach myself a workable knowledge of Latin. I chose the latter, and at night I taught myself Latin.

So there I was: in my late twenties through early thirties, driving around the country teaching roller derby while teaching myself a dead language in order to translate five-hundred-year-old documents to get to the truth behind the witches' ointment.

I forgot all about the wonder child.

~ *October 2013* ~

When I first sent my manuscript of *The Witches' Ointment* to the acquisitions editor at Park Street Press, all I had to go on (so far as writing credits were concerned) was the fact that I had won the Merli, which I desperately highlighted in my introductory letter to this publishing house. "I haven't done shit yet, but look—I won an award you've never heard of! I have potential!" was my presumed "in."

Besides packing up my apartment and putting all the boxes in my mom's attic, writing to Park Street Press was one of the last things I did during my tenure in New York. I wrote the acquisitions editor, Jon, essentially begging him to publish *The Witches' Ointment,* and left my home with no plan other than to skate in the 2013 Men's Roller Derby Association championships. My team, the New York Shock Exchange, took a silver medal. Afterward, I drove around the country teaching roller derby for cash, tacos, or a place to crash. No flight path. No plan. By this time I had built up an extensive underground roller derby network. I loosely crisscrossed the United States based on those locations where a derby team was open to having a visiting coach. I would teach a derby clinic in this city, then drive five, eight, ten hours to that city.

If I didn't know anyone local yet, I'd park in a place that looked like I wouldn't get shot or robbed, and edit my manuscript of *The Witches' Ointment,* refining translations and tightening sentences. My travels eventually landed me in St. Louis, where I spent my time playing roller derby for the GateKeepers, the single greatest team to exist in the history of the sport. Days became weeks, weeks became months; I waited to hear back from Park Street Press. I had no money, except for the little bit I earned teaching derby clinics and selling books and t-shirts. Near penniless, I lived in my friend Vanessa's (a.k.a. "Rumbledore's") closet. After placing a mattress inside, there was just enough room to open the door a quarter of the way so I could squeeze myself through.

Sometime around the spring of 2014, I received an email from Park Street Press—they would publish *The Witches' Ointment!* The publisher's advance gave me enough money to drive back to New York, pack up my research materials, and haul them back to St. Louis.

This began the greatest year of my life. I did nothing except work on my book—knowing that after eight years of researching and writing it would be published!—and skate for my roller derby dream team.

Life was good.

~ *November 4, 2017* ~

I ate half of an eighth of my beloved mushrooms. An hour later, I stood before a room of about three hundred people in the Buchanan A building and launched into my presentation of "The Witches' Ointment" at the Spirit Plant Medicine Conference held at the University of British Columbia. Let me tell you, sometimes after eating mushrooms it can feel like everyone is staring at you.

They aren't.

But this time, *they were*—all six hundred eyes. It was an interesting experience to say the least.

During the dinner break that night, I left the Buchanan A building for a smoke. Walking next to me was none other than Martin A. Lee. Yes, *that* Martin A. Lee. We walked around the beautiful UBC grounds sharing a joint and talking psychedelia—fulfilling a dream of mine. After we turned this way and that, we ended up getting lost. We started attempting—in true stoner fashion—to retrace our steps. It was fruitless! I started to laugh to myself; Martin asked me what was so funny.

I didn't know how to say it at the time, but here's what I was thinking: "I'm fucking high as a kite, lost, and wandering around UBC with Martin Lee!" He asked me about any forthcoming projects. I was wrapping up my second book, *Psychedelic Mystery Traditions,* at the time and told him my plans to revisit my earlier thesis about the phantastic fifties in the coming years.

But then my speaking career started to take off in an unforeseen way. Here's what happened. During my book tour for *The Witches' Ointment* back in 2015–2016, I had taken note of a certain reoccurring theme: when it came time for the Q and A portion of my talk (much to my surprise), audience members were far more interested in my own practices with psychedelics than with anything medieval wise-women were doing five hundred years ago. So as not to unintentionally disappoint when I went on tour for my follow-up book, I wrote a short manual titled *Microdosing Magic: A Psychedelic Spellbook* as I finished the final edits of *Psychedelic Mystery Traditions.* This time around, when I went on tour for *Mystery Traditions,* I would be ready to answer those questions about my own practices with excerpts from *Microdosing Magic.* It worked out well. Many audience members saw *Microdosing Magic* as an extension of *Mystery Traditions*—the former picking up the story of Western psychedelia where the latter ended.

And so I forgot all about the wonder child (this book) . . . again.

Martin and I stayed in touch after the conference and remain good friends to this day. A couple years ago, he made a visit to Portland to give a speech on the benefits of CBD and even crashed at my pad during his stay. That Saturday night we rolled a fat joint and talked endlessly about the history of psychedelics, the failed, ridiculous, wholly idiotic War on Drugs, and how far we had come with the legalization of cannabis (and possible legalization of psilocybin therapy) since he first wrote *Acid Dreams* back in the mid-1980s.

Once again, Martin asked me about my future projects. "Ya know, I still have that old thesis from my graduate days about the LSD revolution of the 1950s," I responded.

"And you're working on it now?" he asked.

Actually, *no,* I wasn't.

"Seems like a good time for it," he said with a large exhale.

He was right. After all, in those days I had been working closely with the legalization efforts for psilocybin therapy in Portland, Oregon—which I am happy to say just passed in November 2020, making us the first U.S. city to succeed in these efforts. I eventually gravitated more toward the decriminalization of all substances in the state at large (which we also won).

Since the recognition of these timeless medicines is finally having its day in the sun, I feel that there are some major lessons that were learned during the phantastic fifties that were later overshadowed by the uproar of the psychedelic sixties. Lessons that I strongly believe will further serve both future legalization and decriminalization efforts. And so it came to pass—fourteen years after writing my graduate thesis—that I updated and expanded it and sent it to Martin to write a foreword. This crazy adventure of the last twenty years was in part influenced by him; it felt only right to have his blessings.

Notwithstanding some minor edits and the backstory you just read, the original thesis introduction went—and goes—as follows.

◎

To many students of American pop culture, substances like LSD, mescaline, and psilocybin mushrooms are associated with the 1960s.

Although psychedelics are forever tied to the 1960s, that decade actually represents the period in history *least* characteristic of what they have meant to many peoples throughout the world. However, this is only because the 1960s represents the first and *only* time in the long history of psychedelic-use when such medicines found employment by a significant number of people as a recreational inebriant; as an "escape" from society. LSD also emerged at a time when American media (yes—it was even biased and useless back then) sensationalized stories about the counterculture. Colloquialisms like "acid," "psychedelic," and "tripped out," tend to evoke mental pictures of 1960s tie-dye art, rock and roll festivals, and a drug-crazed counterculture hell-bent on saving the world via "peace, love, and music." Names like Timothy Leary, Ken Kesey, and Jerry Garcia are often dropped as definitive proof by association of the anti-establishment roots of LSD.

Nowadays, detractors of psychedelia might argue that during the 1960s, LSD disgracefully caused an already restless American youth to go insane; an enthusiast will claim just the opposite—that LSD provided an awe-inspiring revolutionary weapon used to fight the established order. However, a decade prior to the commotion that took place during the latter 1960s, LSD was seen by psychiatrists as a *cure* for insanity, and by the CIA as a weapon *of* the "establishment." By the close of the 1950s, an unknown number of government scientists and a handful of independent psychologists and psychiatrists had dosed thousands of people with LSD in an attempt to uncover the mystery of the psychedelic state and determine how they could best exploit the strange chemical's effects on the human mind. Mixed into this ironic soup was a spice-rack's fill of mystics, spiritualists, artists, and paranormal investigators who believed that LSD could unlock secret powers stored in the brain like telepathy, telekinesis, and extrasensory perception.

There is a story—a history—of psychedelia before the turbulent 1960s. There was a time when LSD wasn't dismissed by the Western scientific milieu, but was actually studied seriously by curious physicians who marveled at LSD's enigmatic properties. There was a time when Western intellectuals recognized and actively sought spiritual experiences with these medicines. There was a time when the U.S. government invested hundreds of thousands of dollars into psychedelics research. This book will explore the progression that LSD, chemist Albert Hofmann's "wonder child," took from being a *psychotomimetic* (meaning mimicker of madness), to being a possible new chemical warfare agent, to finally being recognized as a medicine and a sacrament by philosophers of the mid-twentieth century.

In *DMT: The Spirit Molecule* (2000), University of New Mexico psychiatrist Dr. Rick Strassman wrote that "[t]he natural process within psychiatric research is for scientists to refine research questions, methods, and applications. This never happened with the psychedelic drugs. Instead, their study went through a highly unnatural evolution. They began as 'wonder drugs,' turned into 'horror drugs,' then became nothing."[1] Detractors and enthusiasts alike know the "horror drug" history of LSD during the psychedelic sixties. But most are unaware of the wonder child history of the phantastic fifties. As more and more areas in the United States and Canada adopt the decriminalization policies of over twenty other countries, cities, and states and embrace the awesome power of these medicines, it behooves us to look back to the many lessons and wisdom gained from that disregarded slice of the Western psychedelic story.

The following is the LSD story both detractors and enthusiasts probably don't know.

I would like to tell it now.

Before I forget . . . *again.*

1

Pharmacies of Fairyland

Victorian Psychedelia

No account of the universe in its totality can be final which leaves these other forms of consciousness quite disregarded.

WILLIAM JAMES

STARS OR FIRE FLIES

~ May 24, 1896 ~

After drinking a concoction of peyote, the sacred cactus used religiously by various First Nations peoples, American physician Dr. Silas Weir Mitchell (1829–1914) lay on his bed and closed his eyes. He suddenly felt . . . *aware:* aware of the cosmos crannied between his skin and his clothing; aware of the gaps that lined his clothing and the creases in his sheets; aware of the sheets draped over the mattress; aware of the mattress that rested above his bed; aware of the bed supported by the earth; and aware of the earth that drove into his spine like the fabled princess's pea, which danced along the "unseen millions of the Milky Way," swaying to the beat of the Big Bang and unfolding into the infinities of space and time—all in the comfort of his own home. A Gothic tower of "elaborate and definite design" spiraled up from the floor. The stones of the tower, each bejeweled with an array of crystals, "seemed to possess an interior light" that left Mitchell both dazzled and aphasic. He struggled to define those "magic moments" that the bitter-tasting cactus extract he had drunk conjured in his mind. Despite the poetic prowess of his later report of the experience—filled as it is with delightful musings on the inexplicable awesome—Mitchell felt linguistically barren in that moment—at the mercy of "stars or fire flies" that danced before his eyes.[1]

The visions sped up—delicate, but chaotic; a dream in one instance, a nightmare in the next. Suddenly Mitchell was no longer in Pennsylvania. Through some ineffable miracle of the mind, he found himself across the continent at Newport Beach, California. Wave after wave of foamless tides crashed at his feet, breaking into "myriads [*sic*] of lights"; shades of green, orange, red, and purple ripples poured out of the larger ocean tickling Mitchell's fancy before regressing into the depths of an unchartered abyss.

Then a deluge of memories flooded his psyche. Odd memories, believed to have been boxed and stored in the cellar of his subconscious mind, suddenly burst into the foyer. Secrets long forgotten bubbled up from below, resulting in a feeling of brilliance. Recognizing the opportunity to test his expanded intellect, Mitchell tried to write a medical paper, and then a poem. When neither fleshed out, he tried tackling a math problem. To his dismay, his mediocre math skills mirrored his pedestrian prose. But it bothered him not. This wasn't science, poetry, or math.

This was something else entirely . . .

Physician was an odd career choice for Mitchell, considering he couldn't stand the sight of blood and often fainted while performing surgery. He had first been turned on to toxicology during his mid-twenties while studying medicine in Paris. There, he met Claude Bernard (1813–1878), a Parisian doctor who was a "unique combination of a profound intellect, a superb technician, and a brilliant experimentalist."[2] Bernard's classic book on the philosophy of science, *An Introduction to the Study*

of Experimental Medicine (1865), greatly advanced the steadily grow-ing field of pharmacology. Often considered the "father of physiology," Bernard remarked to the impressionable young Mitchell, "Why think when you can experiment? Exhaust experiment and then think."[3]

Experiment appealed to a person like Mitchell. In 1855 he left Paris and returned to Philadelphia, only a few years before the South would solidify itself under the Confederate banner. Mitchell spent the Civil War years treating Union soldiers. By war's end, he boasted that Turner's Lane Hospital in Philadelphia, where he worked as assistant surgeon, had given "sixty thousand hypodermic injections of morphia" per annum to wounded Yankees.[4] Although he remained off the battle-field, Mitchell took a bullet to the neck by an unknown Confederate soldier. He survived, but it was then that he turned the syringe on him-self for the first time.

THE VIAL MYSTICAL

In the post-bellum world, wounded soldiers and their physicians weren't the only ones using morphine to assuage what ailed them. Many women drank a concoction of opium, spices, and wine called "laudanum" that provided alleviation for "anguished and hopeless wives and mothers . . . [who found] temporary relief from their sufferings."[5] Physicians pre-scribed opium for a variety of ailments. In those days, no one had a monopoly on opium; regular people cultivated raw poppy in their gar-dens for oil and sweeteners.[6]

But some earned a reputation for their opium use. By the late 1800s, many people associated opium smoking with "prostitutes, gamblers, and petty criminals their pimps, apprentices, and hangers-on."[7] In Oxford, during the early nineteenth century, famed opium writer Thomas De Quincey speaks of walking the "harsh, cruel, and repulsive" streets of British society with many girls from that "unhappy class who subsist on the wages of prostitution."[8]

As De Quincey demonstrates, men, too, proved powerless to the allure of Morpheus, one name given to the highly addicting drug morphine, in honor of the Greek god of sleep. De Quincey's autobiographical novel, *Confessions of an English Opium Eater* (1821), solidified the author as the poster child for the degraded opium addict of "polite" society. De Quincey had suffered toothaches in his youth and often submerged his head in freezing water to alleviate the pain. This practice was obviously not without its own risks and, on one occasion, De Quincey wet his head in such a manner and went to sleep. He awoke with "excruciating rheumatic pains of the head and face." Later that day he met a classmate who suggested De Quincey try opium for relief. In London, De Quincey found a pharmacist who sold a "celestial drug" beyond the strength of those concocted by mere mortals. De Quincey suspected that this consciousness-peddler might not be entirely human; existing as "an immortal druggist, sent down to earth on a special mission to myself."[9]

Others used opium to stimulate creativity, a practice that would eventually branch into mysticism. Only most users hadn't initially taken opium to stimulate creativity or spiritual experiences. Their revelations into aesthetics and divine contemplations manifested as completely unforeseen byproducts of opium use. Most artists first took opium to alleviate chronic pain, only later stumbling upon its creative potential and numinous properties. Poet Elizabeth Barrett Browning (1806–1861) was one such artist who drank the elixir contained within—to use her words—"the vial mystical."[10] Browning was neither a desperate housewife nor a prostitute, but rather a sufferer of various cardiovascular ailments due to a spinal injury incurred at age fifteen. Like many other doctors of the time, Browning's primary caregiver prescribed that most regrettable panacea, opium, over and over again.[11]

Such abuses eventually came into question.

Little over a decade after Browning passed, in 1870, English physician Thomas Clifford Allbutt (1836–1925)—who served as commissioner for lunacy in England and Wales in the late 1800s and once lauded morphine as a "marvelous remedy" for indigestion—alarmingly remarked that "the hypodermic use of morphia . . . [has] reached the height of fashion."[12] Mitchell heeded Allbutt's warnings, despite the "endless succession of visions" he received through morphine. After a brief addiction and torturous withdrawal, Mitchell refrained from using any substance at all.[13] That was, of course, until 1894–1895, when ethnographer and anthropologist James Mooney (1861–1921) sent him a box filled with small cactus buttons (recall Mitchell's experience described at the start of this chapter).

~ May 25, 1896 ~

A few days after Mitchell had traversed the more breathtaking corners of his psyche, he gave his friend and colleague, Dr. Eshner, some mescal buttons. Eshner's experience differed from Mitchell's in that he based his report on philology, while Mitchell grounded his essay in psychology.* When he closed his eyes, Eshner saw kaleidoscopic effects; he beheld visual tapestries, decorative geometric mosaics, and "various kinds of scroll work. . . . In none of the images were people or animals or other objects than designs represented."[14] Mitchell, on the other hand, had stumbled into the "pharmacies of fairy land," complete with pipe-smoking dwarfs and a one-hundred-foot-long rotating worm with red and green tentacles. Expressing his gratitude for the buttons, Mitchell wrote a "thank you" note to Mooney while questioning the rationale behind laws forbidding peyote use: "It is really a rather harmless drug as compared with most others which men use, and I think such a law ridiculous."[15]

---

*Dr. Eshner's name appears only once in history, as "Dr. Eshner," in his account with peyote, which was appended to Weir Mitchell's report of his experiment with that cactus in the *British Medical Journal.* Like other names in this book, we simply do not have any other information about him, lifespan or even a first name. See Mitchell, "Remarks on the Effects of Anhelonium Lewinii (the Mescal Button)," 1628–29.

THE MOST VIOLENT OF ALL THE FRUITS

Although Mitchell's report of his own peyote ingestion was probably the first poetically fervent interpretation of the experience by a Westerner, he hadn't been the first American to actually take the cactus. During the Civil War, soldiers from the Texas Rangers and a few U.S. Marshals were said to have imbibed the "whiskey root," which the locals called "white mule."[16] Here and there odd tales depicting the therapeutic potential of peyote buttons would spring up in medical literature.[17] But the first concrete account of an American eating peyote to stimulate a visionary trance is attributed to Texas physician John Raleigh Briggs (1851–1907), who ingested the cactus and gave it an unfavorable review in the 1886 *Medical Register*. The article is both a warning about peyote's effects and also what future researchers would call a "trip report." We can infer that Briggs expected something psychologically bizarre to happen—as he had a pencil and paper handy to record his thoughts; though he wasn't prepared for how unruly the experience would be. His pulse hammered violently out of control, so much so that his heart seemed to be "running away with itself."[18] Struggling to breathe, he rushed to Fort Worth and called for his friend and colleague Dr. E. J. Beall (1836–1921). Beall's prescription for the dry whiskey was, not surprisingly, regular whiskey, and after taking large shots every few minutes, Briggs's heart rate returned to a normal pace. The peyote button was the "most violent and rapid of all fruits," wrote Briggs;[19] he even likened its effects to cocaine and opium.

The *Register* article turned a few heads at Parke-Davis, which was once America's oldest and largest drug maker, founded in 1875. After receiving a formal request for samples of the cactus on Parke-Davis letterhead, Briggs mailed a peyote-filled cigar box to the pharmaceutical giant with an accompanying letter that stated he could procure more, if Parke-Davis would foot the border smuggler's bill. One of the Parke-Davis chemists, Frank Augustine Thompson, discovered the alkaloid materials in the cactus, although he never published his findings, and as a result is not widely known. He sent out samples to different scientists in both the United States and Europe.[20] One man who obtained the buttons was German toxicologist Louis Lewin (1850–1929), who subsequently wrote the first published report that pertained to peyote's alkaloids, and as a result, his work has always overshadowed Augustine's.[21]

LIKE SPIRIT WHISPERINGS

If Briggs wrote the first "bummer" report concerning peyote in America, then it was Mooney, the anthropologist who had supplied Mitchell with peyote and was now serving as domestic ambassador for the Bureau of American Ethnology, who, six years later, wrote the first favorable one. Mooney had eaten the buttons not in his home, but as a partaker in a peyote rite. How Mooney ended up in such an alien position—a white man participating in an indigenous custom, tuning into the "spirit whisperings" that filled the air—is a story in itself.[22]

Mooney had cultivated a fascination for the exotic customs of First Nations peoples at least as far back as his preteen days, when he made a list cataloging all the known tribes of the time. As a young lad, Mooney had witnessed the last First Nations peoples of the eastern seaboard saunter westward to break away from imminent domination by this strange, ever-expanding United States. During his valedictorian address at Richmond High School in Indiana, Mooney used the pulpit as a soapbox and discussed the unfairness of the First Nations peoples relocation program. His passion for justice was so strong that later in life, the Cherokee and Kiowa embraced him as a friend, the latter inviting him to witness a peyote ceremony that they had recently adopted from the Comanche.

Much of the information Mooney obtained while visiting with the Kiowa came from his friend Paul Setkopi, a Kiowa who impressed Mooney both as "an excellent interpreter" and "faithful above average."[23]

One particularly cold and rainy night, Mooney prepared himself to observe a peyote ceremony; Setkopi rode twenty miles to meet him and assured him that he would explain in detail the nature of the rite—just as he had always done. Setkopi had already participated in a rite the night before and, through undisclosed avenues, caught wind of Mooney's involvement in a neighboring community's ritual. Mooney, considering the health of his friend and the steadily dropping temperature, stressed that it was in Setkopi's best interest to just go to sleep. "I will stay with you. . . . I shall eat mescal [peyote], and soon I shall be alright," replied Setkopi. The ceremony lasted the whole night. Setkopi "sang his song like the others." And when the ritual ended, Setkopi, running on two successive days without sleep, "came out as fresh as [the others] in the morning."[24]

Until 1891, Mooney had only participated in at least one (possibly two) peyote ceremonies, but hadn't partaken in the rites by ingesting the medicine himself. That year, however, he finally ate seven buttons from the sacred cactus. After his experience, Mooney sent an article to the *Therapeutic Gazette* in which he claimed that the peyote-using peoples "regard mescal [the cactus] as a panacea in medicine . . . the key which opens to them all the glories of another world."[25]

At the time, Mooney had to watch his words. The rise of the temperance movement had gained momentum. He cautioned against writing too explicitly about the intoxicating effects of peyote, for fear that his indigenous friends would come under attack by those who knew nothing of the ceremony. What mattered most, said Mooney, was context—the setting and the ritual. "The psychologic [*sic*] effect is perhaps the most interesting . . . this is undoubtedly due to the ceremonial accompaniments of prayer and song, the sound of the drum and rattle, and the glare of the fire."[26] Commenting on previous experiments by D. W. Prentiss and Francis Morgan that resulted in "horrible visions and gloomy depression," Mooney extolled the ritual as a useful combatant to such dejection.[27] "One seems to be lifted out of the body and floating about in the air like a freed spirit," he wrote. "The fire takes on glorious shapes, the sacred mescal upon the crescent mound becomes alive and moves and talks and you talk to it and it answers."[28]

MELTED INTO UNITY

Famed psychologist William James (1842–1910), a man widely credited as the father of modern American psychology, is also known to have dabbled in altered states of consciousness. "Modern" is the key word here; although psychology can be traced back to the ancient Greeks, most psychological works were, as James wrote to his brother Henry on June 4, 1890, "ante-scientific . . . predestined to become unreadable old medieval lumber."[29] Though, unlike some of his more scientifically minded contemporaries, James cultivated a deeply spiritual side—his collection of lectures, *The Varieties of Religious Experience,* remains a literary milestone in the equally philosophical and scientific quest to find God in the mind. One way of obtaining a vision of this God was through an altered state of awareness brought about by inhaling nitrous oxide. James was well aware of the risk academics of his day took in contemplating the supernatural. In one such oration, he recognized that "mysticism," as understood by many of his cohorts, was an expression "of mere reproach . . . vague and vast and sentimental, and without a base in either facts or logic."[30] He defined mystical states as quantifiably realistic if the right equations were applied that could marry the inexplicable to the measurable.

Mitchell didn't go for his friend's unscientific claims of spirituality, once remarking on a séance that he and James attended as "inconceivable twaddle."[31] And yet, he may have been surprised to find out that his first experience with mescaline fit almost perfectly into James's definition of mystical consciousness! Such states, reasoned James, included four parts: *Ineffability:* "The subject of it says that it defies expression . . . mystical states are more like states of feeling than like states of intellect." Mystical states would also bear a *Noetic Quality,* meaning they "carry with them a curious sense of authority for aftertime." *Transiency* meant that even after the experience wore off their qualities could but "imperfectly be reproduced in memory."[32] The only point of James's four-part paradigm of which Mitchell fell short was the final one, *Passivity*. After the peyote subsided, Mitchell did not feel "as if he were grasped and held by a superior power."[33] There was no divine awakening, just pipe-smoking dwarfs—beings peyotists would have surely interpreted as "spirits," either for good or ill. But Mitchell came from a different cultural time and place. And although James's mystic-model might have carried weight with other theologians of his day, there was a stronger paradigm—one of scientific reason—that Mitchell was unable to transcend.

Sadly, James is no help here; for he never got to contemplate the wonders of the cactus. It is known that Mitchell sent buttons to James, but the buttons caused James nothing more than twenty-four hours of feeling "violently sick" followed by a rough *katzenjammer*, or "hangover." James's trial with the buttons was so unsettling that he decided he would never ingest them again. Instead, he wrote to his brother Henry that he would evade further experimentation and "take the visions on trust."[34]

Even before Mitchell mailed him the stale buttons, James had already harbored an interest in altered states of awareness—probably why Mitchell decided to send him the buttons in the first place (despite their frequent intellectual head butting). James's first encounter with his unconscious occurred in 1875 while teaching at Harvard. A fellow professor, Charles Loring Jackson (1847–1935), had been experimenting with amyl nitrate (the active ingredient in "poppers," the dance-drug of the disco era), which he claimed caused him to sing and dance. James's curiosity got the best of him and he tried the gas right then and there. He wanted to know how changes in one's bodily processes distorted their mental counterparts.

◎

"Oh! How queer I feel!"[35] exclaimed James after inhaling the gas. He wanted to know if his face had flushed—a sign that his physical state had directly influenced his mental one. He did not write a significant account detailing how he felt about the incident, but we can infer that it had a considerable impact on his psychological life; from then on, James adapted a not-immodest view pertaining to altered states of consciousness. Alcohol, he felt, was "the great exciter of the Yes function in man," yet his mind expander of choice was nitrous oxide, which he inhaled "to stimulate the mystical consciousness in an extraordinary degree." Of nitrous oxide, James claimed:

> Depth beyond depth of truth seems revealed to the inhaler. This truth fades out, however, or escapes, at the moment of coming to. . . . Nevertheless, the sense of a profound meaning having been there persists; and I know more than one person who is persuaded that in the nitrous oxide trance we have a genuine metaphysical revelation. . . . Yet they may determine attitudes though they cannot furnish formulas, and open a region though they fail to give a map. . . . Looking back on my own experiences, they all converge towards a kind of insight into which I cannot help ascribing some metaphysical significance. . . . It is as if the opposites of the world, whose contradictions and conflict make all our difficulties and troubles, were melted into unity.[36]

However, the pragmatist in James also observed that simply inhaling nitrous oxide didn't automatically default to a "tremendously exciting sense of an intense metaphysical illumination," and conceded that "the effects [of the gas] will of course vary with the individual, just as they vary in the same individual from time to time."[37] A physiologist with a penchant for the "new science" of psychology, James had for several years struggled to wed science and theology into an innovative discipline between positivism, which "naively espoused faith in scientific naturalism," and spiritualism, which "let religious belief close off inquiries into the body's operations."[38] James' antidote for this dilemma caused him to swan dive into the depths of his own consciousness. In this respect, he opened himself to either authority, theological and/or scientific, with "no odds given and no favors shown."[39]

James had decided to experiment with chemically induced mysticism after reading *The Anaesthetic Revelation and the Gist of Philosophy* (1874) by Benjamin Paul Blood (1832–1919), a poet/philosopher who discovered the "unhinger" of visions while inhaling nitrous oxide during a dental procedure. An eccentric man, Blood described the "Anaesthetic Revelation" as the "Initiation of Man into the Immemorable [*sic*] Mystery of the Open Secret of Being, revealed as the Inevitable Vortex of Continuity."[40]

One person particularly turned on by Mitchell's descriptive tone was poet and psychologist Henry Havelock Ellis (1859–1939). Ellis existed philosophically between Mitchell and James: like Mitchell, Ellis preferred writing poetry to writing prescriptions; yet his Jamesian curiosity sought compatibility between science and religion: "Religion cannot live nobly without science or without morals," he wrote. "It is only a strenuous devotion to science, by a perpetual reference to the moral structure of life, that religion . . . can be rendered healthful."[41] In the past, Ellis had been intrigued by such blissful intoxicants as hashish. Therefore, it comes as little surprise that Mitchell's account of mescaline in the *British Medical Journal* inspired Ellis to seek the visionary cactus for himself. Ellis wrote about his mescaline experiences four times (first in *The Lancet* in June of 1897), although it is his third journal entry that gets the most press. The third caused a stir among the editors of the *British Medical Journal;* it is also the report that discusses the more profound visionary states not only induced in Ellis but also several others to whom he gave the buttons.

Ellis was quick to discount the similarity between an alcoholic stupor and the effects of the mescal button. "Mescal," he wrote, "must not be confounded with the intoxicating drink of the same name . . . yet, as we shall see, it has every claim to rank with hasheesh [*sic*] and the other famous drugs which have procured for men the joys of an artificial paradise."[42]

◎

Besides the mystical and recreational interpretations of these otherworldly states, a third paradigm also formed, specifically in Europe: that of the medical model, specifically helping the mentally deleterious by trying to understand their thought processes. For nineteenth century French psychiatrists, insanity was as steeped in Christianity as confession and communion. The public tended to view madness in religious terms, and psychiatrists were a "species of missionary whose job was to save souls for Reason."[43] The doctor credited with pioneering—or, if not that, then certainly cheerleading—the use of cannabis to study psychosis was undoubtedly Jacques-Joseph Moreau, (1804–1884). In his youth, Moreau had "longed to see foreign countries."[44] While traveling through Islamic lands during the 1830s, Moreau was struck by the lack of mental health problems in places like Egypt, Syria, and Palestine. These people, due to religious restrictions, eschewed alcohol in favor of hashish. The whole thing fascinated him. He studied, inquired, and took notes, and upon his return to France decided to try the plant medicine himself. It was only then that he realized Islamic hashish users disengage from society not because they are empty-headed, but rather because their minds were so overwhelmed with thoughts, feelings, and sensations brought on by cannabis that a regular life seemed boring.[45]

Cannabis wasn't alcohol. It wasn't even opium, which, despite its well-known ability to produce fantastic visions at first, usually left the user incoherent and sluggish. Hashish was different: it left the mind perfectly intact and able to adjudicate, rationalize, and discuss the flurry of visions encountered by the sacred herb. This was exactly what Moreau was looking for—a "halfway" point between psychosis and sanity. As he saw it, there existed degrees between the two extremes. Cannabis could safely ferry a person from one end of the spectrum to the other, allowing a sane individual to experience madness for a short while and then return safely to reason.

Working off this hypothesis, Moreau joined the staff at les Hôpital Universitaire la Pitié-Salpêtrière in 1840, where he used cannabis to induce madness in his patients. He didn't believe that cannabis actually caused true madness, just that the two states were similar enough for research purposes. Five years later, he published his findings in *Du Hachisch Et De L'aliénation Mentale: Études Psychologiques* (*Hashish and Mental Illness,* 1845).

His colleagues protested. Since Moreau had taken hashish, he was "not keeping with strict scientific claims for objectivity."[46] But for Moreau, his skeptical colleagues' lack of experience with hashish left their claims barren of objectivity.* Still, for Moreau, hashish proved therapeutically indispensable for giving an otherwise sane person insight into insanity. Others agreed. By 1900, various doctors had published over one hundred articles on the medical use of cannabis.[47]

But there was another natural substance—not cannabis nor opium nor peyote—that caught a number of scientists' attention in the mid- to late 1800s. Mind you, it did not cause a stir due to its visionary properties, despite its ability to invoke them intensely. This particular fungus has a long history as both a medicine and a purveyor of death, to say nothing of its role in medieval and early modern witchcraft.

This fungus called "ergot."

---

*Such disagreements still exist today. I speak at both psychedelic conferences and medieval conferences. At psychedelic conferences, I am told that unless I've eaten the *Amanita muscaria* mushroom (I have, by the way), my arguments against ridiculous ideas like the "scared mushroom" conspiracy (which holds that the *Amanita muscaria* appears secretly in Christian art) are bogus. At medieval conferences, I am told that *because* I use plant medicines, my arguments for the witches' ointment are bogus. Go figure.

2
Mother's Grain
A Brief History of the Ergot Fungus

Ergot . . . is so powerful a drug that in the hands of amateurs . . . it sometimes leads to psychical disaster and death. In skilled hands, however, it can be a valuable medical tool.

LUCY KAVALER

A LOATHSOME ROT

~ *Sometime in the Sixth Century BCE* ~

An unknown Assyrian scribe pressed the cuneiform characters "noxious pustule in the ear of grain" onto a wet clay tablet, giving us our earliest surviving reference to ergot.[1] Another reference from not long after speaks of noxious grasses that cause pregnant women to "drop the womb."[2] Ergot, a fungus that grows on diseased rye grain, has been the cause of plague-like outbreaks of ergotism throughout European history, appearing in one of two forms: convulsive and gangrenous.[3] Both suck. Gangrenous ergotism includes nausea and vomiting, while extremities like fingers and toes slowly decay and splinter off the body; beneath the skin, a fire roars so massively it as if the devil himself stoked the blaze. Convulsive ergotism attacks the nervous system, resulting in seizures, hallucinations, and psychosis. One anonymous writer living in the mid-ninth century CE chronicles with much despair, "A great plague of swollen blisters consumed the people of a loathsome rot."[4]

◎

But ergot also proved to have medicinal value, provided the right person worked with it, preparing the fungus properly to cure, not to kill. Hippocrates (c. 370–470 BCE) would recommend ergot as a way to suppress postpartum hemorrhaging.[5] For centuries thereafter, midwives and physicians would employ ergot to speed up muscular contractions in the uterus and thus facilitate childbirth. Other times, they used ergot to abort the pregnancy, resulting in one (of many) of its Germanic names, *mutterkorn,* or "mother's grain." Medieval lay-physicians, or "leeches," wrote of ergot's medicinal properties in their leech books, where it found employment as an alleviator of "ear worms," upset stomach, runny nose, and even as an acne cream.[6] And yet ergot is most notorious as the cause of outbreaks of ergotism that pepper the European historical landscape.

Ergot—the schizophrenic fungus: a medicine one day, human raze the next.

Excruciating death and lifesaving medicine aside, certain classical names for the fungus also point toward our ancestors understanding its intoxicating properties (granted it is prepared properly and served in a small dose). For example, the French referred to ergot as *seigle ivre,* or "drunken rye." *Tollkorn,* or "mad grain," confirms that medieval Germans also knew that this particular grain parasite deeply affected the mental state of those who ingested it.[7] One medical student, Johannes Gotofredus Andres, even remarked about an ergotism outbreak that took place in Silesia, Poland, in 1717. Some of the afflicted acted "like ecstatics" who fell into deep sleeps and, upon waking, "told of various visions."[8]

For its psychoactive properties, it seems ergot also found employment in magic and witchcraft. Several cases from Finnmark, Norway, certainly point in that direction. In late 1684, the district governor, Hans Hanssen Lilienskiold (1650-1703) decided to catalogue the various trials for witchcraft that had taken place in the district since 1620. Among a host of offenses, Lilienskiold listed seventeen cases that implicated mixing black pellets "the size of barley grains" into milk, and giving the beverage to drink. The Norwegian women who were mixing these ergot potions had somehow figured out how to suppress the negative, gangrenous effects and amplify its visionary properties,* as Lilienskiold records that some people "learned [witchcraft]" through imbibing these pythiagenic† cocktails.[9]

Other times, ergot-like symptoms appeared in places where rye provided the staple food of commoners. Take Norfolk, England, which saw two mysterious outbreaks of *something* in 1600 and 1621. Many local cattle died, while some villagers suffered ailments like fits, hallucinations, manic behavior, and one person even developed gangrene. Another case from Warboys, Huntingdonshirek, 1589, featured some undesirable pestilence infiltrating Robert Throckmorton's house. Not only did other villagers suffer ergot-like maladies, but Throckmorton's seven servants and five daughters developed "fits, hallucinations . . . temporary blindness, deafness, and numbness"—all common symptoms of ergotism. Here, we can surely make a good case for ergot poisoning, for which a victim of the loathsome rot could easily launch a charge of witchcraft against an eccentric individual living on the outskirts of Warboys.[10]

We also find additional evidence for ergot-induced witch persecutions on continental Europe. Historian Erik Midelfort marked the number of witch trials in Swabia against the fluctuation of rye prices in Augsburg between the years 1550–1689. He found that during this

---

*The only real evidence we have for this is the fact that the women who mixed these drinks did so without intending to kill the imbiber. Wasson also notes in *The Road to Eleusis:* "The separation of the hallucinogenic agents by simple water solution from the non-soluble [toxic] alkaloids was well within the range of possibilities open" to the ancient Greeks (43). Perhaps these women in Finnmark had discovered this process as well?

†Pythiagenic: to generate magic using psychedelics. See Hatsis, *Psychedelic Mystery Traditions,* 11.

time, the impoverished masses subsisted on "grain of questionable quality."[11]

Some researchers have suggested other areas in history where ergot might have reared its fungally little head. For example, ergot may have also helped inspire several mystical Jewish movements, as present-day psychiatrist Sharon Packer maintains, noting the correlation between outbreaks of ergotism and the rise of mystical groups like the Ashkenazi Hasidim of the Rhineland in the tenth century; Sabbateanism, which spread across Eurasia in the mid-seventeenth century; and Hasidism in late seventeenth century Ukraine.[12] Of the Ashkenazi Hasidim, Packer writes, "whole towns were infused with such religious fervor. . . . Ecstatic seizures and religious visions became commonplace occurrences and were incorporated into semi-official rabbinical teaching." Some followers of Sabbatai Zevi, founder of Sabbateanism, "fell into trances, convulsed and burst into paroxysms of joy during synagogue service. Enthusiasm peaked during the early summer Shavuoth celebration, when freshly-harvested grain harbored the most potent ergot." Finally, of the Hasidic, Packer states that their "emphasis on transcendence faded after the death of . . . Rabbi Nachman of Bratslav.* This shift also coincided with the decline of endemic ergotism."[13]

While this certainly remains a possibility, too much time and distance has passed—and far too little information survives to gauge validity—that we can do little more than speculate about such possibilities over adult beverages at psychedelic conference afterparties.

With this in mind, it is an easy and short step to attributing all medieval and early modern witch activity to plant-based elixirs. And in some cases, ergot may have caused a kind of uproarious societal disorder that authorities misattributed to witchcraft. But only *some*. The majority of times, other historical realities roll such conjectural waves back out to sea. For instance, in my last book, I made the case that while we will likely never even know *if* an entheogen played a role at the Rites of

---

*The great grandson of the Baal Shem Tov, founder of Hasidic Judaism.

Eleusis in the first place, supposing one did, said entheogen probably wasn't ergot (as is popularly believed).[14] But ancient Eleusis is not the only place where ergot has been, I believe, misapplied.

THE SALEM INCIDENT

~ *March 1, 1692* ~

The chains around Sarah Good's legs scraped both the flesh on her ankles and the wooden floor as she entered the trial room of the courthouse.

The sweat of fury forming on his brow, the prosecutor examined Sarah Good. Did she hurt the children?

"I scorn it," Good testifiied.

Did she employ familiar spirits?

"I scorn it. . . . You bring others here and now you charge me with it? You brought two more!"[15]

Unfortunately for Good (1653–1692), the magistrates were not content with these answers. Whenever she would speak, the children—a group of young girls, aged nine to twenty—would thrash their bodies and bellow with pain. Indeed, they had been suffering convulsions (on and off) for a few weeks now; Sarah Osborne (a social outcast), Good (the beggar woman), and Tituba (the slave woman) had bewitched them. As the girls sat in judgment of the accused, they couldn't help but demonstrate the effects of bewitchment at the sound of Good's voice. Whenever the magistrates spoke, the holy word on their tongues, the young girls—thank God!—returned to normal. The judge, the bailiff, the audience—everyone—wanted to know far more about this beggar woman, Good. For instance, villagers often heard her mumbling to herself as she walked away from the homes of the upper class, should the residents deny her their charity. This certainly raised suspicions of witchcraft and could easily explain the girls' possession.

But those mumbles weren't curses. "It is the [ten] commandments I say. I may say my commandments, I hope," Good testified. Between the lines, she was begging for her life. She knew *exactly* what a charge of witchcraft meant.[16]

When asked to recite the commandments, Good could only recite gibberish, notwithstanding a few lines from the psalms and an accusation against Osborne of the very crimes for which she stood trial.

Osborne trembled in her shackles as she heard Good drop her name. For she was waiting in the parlor for her turn to be called to judgment, wholly innocent of whatever charges (and Good's indictment) awaited her.* She had been ill, too sickly even to get out of bed. The ministers present had to help her into the room and then into the chair in which she sat. She looked damn near bewitched herself. She rambled on about her dreams, interrupted only by the screams and writhing of a few young girls if she looked in their direction. But she was so out of sorts that it seemed almost cruel to continue the inquest; the magistrates removed her from the courtroom. The girls' convulsions stopped.

Finally, it was time to question Tituba, the slave woman who started it all.

Some researchers in our own day have pointed to ergot poisoning as a possible explanation for the Salem witch trials of 1692, beginning with the publication of Linnda Caporael's "Ergotism: The Satan Loosed in Salem?" (1976). Caporael focused on two pieces of evidence: weather conditions and the behavior of the "possessed" girls. On the former, she claims (correctly) that ergot favors "warm, damp, rainy springs."[17] However, she provides no evidence that such a spring occurred. On the latter, it is true that the girls exhibited *some* signs of ergotism like "mania, melancholia, psychosis, and delirium," but lest we fall into thinking that correlation equals causation, we might take a closer

---

*In the United States today, we often take for granted that an arresting officer will tell us the charges brought against us (should we find ourselves in such a position). To those unfortunate innocents living in Salem, say around 1692, no such right existed. Without warning, they were plucked from their lives and brought before judges in chains.

look at what took place in Salem that most unfortunate year of our Lord, 1692.

Around a decade after Caporael published her article, historian Mary Kilbourne Matossian added weight to her hypothesis by including firsthand accounts (that Caporael did not provide) that sounded much like ergot poisoning from in and around Salem Village in her *Poisons of the Past* (1989). Take this example from Sarah Abbott, who testified on August 3, 1692, "My husband Benjamin Abbott has not only been afflicted in his body . . . but alsoe that strange and unusual thing have happened to his Cattle, for some have died suddenly and strangely, which we could not tell any natural reason for." There was also the testimony of Hannah and John Putnam, whose daughter died after experiencing "strange and violent fitts . . . it continewed in strange and violent fitts for about Two day and Two nights and then departed this life by a cruell and violent death being enuf to piers a stony hart."[18]

There is no doubt that this all reeks of ergot poisoning.

But there are some problems. The first of which is that none of the firsthand accounts Matossian offers originate before January 1692, when the first whispers of witchcraft started to stir in Salem Village. Not only that, but while some of the girls' symptoms aligned with ergotism, other symptoms most certainly did not.

Young girls had few outlets in the seventeenth century.* Some however, found delight from hearing about the damnations of those in Hell. How did they suffer? What merciless tortures did Satan visit upon the sinner? How exactly did the demons torment the damned? Sickness? Isolation? Restlessness? Hallucinations? It was all so exciting!

At least it was exciting for Abigail Williams (b. 1680), who delighted in these tales. She couldn't wait for the day when she would join the others in Heaven and actually get to watch the anguish of the damned.

---

*And pretty much all of human history.

How can we blame her? She was an eleven- or twelve-year-old girl living in Salem Village in 1692. She was ignored. Belittled. Expendable. Bullied. *Frustrated.* She found herself at the parsonage of her uncle, the Reverend Samuel Parris (1653–1720), playing around with his daughter, nine-year-old Elizabeth Parris. They were enamored with the Caribbean magic of Tituba.

We know little of Tituba before the Salem witch scare of 1692. She came to Salem via Reverend Parris, who acquired her while taking a break from his theological studies at Harvard to visit Barbados. His father, Thomas Parris, a cloth dealer from London, had recently died, leaving Samuel his twenty-acre cotton plantation in Barbados. Tituba arrived in Massachusetts with an exotic form of (what was probably) an echo of voodoo. Casting these spells with Betty and Abigail provided a living memory of her homeland, her family, her traditions, and a much-needed outlet from the unbearable suppression she endured on a daily basis.

But these spells, this magic, was well-known to the young girls to be sacrilegious. Reverend Parris often preached about the Hell that awaited those who dabbled in the very acts that his daughter engaged while at the parsonage with Tituba and Williams.

But it didn't end there. For Parris and Williams were hardly the only overlooked, bored, frustrated girls in the surrounding area. Every Sunday their friends would come in from the outskirts of Salem Village to hear both Mass and Parris and Williams' tales of Tituba's strange practices. Eventually, these girls developed their own excuses as to why they needed to visit the parsonage after Sunday Mass. They likely told their parents any number of tales—anything—just to meet the grand witch herself, Tituba.

One of those girls was twelve-year-old Ann Putnam (1679–1716). Her visits to the parsonage were more of a reconnaissance mission for her mother (also named Ann), who had suffered the loss of her sister, several of her sister's children, and even some of her own children. Her daughter Ann (the eldest surviving child) often fell sickly, surviving only until the age of thirty-seven, the residues of an unhealthy bloodline.

At times, deceased family members would visit Ann (senior) in dreams. She would tell the younger Ann the minutest details about these dreams and then send her to Tituba to see what it all meant—maybe even reconnect with the departed. Ann is important to this episode as it was her firm belief in the reality of Hell, her mother's dreams, and Tituba's powers that kicked off the witch scare. Most unfortunate for the people of Salem, just as Ann fell in with Tituba's magic circle at the parsonage, her transition into puberty came with especially horrific pains and aches—pains and aches separate from her usual illnesses. Pains and aches that witches were well-known to inflict upon little girls.

And so the younger Putnam received attention—attention that no one ever gave her; attention that adolescent girls simply didn't receive in Salem Village (or anywhere else) in 1692. The attention made her feel alive; it put her on the sunny-side of afterlife possibilities—the diametrical opposition between herself and the devil's subjects meant *she couldn't be* one of the devil's subjects. And lo! To everyone's surprise (and retrospectively, to *no one's* surprise) suddenly Williams fell under this same spell, only with new symptoms, as yet undiagnosed in Parris. Williams got on all fours and started climbing on and under furniture like an animal, braying and whinnying, only to suddenly stop frozen in her tracks, convulsing and flailing about on the floor; other times she would make "as if she would fly, stretching up her arms as high as she could, and crying 'whish, whish, whish!' several times."[19] The girls met the prayers said for them with wild screams and agonized bellows. In fact, at one point, young Parris even threw a Bible across the room. As news spread of the odd suffering of Parris and Williams (and the devoted attention they received), other girls in Salem Village like Susanna Sheldon and Mary Walcott started to suffer as well.

Witchcraft certainly offered a plausible explanation for the girls' odd behavior. To the devoutly religious sensibilities of the Salem population in the late seventeenth century, case closed.

But how do we adjudicate such claims in the early twenty-first century?

Let's investigate.

◎

Obviously, there was a lot more to the Salem witch scare beyond the brief outline above. The whole of the Salem affair is not the subject of this book and, quite frankly, there are too many books about it anyway. I merely wanted to show how the whole Salem scare initially unfolded. For if ergot truly spurred the witch scare, that's where we will find it—in the *beginning*. So that's the beginning: a string of young girls, one by one, came down with a strange malady that no one else in the village endured.

With this in mind, let's explore the plausibility of the ergot hypothesis.

For starters, the ergot that possibly grew in the Salem fields would have to have behaved unlike every other strand of ergot in history. Ergot epidemics do not discriminate by race, gender, or age demographic. Ergotism is a mean, harsh killer. Children, who are most vulnerable to ergot poisoning, die gruesome, horrible deaths. And yet, not only did every girl survive her seizures (none showing a single *outward* sign of ergotism*), perhaps most bizarre, all the girls—post-screaming, post-writhing, post-convulsive fits, post-agony—seemed "little the worse" once they returned to baseline. Some even looked "positively refreshed."[20] Somehow, between receiving unyielding prayerful attention and feeling worn out from all their spasms and fits, the girls found long stretches of respite from their afflictions.

Somehow . . .

Next, there is the problem of *when* their symptoms showed. Isn't it strange that the convulsions and outcries took place at odd times here and there? And why did the bulk of their ergotism-like symptoms

---

*Gangrene, loss of eyesight, vomiting, loss of consciousness, skin peeling.

appear in the presence of the accused? Or when an adult prayed or mentioned holy names? That's mighty *specific* for ergotism.

But it's even more specific for young girls with big imaginations, whose daily reminders of the realities of Hell gave their young and fertile minds a firm understanding of what demons and demon possession looked like. They knew from Sunday sermons, from Parris's own father, the very man in whose parsonage this had all began, that demons hated holy words. They could easily play along.

And so they did.

In fact, two of the elder girls grew fearful that some of the younger girls were overdoing it, taking the act a little too far, and so quickly decried them.[21]

None of this is consistent with ergot poisoning. The demographic of the afflicted, how said affliction spread, how the symptoms manifested and when, and the *scripted* nature of it all waxes more toward a group of mostly teenage girls (at least one deeply disturbed) enjoying a rare and coveted attention than anything like ergotism. So while the ergot hypothesis is technically plausible (as it has happened in history before), there seems to have been different forces and circumstances at work in Salem, Massachusetts, during that cold, foul winter of 1692.

A FINE BOGEY TALE

About a century before the Salem affair, in 1582, ergot had found its way into the *Kräuterbuch,* or *Book of Herbs,* of Adam Lonitzer (1528–1586), a physician and botanist from Frankfort City, Germany. Lonitzer didn't describe ergot as a witches' poison used by malevolent crones to cause madness and death, but quite antithetically, as an ecbolic—a facilitator of child delivery, as midwives had used in different places and at different times.[22] Just seven years before the Salem incident, Gaspard Bauhin (1560–1624) would leave us our earliest surviving illustration of ergot growing on rye grass in his posthumously published *Theatrum Botanicum* (1658). Later, a French physician, Dr. Louis Thuillier

(1856–1883), pinpointed the origins of ergotism by noting that peasants ate the infected rye while the upper-class did not. Common people thought the ergot harmless, just a byproduct of the rye grain.[23] In the early 1800s, the Scottish physician Adam Neale (d. 1832) had reviewed 720 cases of ergotism in both Europe and America. Not long after, in 1875, French pharmacist, Charles Tanret (1847–1917) extracted and classified a variety of the ergot alkaloids: ergometrine, ergocryptine, ergosterol, ergotamine, and ergotine, to name a few.

~ *August/September 1885* ~

Fanny Stevenson (1840–1914) watched in bewilderment as her husband, the novelist and poet Robert Louis Stevenson (1850–1894), whom Fanny called Louis, began feverishly formulating plot ideas and scribbling notes on loose sheets of paper. Two weeks earlier, Louis's physician had injected him with the drug *ergotine,* presumably to suppress the bleeding in his lungs. Louis suffered from tuberculosis, and ergotine was a staple alleviator in many Victorian doctors' kits during the latter-half of the nineteenth century. At some point during the bizarre episode, Fanny penned a letter to Louis's literary agent and friend, Mr. William Henley. The letter outlines Louis's tormented bout with muscle spasms and visual disturbances. Fanny also describes "Louis's mad behavior," and concludes, "I think it must be the ergotine that affects his brain at such time." The delirious Louis insisted that he "be lifted into bed in a kneeling position, his face to the pillow."[24]* Ignoring these irrational pleas, Fanny simply waited out the bizarre episode.

One night during Louis's psychic bout with ergotine, Fanny, shaken by her husband's tormented screams, stirred him from his sleep. He had been dreaming a most novel nightmare—that of a doctor who created a potion that would suppress his shadow-side. However, instead of calm-

---

*Whether he felt the position would stifle his muscle spasms somewhat or if he was asking his wife to smother his face in the pillow to assist him in suicide is unknown.

ing his baser instincts, the potion transforms the doctor into the physical manifestation of his shadow, an alter ego named Edward Hyde.

"Why did you wake me?" Louis asked Fanny. "I was dreaming a fine bogey tale."

Louis would later title that bogey tale *The Strange Case of Dr. Jekyll and Mr. Hyde,* which became a bestseller after *The Times* lauded it in their January 25, 1886, edition. The novella explores the duality of good and evil in the human psyche. A year after its publication, the actor Richard Mansfield (1857–1907) and playwright Thomas Russell Sullivan (1849–1916) adapted the novella as a "shilling shocker" for the stage.[25] The term "Jekyll and Hyde" has become commonplace to describe bipolar tendencies in people since then.

Let's return for a moment to Tanret, the French pharmacist who first isolated ergotine and all those other ergot derivates. One of these alkaloids, ergotinine, had not been isolated purely, and proved inactive in Tanret's lab. This changed in 1917 when Arthur Stoll (1887–1971), working at Sandoz Laboratories in Basel, Switzerland, isolated pure ergotinine. Not three years later, he followed up by isolating ergotamine. Once deemed safe for human consumption (sort of), ergotamine found use as a uterine stimulant. This changed in 1925 when Ernest Rothlin (1888–1972), another Sandoz chemist, gave ergotamine to a person who suffered migraines. It worked so well that the medical marketing team at Sandoz quickly switched gears: ergotamine, while useful for stimulating the uterus, made a much better migraine suppressant. Though it still had its dangers: some patients experienced gangrene. Some modifications in dose sizes eased that problem and ergotamine still finds employment today as an alleviator of cluster headaches.

It seemed that the magic engendered in ergot had all but been demystified.

3

A Peculiar Presentiment

Birth of the Wonder Child

*I luxuriated in the colors of the altar of Isenham, and
knew the euphoria and exultation of an artistic vision.*

WERNER STOLL

DAS WUNDERKIND

~ *April 19, 1943* ~

"[Am] I dying? Was this the transition?" the terrified chemist lamented.[1]

He lay down on his bed, closed his eyes, and died.

And then . . .

And then he was reborn.

~ *April 16, 1943* ~

Albert Hofmann (1906–2008), a Swiss chemist who was working
with ergot at Sandoz Pharmaceuticals in Basel, Switzerland, decided
against taking his lunch break in the company cafeteria, opting
instead to remain in his laboratory. He wondered if a recently synthesized compound, derived from ergot and known as 25-*lysergic acid
diethylamide*—or LSD-25—might display similar effects observed in
another derivative of acid diethylamide, Coramine, a popular circula-
tory stimulant of the time; the similar chemical relations between the

two substances encouraged such possibilities. After washing down a honey and butter sandwich with fresh milk delivered by the Sandoz agricultural research farm, Hofmann began to pace vigorously around the lab.

In those days, Sandoz chemists held an illustrious reputation: that of unweaving the stitches of nature's handiwork by isolating the active principles of known medicinal herbs—even modifying and synthesizing those that showed promise for easing a variety of ailments. Hofmann had been attracted to ergot and Sandoz Pharmaceuticals for the same reason: both allowed him "the opportunity to work on natural products."[2] As he described it, working with raw compounds allowed "Nature [to be] altered in magical ways." Hofmann had already turned down several other employment offers that dealt only with synthetic chemistry. After several years of studying the active compounds of Mediterranean squill (a bulbous herb used as a diuretic and cardiac fillip), Hofmann developed Methergine, a drug that, to this day, is still the foremost suppressant of postpartum hemorrhaging. Hofmann's efforts with squill nearing completion, his boss, Stoll, suggested he take a crack working with ergot.[3] Ergot studies had recently blossomed in Europe. So much so that—much to the surprise of a medieval peasant—ergot was now consciously cultivated for experimental purposes. As one example, Hydergine, a Sandoz creation derived from ergot, stifles senility in geriatrics. As Stoll later commented, "An enemy of man has transformed into a friend."[4] Noticing ergot's resemblance to Coramine, Hofmann hoped to fashion a new migraine analeptic.

Only Hofmann couldn't score a win with ergot—not even by his twenty-fifth attempt. Eventually dubbed "pharmacologically uninteresting" by the heads of Sandoz, LSD-25 tests ceased, the chemical forgotten.[5]

Almost.

"On a hunch," Hofmann reopened the case for LSD-25 five years later.[6] He had been unable to shake the "strange feeling" that he had overlooked something back in 1938. He whipped up a new batch of the twenty-fifth synthesis of the failed chemical. This was an odd practice; at Sandoz, the rule regarding new synthetic modifications stated that if a chemical proved "pharmacologically uninteresting," it was completely discarded. What *exactly* compelled Hofmann to brew LSD-25 again (after jettisoning the first batch) remains uncertain; but those decisions would one day cleanse the doors of perception for millions of people.

Sometime thereafter, Hofmann's initial "strange feeling" manifested into an exceptionally *weird* feeling characterized by a "remarkable restlessness, combined with slight dizziness."[7] Deciding to take the rest of the day off, he made his way home into bed and fell into a "dream-like condition . . . [that] was rather agreeable."[8] After a few hours of watching an "uninterrupted stream of fantastic pictures" coupled with a "kaleidoscopic play of colors," the odd condition started to wane and soon faded lucidly into memory.[9]

And that was perhaps the strangest part.

LSD, for all its powerful effects on the mind, did not damage it one iota.

Hofmann was meticulous about the sterility of his laboratory conditions. Yet he couldn't help but wonder if he unintentionally absorbed something back at Sandoz that had caused such peculiar sensations. He decided that following Monday to take some dichlorethylene—a substance similar to chloroform—which he had used as a solvent while preparing LSD. The effects proved negligible. Hofmann then reasoned that the psychic disturbances could have only come from one other place—the only other chemical he had worked with that day—LSD-25.

But how? He hadn't tasted anything, so he couldn't have swallowed an amount sufficient to have caused Friday's bizarre episode. Maybe a small amount found its way onto his hands and he subsequently rubbed his eyes or wiped his mouth? In any event, this new creation, this LSD, wielded tremendous power over the mind in infinitesimal doses—a mere pencil-point worth.

~ *April 19, 1943* ~

Hofmann matched his cleanliness with cautiousness; as such, he decided to imbibe a fraction of what he believed to be a strong dose of the chemical that following Monday. Telling no one of his intention* except his twenty-two-year-old lab assistant, Susi Ramstein (1922– 2011), Hofmann began with 0.25 milligrams—about half the size of a grain of salt—and anticipated upping the dose over time in small increments. He did not even think the first dose would have any effect.[10] At 4:20 p.m. that day, Hofmann took the first deliberate dose of LSD. But this moment was not without its folly, for Hofmann didn't yet understand the psychic power contained in microscopic amounts of the chemical. As the first symptoms began to materialize and then mesmerize, Hofmann authored the first LSD trip report in history. It is a paradoxical document: Hofmann writes about his "desire to laugh," while in the midst of "feeling[s] of anxiety [and] . . . symptoms of paralysis"—these last words taking all the effort he could muster to push pen to paper. He quit writing shortly thereafter and began to feel that familiar dizziness.[11]

Fearing he had overdosed, Hofmann requested that Ramstein accompany him home, lest the worst should happen. But she was in a bit of a bind. How exactly would she get Hofmann home? Taking a streetcar courted any number of hazards, as no one yet knew exactly what LSD would do to Hofmann's mind. Driving a car was not an option, as Hofmann did not own one. And while others employed at Sandoz owned cars, the Swiss Parliament barred citizens from driving them, routing all gasoline toward the war effort. Even the city's taxi services had shifted away from serving civilians to serving Parliament's needs. The world that awaited Hofmann when he walked outside wasn't the fine spring day he had met earlier that morning when he first entered Sandoz. Despite the radiant glow of the afternoon sunshine and a glitter in the air that echoed in him one of an

---

*Deliberate, in-house self-experimentation was frowned upon at Sandoz.

"enchanted" childhood memory, Hofmann had fallen into "a strange state of consciousness," a mere speck in the "strange new universe" that awaited him.[12] It was then that Hofmann made what was probably the most famous bicycle ride in history—"Bicycle Day" is still celebrated in Switzerland (and now San Francisco, California, and Portland, Oregon, among other cities) to commemorate that fateful event. After mounting his bicycle, Hofmann pedaled as swiftly as he could, yet complained to Ramstein that he could not get the wheels to turn.

But Albert, Ramstein must have thought, *you are moving—and quite rapidly!* Now she was in quite the peculiar presentiment, indeed: balancing Hofmann on his bike while maintaining her own. By the time Hofmann arrived home, the world as he knew it had descended into a deluge of terror and wonder. The chairs breathed; walls moved as if driven by an underlying possession. Some unknown force animated every corner of Hofmann's surroundings. But it didn't just end with his furniture; Hofmann, too, felt the pull of some unknown power bludgeoning his senses from within. "A demon had invaded me, had taken possession of my body, mind, and soul," he feared. "[Am] I dying? Was this the transition?"[13] Questions like these plagued his mind. Ramstein placed two phone calls: one to Anita Hofmann, Albert's wife, who was visiting family with their three children in Lucerne, and the other to Dr. Werner Stoll, a physician and the son of their boss. The younger Stoll, almost as perplexed as Hofmann, could not find anything wrong with Hofmann physically—his galaxy-sized pupils notwithstanding. As an "unspecific detoxicant," Hofmann drank two liters of milk delivered to him by his neighbor.[14] Only his neighbor wasn't kindly old Mrs. R, as she was normally known, but rather a "malevolent insidious witch," who only exacerbated the overwhelming anguish of the poor chemist. Hofmann recalls:

My fear and despair intensified, not only because a young family should lose its father, but also because I dreaded leaving my chemical research work . . . unfinished in the midst of fruitful, promising development. Another reflection took shape, an idea of bitter irony: if I was now forced to leave this world prematurely, it was because of this lysergic acid diethylamide that I myself had brought forth into the world.[15]

It seemed to be all over for Hofmann, whose wife and children, he was certain, would come home the next day to find him permanently deranged—or dead.

But he didn't die.

He calmed down and "began to enjoy [the] wonderful play of colors and forms, which it really was a pleasure to observe." The impending feeling of doom shifted to a state of tranquility and serenity. He had made it through the peak into a gentle plateau. Eventually he drifted off to sleep. The next morning, he awoke not in a maddened state, but in a renewed one. He would later recall, "I had the feeling that I saw the earth and the beauty of nature as it had been when it was created . . . it was a beautiful experience! I was reborn, seeing nature in quite a new light."[16] A rejuvenated Hofmann biked back to work. He wrote a report of the experience and sent one copy to his boss, and another to Rothlin, head of the Sandoz pharmacology department and the chemist who isolated ergotamine and discovered its usefulness for treating migraines.[17]* Thinking Hofmann had made a mistake in measuring his dose—how could a drop of LSD cause such wild aberrations?—both Stoll and Rothlin immediately (and independently) phoned him.

"Are you certain you made no mistakes in the weighing? Is the stated dose really correct?" asked Stoll.[18]

Hofmann replied in the affirmative.

---

*At other times, Hofmann claims that Stoll, not Rothlin, isolated ergotamine. See Albert Hofmann, *LSD and the Divine Scientist* (Rochester, Vt.: Park Street Press, 2011), 15. A copy of the patent proposal drafted by Stoll and Rothlin, submitted April 18, 1933, lists both men as the creators almost ten years to the day before Hofmann's famous bike ride, 19 April 1943.

Stoll had a right to suspect an error, for up until that day no substance had ever been known to work in such small doses *and* also prove profoundly effectual. Rothlin even accused Hofmann of exaggerating the effects of LSD, insisting that using willpower alone he could thwart any intoxicating effects.

Right.

Rothlin ate those words after he swallowed 60 micrograms of LSD—a fraction of what Hofmann had ingested. Hofmann burst into hearty belly laughs when Rothlin started speaking of "fantastic visions" within a few hours of taking LSD.[19] Stoll followed suit. His initial two experiences with LSD perfectly capture its dualistic nature. The first brought Stoll into the world of "romanticists and dreamers." As for his second run with LSD? "I was depressed and thought with interest of the possibility of suicide."[20] Ramstein became the fourth (and youngest) person to take LSD (opting for 100 micrograms). All three confirmed Hofmann's findings.

And thus, LSD, Albert Hofmann's wonder child, was born.

OF MICE AND MEDICINE

LSD raised more questions than it answered. Initial tests in animals failed to turn up anything substantial back in 1938. But in 1943 the situation was different; Sandoz chemists now had something to look for: *nuance.* Indeed, a higher-thinking animal had now seen how LSD affected the mind; subsequent animal tests would be observed through a more scrupulous eye. Rothlin oversaw the first animal studies, conducted by Aurelio Cerletti (1918–1988). Situated in Sandoz's pharmacology department, Cerletti dished LSD to arachnids and fish. Additionally, mice received injections of LSD and "were sacrificed at various time intervals" to see if and how "LSD-25 penetrated the brain."[21]

Still, LSD intoxication in these creatures turned up nothing interesting. For instance, the chemists observed how the spiders spun webs before and after exposure to LSD. Pre-LSD, the spiders produced webs that one might expect a spider to create—a more-or-less octagon-like mesh that spiraled into itself with minor imperfections. Spiders who were administered small doses of LSD weaved more finely geometric webs; but they became lethargic and indifferent to constructing webs altogether when given higher doses.

On the aquatic front, Siamese fighting fish swam slowly around the tank. Trance-like states were reported, though it seems unlikely that a person would be able to make a valid discernment between the actions of a tripping fish and a lucid one. Guppies, however, showed odd behavior. They would swim to the wall of the tank and keep bumping into it as if they were trying to break through the barrier of their environment.

Cerletti soon realized that the further up the evolutionary scale one ascended, the more perplexing the reactions to LSD. A certain "phenomenon" formed among the laboratory mice characterized by "motor hyperexitation." Hofmann had already confirmed back in 1938 that mice showed only disturbances in movement, nothing more. Cats displayed piloerection and apparently signs of hallucinating, as evidenced by their apparent gazing at unseen forces (though cats tend to do that anyway). Most curious, some cats even cowered before mice. Some peculiar reactions occurred in chimpanzees. A chimp removed from its community, exposed to LSD, and then returned, showed no signs of physical discomfort or anxiety. However, the chimp would cause quite a stir in the cage by ignoring all the social laws of the primate hierarchy. The other chimps ostracized their nonconformist member.[22]

But the most profound discoveries were observed in another kind of primate—the thinking ape. Humans. *Us.* While Hofmann made his way to Burghölzli Hospital in Zurich to test LSD on five schizophrenic patients,[23] Sandoz sent LSD samples to the University of Zurich where Werner Stoll (Arthur Stoll's son) worked in the psychiatric clinic. Stoll gave LSD to both the mentally healthy (*Normalpersonen*) and the mentally troubled (*Psychotikern*), his work often interrupted for military service. Stoll published the results of his studies in the *Schweizer Archiv* *fur Neurologie und Psychiatrie* (1947) the first of more than a thousand medical articles researchers would pen about LSD over the next decade. Stoll felt that the "euphoria" (*Euphorisierung*) experienced by volunteers and patients under LSD "could support a therapeutic effect."[24] Working alongside Stoll in the psychiatry department at the U. of Zurich, Dr. Gion Condrau (1919–2006) gave the chemical to thirty psychiatric patients and seven "normal individuals." Dose sizes hovered around 100 micrograms* (with one patient receiving 280 micrograms). Condrau also noticed that the psychiatric patients did not respond to LSD as obviously as had his healthy volunteers: "The disturbances in perception, consciousness and personality, were less marked in the psychotic than in the normal subjects and the LSD intoxication was milder," he noted.[25] This single line would color the LSD paradigm for the next decade; since psychotic patients felt the effects of LSD far less than regular people, Condrau proposed a novel (albeit grossly mistaken) hypothesis: "the question arises whether a substance similar to LSD is etiologically involved in psychosis."[26] *That* perhaps explained why psychotherapeutic subjects remained so resistant to the drug's effects—the chemical brains of those individuals, so the logic went, had already been flooded with whatever LSD-like chemical caused their illnesses. Adding LSD amounted to little more than pouring water into an already overflowing bucket. He closed his investigation with these sentiments: "LSD . . . offers nothing of direct promotional value. It is possible that the drug may eventually find use for experimental induction of psychotic states."[27] In other words, LSD's biggest promise rested in allowing the mentally fit to experience insanity for a few hours. Just as Jacques-Joseph Moreau had hoped cannabis would do in the previous century.

Stoll and Condrau's work at the U. of Zurich owed much to another article published several months earlier. G. Tayleur Stockings, a psychological medicines specialist at the City Mental Hospital in Birmingham,

---

*Condrau says that nineteen of the thirty patients took 100 gamma (micrograms); the 280 gamma dose notwithstanding, he says nothing more about the amounts of LSD taken by the other ten patients.

Alabama, had worked first with Pyrahexyl, a synthetic marijuana-like derivative that, when taken every morning, was said to make even "the saddest sack happy." Stockings gave Pyrahexyl to fifty manic-depressive persons who had been unresponsive to traditional psychotherapy. Of the fifty, thirty-six "felt much better, forgot their vague aches and pains [and] took a cheerful new lease on life."[28] The only problem, it seemed, was that Pyrahexyl caused psychological dependence when given in high doses. Perhaps a drug could be found that displayed similar effects in people but wasn't habit-forming.

◎

Behind the scenes of academic professionalism and peer-review studies, irresponsible use also ran through the psychiatry department at the U. of Zurich. One of the younger Stoll's colleagues had dosed another doctor's morning coffee with LSD as a prank. But pranks become problematic when they deal with the delicate intricacies of the mind. The poor fellow had a bad reaction and tried to swim Lake Zurich at below freezing temperatures. His colleagues quickly intervened before he reached the icy water. Apparently, there was more to LSD than just visual kaleidoscopes and auditory distortions.

Not all tests took place within the serene beauty of a sterile clinic. Hofmann also took LSD home for further experimentation. Although the terms "set" and "setting"* would not be coined for some time, that was exactly what Hofmann sought to test. "Around 1949 to 1951, I arranged some LSD sessions at home in the friendly and private company of two good friends of mine, the pharmacologist Professor Heribert-Konzett, and the writer Ernst Jünger," reflected Hofmann to a *High Times* reporter in 1976; "I did this in order to investigate the influence of the surroundings, of the outer and inner conditions on the LSD experience."[29]

---

*"Set" refers to the mindset of the person taking LSD (or related medicines). "Setting" refers to the environment in which the LSD (or related medicine) is taken.

◎

Hofmann's discovery was but one small part of a larger medical revolution happening throughout Europe. Over the course of the early twentieth century, considerable advances had taken place in medicine; new drugs emerged as ways of curing old ailments in new ways. On the other side of the Atlantic, American scientists followed close behind the European vanguard. Cannabis and opium usage, both sometimes mixed with each other and plants of the Solanacae family—the nightshades—like mandrake and henbane, steadily increased among the populations as a healthy form of mental escape. This trend continued into the twentieth century; by the Prohibitive 1920s, newer pharmaceuticals like barbiturates (first created in 1864) and amphetamines (1887), once used only to alleviate pain in the sick, increasingly replaced alcohol consumption as social and recreational drugs among the healthy. The following decade, appropriately remembered as the Great Depression, accelerated the process of turning medicine-taking into merriment-making. In 1935, French visitor and writer Andre L. Simon remarked in his *First American Impressions* that "millions of unfortunate people . . . at present live on their nerves and pills."[30] By the dawn of the 1950s, cigarettes, caffeine, barbiturates, amphetamines, and various other downers and uppers had found their way into American life. "The craving for ethyl alcohol and the opiates," wrote famed author Aldous Huxley (1894–1963), "has never been stronger, in these millions, than the love of God, of home, of children; even of life."[31] Although the use of psychedelic plants is as old as civilization, the twentieth century offered a pharmacopeia of new substances more readily available to people than at any other time in history.

LSD was one of these substances. First listed as an Investigational New Drug (IND) under the U.S. Food and Drug Administration's Food, Drug, and Cosmetics Act of 1938, LSD soon found favor among researchers applying for federal grants.

The senior Stoll and Hofmann proposed a therapeutic model during their pilot tests with LSD at Sandoz. It was after one of their volunteers had articulated a most inspiring thought; a thought that would create a paradigm for LSD just as Sandoz prepared to ship it out to foreign doctors for study: "I can watch myself all the time as in a mirror and realise my faults and mental inadequacies," the volunteer revealed.[32] This perspective would carry as much weight as Condrau's observation that LSD produced psychotic-like symptoms. The pamphlet that Sandoz sent out to physicians for study reflected both positions—that of Condrau and that of the volunteer; it stated that doctors might use LSD for either an adjunct to psychotherapy in hopes of "elicit[ing] release of repressed material," *a la* the previous volunteer's comments. This phenomenon—when a person recalls deeply subdued and/or forgotten memories—psychiatrists call "abreaction." Furthermore, the pamphlet echoed Condrau: "By taking Delysid . . . the psychiatrist is able to gain an insight in the world of ideas and sensations of mental patients. Delysid can also be used to induce model psychoses of short duration in normal subjects, thus facilitating studies on the pathogenesis of mental disease."[33] Sandoz quickly trademarked the artificial indole ring,* naming the experimental product "Delysid," after Hofmann's suggestion.[34] To Hofmann and Sandoz Laboratories, Delysid would soon become another mental health supplement that one would only need a prescription to obtain.

History would unfold . . . *differently.*

---

*Most psychedelics contain variations of biological substances called indolamines. These indolamines contain the indole ring, which is a six-membered benzene ring alloyed to a five-membered ring containing nitrogen. One endogenous indolamine in humans is the molecule serotonin. The variations in indolamines combine with methyl groups, a joining that makes the molecules more fat-soluble (lipophilic) and enables them to pervade the fatty membranes that cushion nerve endings. The molecules can now more easily pierce the central nervous system. Synthetic substances, like LSD, psilocybin (the psychedelic compound in "magic" mushrooms), and others, contain an indole ring or something molecularly similar.

4

Delysid

Seeking a Model Psychosis

*On the day after the LSD experiment I felt myself to be . . .
in excellent physical and mental condition.*

ALBERT HOFMANN

THE STRANGE CASE OF
DR. RINKEL AND MR. HYDE

~ *c. November 1949* ~

The assistant superintendent at Boston Psychopathic Hospital, Robert
Hyde (d. 1976), grew suspicious—paranoid even—but he could not
let his colleagues, Drs. Max Rinkel (1895–1966) and Herbert Jackson
DeShon (1901–1984), know. He sped up his pace, thinking maybe he
could lose them down some long hallway. But Rinkel and DeShon, ever
curious, matched Hyde's speed. Hyde's suspicion soon turned to frustra-
tion. *Why can't they just leave me alone so I can make my rounds through
the hospital unbothered? How can I possibly keep my mind on my tasks
with the sound of their footsteps tapping close behind?*

*Wait . . . their footsteps . . . are they louder than usual? And the sound
itself . . . is the echo of sole to linoleum almost . . . symphonic? Can clomps
create concerto? And their eyes . . . their eyes burrow holes into the back of
my head. Can I feel the gaze of eyes now?*

No . . . of course not.
That's crazy.

◎

But "crazy" seemed to be all the rage in the late 1940s—at least if measured by the amount of psychologists and psychiatrists being churned out of American universities between 1920 and 1940. For a variety of reasons (including the First Great War and the first Great Depression), a fascination with the mind began to evolve among many Americans. Jungian and Freudian lingo—once reserved for professional psychiatrists and psychologists—could now be found around common American dinner tables and discussed between clinking glasses at cocktail parties.[1]

The National Mental Health Act of 1946 instigated a second boom in the growth of mental health awareness; at the beginning of the forties decade, not even three thousand psychiatrists existed in America. By 1956, that number shot up to fifteen thousand. Still, even this most rapid explosion was not quick enough to keep up with the growing list of "conditions" discovered among the average person. In those days, a doctor could rather ingeniously transform even the mildest idiosyncrasies into some form of psychosis. As one historian notes of this era, "[h]appiness became euphoria; enthusiasm, mania; creativity was a socially approved outlet for neurosis, while homosexuality and other forms of deviant bedroom behavior were an indication of psychopathology. . . . Old age became senile psychosis."[2]

In the backdrop of all this brain activity was the surprising realization that biochemist Johann Ludwig Wilhelm Thudichum (1829–1901) had been right. Criticized for theorizing that the brain was largely a chemical soup (and penning the controversial *A Treatise on the Chemical Constitution of the Brain*, 1884), Thudichum dealt with the slings and arrows of popular scholarly consensus of his day. The accepted view held that the brain was a "single giant molecule" that experts called Protagon. Thudichum's heresy rocked the biochemistry world—his claims so brazen that his enemies eschewed respectful disagreement, dubbing him a "liar and falsifier."[3] Then in 1946—the same year Congress passed the National Mental Health Act—Swedish biologist Ulf von Euler (1905–1983) discovered norepinephrine, one of several chemicals that rouses the body to action against danger (part of our "fight or flight" response). The brain, indeed, was not a solitary, oversized molecule; and chemistry certainly played a part in how it functioned.

A new possibility emerged. If the brain had endogenous chemical components, might exogenous synthetic agents influence both perception and perspective? What if madness itself was the result of an imbalance of natural brain chemicals; could synthetic chemicals correct the imbalance? Equally intriguing was another possibility—could doctors trigger something like schizophrenia in an otherwise healthy person (presumably another doctor) to gain insight into the world of their patient?

Could doctors generate a model psychosis?

Hyde knew nothing of this strange new chemical—other than it supposedly made a sane person crazy for a few hours. That can be a tricky space to navigate. How does one properly prepare for such an ordeal in 1949? (Remember, Hyde didn't enjoy the same psychedelic contexts we know today: no Sergeant Pepper, no Summer of Love, no copy of Huxley's *The Doors of Perception* to turn to for a relatable passage to read. Even the CIA, which would soon develop a clandestine operation called MKUltra to study a variety of natural and synthetic chemical agents, knew nothing of LSD yet. Hyde had to keep himself together; he could not let on that he was indeed beginning to feel the first effects of 100 micrograms of Delysid.)

One hundred micrograms for a volunteer's initial LSD experience with a still relatively unknown substance? This was highly unusual. Sandoz had been clear that subjects taking LSD should start with small amounts and only gradually increase the dose.[4] Early studies with

Delysid in Europe, notably those of Stoll and Becker, were very clear on this point. But Rinkel, who supplied Hyde with the LSD, decided to avoid the microdoses and go for the throat; after all, it wasn't *his* mind on the line.

LSD can sneak up on a person.

One moment Hyde was telling himself he was fine; the next moment he started to grow anxious. He eventually lost his cool, snapping, "[Sandoz] cheated us . . . [they gave] us plain water." He proceeded to berate Rinkel and DeShon. This startled the two doctors. Hyde was usually a "friendly, pleasant man."[5] But at least for the while, Hyde's reprimands caused Rinkel and DeShon's feet to stop clomping and their eyes to sheepishly recede into their sockets.

NEGATIVE LOGIC

Although it is possible that an American ingested LSD before Hyde did in 1949, his is the first documented case.* Hyde had not sought the LSD experience nor wondered about using the chemical to unlock the secrets of the cosmos; neither had Rinkel. Both were interested in Delysid's ability to cause "a transitory psychotic disturbance" in an otherwise healthy individual.[6] But not so that they could have a better understanding of their patients' afflictions or help them abreact (as the Sandoz pamphlet recommended), but rather to find a cure for insanity. Rinkel informed his research with a "negative logic." He wanted to know how LSD worked in hopes of finding a way to reverse its effects.

---

*In Ellens and Roberts, *The Psychedelic Policy Quagmire,* Dr. Ben Sessa (for whom I have unyielding love and respect), in his wonderful essay "A Brief History of Psychedelics in Medical Practices," mentions Dr. Nicholas Bercel from the University of Southern California Medical School's Department of Physiology, who also took LSD in 1949 while visiting Sandoz, in Basel, Switzerland. Sessa writes that Hyde was only "the first person in America" to sample LSD, and that Bercel was actually the first American to try LSD, albeit not on American soil. However, despite his employment at an American university, Bercel was Hungarian (born and raised), leaving Hyde as the first American in the United States—so far as we can tell—to take LSD.

If the chemical truly induced a "model psychosis," and he could discover an antidote for it, then perhaps a similar medication could be produced that would eliminate comparable afflictions experienced by schizophrenics.

It could change the world.

◎

Rinkel had taken a job at the Boston Psychopathic Hospital in early 1949. Not long after, a couple of serendipitous meetings with two other doctors steered Rinkel toward Delysid. First was a "chance remark" made by the Director of Boston Psychopathic Hospital, Harry C. Solomon, to Rinkel that "we would know a great deal more about psychiatry if we were able to produce a psychosis experimentally."[7] Second, around the same time, was a speech Rinkel attended about LSD delivered by a professor of psychiatry at the University of Vienna, named Otto Kauders (1893–1949), who had visited the United States seeking grants for his research. It was Kauders who first promoted Hofmann's story on the western side of the Atlantic and the original Sandozian prescription that LSD rendered a person temporarily crazy.[8] Meeting with Rinkel after the speech, Kauders "insisted that [he] carry on experiments with [LSD]."[9] Kauders's influence on Rinkel was evident in the considerable amount of Delysid that Hyde had received—the Viennese psychiatrist believing that LSD's true power rested with the higher doses.[10]

The timing was nothing short of paramount.

Kauders passed on not long after, but presumably not before telling Rinkel how to obtain Delysid. Like any other doctor with the proper credentials, Rinkel need only fire off a letter to Ernest Rothlin, director of pharmacological laboratories at Sandoz Pharmaceuticals. Within a few weeks, Rinkel had his very own supply of Delysid. Within a few years, he had given that supply of Delysid to over one hundred (as he put it) "normal—as far as anyone can be considered normal" volunteers.[11]

Rinkel's protocol was simple enough. First, there were prescreens and a "pre-experimental evaluation" of every volunteer. Prescreening each volunteer not only weeded out those unfit for experimentation but also, so Rinkel believed, "allowed predictions of expected actions." "Normal subjects" received between 20 to 90 micrograms. "Psychotic patients" received higher doses, as "unanimous reports in the literature" demonstrated that these individuals "were particularly resilient" to LSD.[12]* Every volunteer had to drink their dose of Delysid mixed in water at 8:00 a.m. on test days; this way, no one knew who had received it. Occasionally, Rinkel kept the nurses and other medical observers in the dark about who drank the Delysid as well. The volunteer would then undergo a series of seven experiments throughout the week—from Rorschach tests to Draw-A-Person analyses.[13] However, this was not as simple as it sounds. Who exactly wants to take a test while in the throes of a psychedelic experience? One early Delysid subject in Baghdad, Iraq, complained of such exams: "I hate to really focus on anything closely. The air is full of shimmer like a heat wave."[14] Even the literary great, Aldous Huxley, who we will meet more in-depth in later chapters, commented during his first psychedelic experience: "The mind was primarily concerned, not with measures and locations, but with being and meaning."[15]

Can one really blame them?

THE GIRL WE'D LIKE TO GET TO KNOW

Her descent had evolved over a lifetime.

One moment she was yelling at her parents, the next she was proclaiming to her mother, "Last night I married God."

Twenty-three-year-old Marion Enders† (b. 1927) "laugh[ed] easily," and had a penchant for tweed skirts and a young man employed by the gas company. Within only a few months, she was "alternatively

---

*Doses depended on body weight. "Normal" patients received one gamma of LSD per kilogram of body weight; "psychotics" received three gamma of LSD per kilogram of body weight.

†Marion Enders is the name given to this woman by the author to conceal her identity.

moping in the wardroom of a mental hospital or screaming invitations to her funeral." The doctors were losing her; she was drifting deeper and deeper into the "horror tale" of schizophrenia.[16]

Enders grew up the younger sister of two elder brothers, born to wealthy parents in a New York suburb. She was precocious, both walking and talking at an earlier age than usual. But she was also stubborn, a characteristic her mother often pointed to as proof that Enders took after her father. In her preteen years she preferred books to boys, often going unkempt and making provocative statements at dinner. By fifteen, she was an honor roll student, but showed no interest in making friends with anyone, and still paid no attention to young men. One of her brothers took her to the prom. Just below her high school yearbook picture someone inscribed the words, "The girl we'd like to get to know."

After numerous treatments failed to impede Enders's symptoms, she finally found relief with histamine. Histamine is synthesized from histidine, an amino acid in the human body, and was used as a way to balance the endocrine system. Tests with histamine had started in the 1930s, but successes in the 1940s led one author to claim by 1950, "The development of histamine therapy and other recent experiments have stirred the hope that insanity can be prevented, perhaps cured by drugs and chemicals. . . . Therefore a world-wide effort is being made to discover the physical causes of mental disease and to find new, helpful drugs."[17]

The longest running study with histamine had started in 1945 and terminated in 1950. Conducted by a group at Creedmoor State Hospital in Queens Village, New York, histamine found employment as a way "to arrest the relentless psychotic processes which cause the brain of the schizophrenic to deteriorate." The results proved encouraging to say the least, as the Creedmoor group reportedly "doubled the number of patients who could be released." Schizophrenics "particularly benefited" from the treatment, as did "neurotics" who found "immediate relief" from "acute anxiety and tension."[18]

⊚

Dr. Rinkel first announced the strange case of Mr. Hyde and subsequent tests with "normal" subjects at the 106th annual meeting of the American Psychological Association's (APA) Convention at Detroit's Book-Cadillac Hotel in May 1950. The APA had just seen a recent boom in membership—569 new constituents had joined since January, bringing the association to 5,247 members.[19] The Creedmoor doctors also spoke at the meeting. They impressed Rinkel, who listened to their presentation on histamine and schizophrenia with "great respect and attention."[20] But he was also excited to tell his colleagues about the "different angle" he and the others at Boston Psychopathic Hospital currently pursued. Sure, histamine calmed aggressive symptoms in some mental disorders. But what if that were just putting a band-aid over a bullet wound? What if understanding mental disease from *within* could give insights that went beyond histamine? Rinkel addressed the congress:

> In order to understand a disease, or a psychosis, it would be of great advantage if one could experimentally produce a psychosis. We are in the fortunate position to have a chemical . . . with which we could produce a transitory psychotic disturbance.

Drawing attention to the fact that both histamine and LSD derived from ergot, Rinkel then noted this was where the similarities ended.

> While with histamine treatment the patient thought more clearly, our patients had difficulty in thinking. . . . They had strange sensations; their limbs felt like lead. . . . They had illusionary experiences. . . . They saw figures on the wall, and the walls were moving. Some became quite silly, laughing without being happy or gay, and some became very talkative. However, the content of what they produced was very shallow.

Rinkel's team had even decided to record the LSD sessions, though he is quick to admit that some of the recordings are "almost gruesome to listen to."[21]

Dr. Frank Co Tui, a Creedmoor chap who had earlier cofounded the American Bureau for Medical Advancement in China, was intrigued. "Is it a form of drug intoxication—a type like that of cocaine poisoning?" he asked.

Rinkel answered confidently that he knew of no other chemical that caused such bizarre symptoms in only microscopic amounts.

Raymond Sackler, another Creedmoor fellow, was curious about LSD's physiological effects. Besides lowered blood pressure, dry mouth, and clamminess, Rinkel mentioned certain "subjective symptoms, which objectively could not be corroborated."[22]

But none of the tests with Delysid at Boston Psychopathic Hospital had terminated yet, leaving Rinkel enthusiastic, but coy. He says no more about LSD at the conference—at least nothing recorded in the minutes; as exciting as Delysid struck him, funding did not yet match enthusiasm.

By the following year, that would change. In Rochester, New York, the owners of one of the most successful family-owned department store chains of the twentieth century, the McCurdy Company, developed an interest in LSD. We do not know which McCurdy family member found LSD a worthwhile endeavor, or what they hoped the research would accomplish. I will offer my own speculations on this matter in a later chapter, where the topic comes up again; for now, let's just say that someone at the McCurdy Company, for some unknown reason, granted Rinkel and Hyde a large enough sum of money to keep tests with LSD operational for a while.

And it certainly paid off.

Due to the McCurdy grant, Rinkel had much more to say about Delysid and so-called "transitory psychoses" the following year, in May 1951, at the 107th annual meeting of the APA: "Clear-cut blunting of affect and suspiciousness, as often seen in schizophrenic patients were outstanding. These symptoms frequently led to feelings of indifference and unreality. . . . The subjects experienced hostility and resentment, and on rare occasions ambivalence." In only one instance did Rinkel's team observe a volunteer experience an auditory hallucination—the volunteer heard bells, though no one else did. Two patients (a male volunteer and a female schizophrenic) thought they peed themselves while on Delysid but hadn't (although, the woman later did wet her bed). One schizophrenic woman (who took an unknown amount of Delysid*) first stared blankly around the room. She then got on her knees, "kissing the wall, the floor, the examining table," eventually ripping her clothes off and turning loud and unruly. Deciding to terminate the experiment, Rinkel had her injected with sodium amytal, a depressant to counteract the effects of LSD.[23]

These were the kinds of experiences Rinkel reported to his colleagues. At no point, he maintained, did his team "observe the happy and dreamy feeling of ecstasy as it has been described by other authors who experiment with L.S.D." In fact, quite the contrary, "[m]orbid ideas were common." Though, we should note that Rinkel gave nonpatient volunteers "relatively small" amounts of Delysid—not enough to promote a deep, visionary state. Even the kind of visual that could trigger a mystical experience—like a wall thermostat morphing into a crucifix—Rinkel recorded as merely "an illusion."[24]

As we now know, a person who takes LSD is highly susceptible to environmental factors. More importantly, with the Boston Psychopathic Hospital team seeing the LSD experience through the lens of a "model psychosis," we are left wondering how many people—both patient and volunteer—might have had a truly enlightening experience, which Rinkel recorded as one of two subtypes of schizophrenia: hebephrenic and hypomanic. Briefly, hebephrenics—named for Hebe, the ancient Greek goddess of youth—tend to act inappropriately in social situations;

---

*Rinkel tells us she drank three gamma per kilogram of body weight, but we have no idea how much she weighed.

this is also called "disorganized schizophrenia." Laughing, giddiness, spontaneity, and dulled emotions furnish the psyche of a hebephrenic whether they are at a rock concert or a funeral. Hypomania refers to those with narcissistic personality disorders or bipolar disorders (in other words, they shift from happy to sad at a moment's notice).

◎

Reports from other researchers steadily accumulated, bolstering some of Rinkel's theories while challenging others. One of the more notable experiments emerged via the research of Drs. Anthony Busch (b. 1906) and Warren Johnson (1923–2014) at the St. Louis State Hospital in the Washington University Medical School in Missouri, which had begun in earnest as early as 1950. Notwithstanding the Boston Psychopathic Hospital team, Busch and Johnson were some of the earliest Americans to work with Delysid. Their first major exploration into the effects of LSD dealt with giving it to twenty-nine patients. They subdivided these patients into two groups: Group "A" numbered twenty-one "psychotic" females and Group "B" numbered eight psychotherapeutic patients (two males and six females).

Upon taking LSD, those in Group A exhibited a wide spectrum of disturbances in their minds and bodies. Most became excitable; others fell into "short periods of confusion and distortion and . . . transitory visual hallucinations . . . most patients exhibited some degree of euphoria."[25] Nausea, rapid pulse rates, and gastric distress accompanied by vomiting also occurred.[26]* The vagueness of the reactions puzzled the doctors.

---

*These physical symptoms (such as nausea, vomiting, rapid pulse, etc.) run counter to tests conducted by Gordon R. Forrer, M.D., and Richard D. Goldner, M.D., at the Ypsilanti State Hospital in Michigan. Their tests included six schizophrenic patients who had been chosen "on the basis of poor prognosis and failure to respond to other types of therapy." Each patient received LSD seven times for a total of forty-two treatments. The doctors wrote in their report: "Contrary to the findings of other investigators, nausea, vomiting, and anorexia were not prominent in the present group of patients. In a total of 42 treatments vomiting was experienced three times." Forrer and Goldner, "Experimental Physiological Studies," 583.

Busch and Johnson's eight psychotherapeutic patients (Group B) experienced very different reactions to those recorded among the psychotic patients (Group A). Those in Group B took LSD and apparently circumvented the "disturbing barrier of repression . . . permitting re-examination of significant experiences of the past, which sometimes were relived with frightening realism." The abreaction theory of Delysid once again proved fatidic. An unspecified number of these eight patients were able to "re-evaluate emotional meaning of their symptoms and were improved. Most were better able to organize their ideas. Two patients [improved] sufficiently to discontinue treatment."[27]

Still, like Rinkel, Busch and Johnson were stuck in the original Sandozian model: LSD caused "a transitory delirious state";[28] nothing more.

What Busch and Johnson had witnessed in their Group B patients—LSD acting as a key that possibly unlocked the Freudian unconscious—would be looked at throughout the 1950s as a psychological breakthrough. To some early researchers, LSD pierced the veil that blocked the subconscious and allowed "recall of experiences provoking anxiety and fear without sluggishness of speech . . . or marked confusion." And although it was still highly questionable, Busch and Johnson postulated that LSD "may serve as a new tool for shortening therapy."[29] Perhaps there was a way to stop patients like the eight subjects in Group B from descending into the perpetual madness that made up those in Group A.

ENTER ADRENOCHROME

~ Sometime in 1952 ~
Humphry Osmond (1917–2004) and John Smythies (1922–2019), two psychiatrists working at the Weyburn Medical Hospital in Saskatchewan, Canada, readied themselves to ingest mescaline for the first time. They took the mescaline for two reasons. Like other researchers of the time, Osmond and Smythies believed it would allow them

access into the mind of a schizophrenic. What other researchers had overlooked in their quest to find the best synthetic mind drug was—oddly enough—*natural* mind drugs. A book by Alexandre Rouhier, *Le Peyotl,* described in detail the Mesoamerican shaman's divine cactus of visions, peyote, which Smythies had recently heard about through another colleague. Flipping through the pages, he and Osmond found pictures and diagrams of peyote. The molecular design of mescaline, a synthetic derivative of peyote's active alkaloids, caught the doctors' attention. They noted the molecular similarities between mescaline and the endogenous human hormone adrenaline, which is part of the "fight or flight" reaction to stress. With that in mind, Osmond and Smythies hypothesized a possible connection between the schizophrenic state and naturally occurring adrenaline in some psychotic patients. This was their second reason for taking mescaline . . .

Osmond had always been "a real pioneer in research ideas," as his colleague and frequent writing partner Abram Hoffer (1917–2009), a research psychiatrist who worked at the University Hospital of Saskatoon, recalls.[30] Writing on his experiences with mescaline (and later LSD and psilocybin—the psychedelic compound in "magic" mushrooms), Osmond wrote:

> [E]ven the best written book must fail to transmit an experience that many claim is incommunicable, and the doctor often wishes that he could enter the illness and see with a madman's eyes, hear with his ears, and feel with his skin. This might seem an unlikely privilege, but it is available to anyone who is prepared to take a small quantity of the alkaloid mescaline or a minute amount of the ergot-like substance lysergic acid diethylamide, which transmits the taker into another world for a few hours.[31]

Osmond had begun his research within the *psychotomimeticist* school of thought and opined that natural chemicals caused schizophrenia. His conjecture, dubbed the M-factor theory, posited that the overproduction of a structurally similar chemical to mescaline and/or LSD in the brain might cause psychosis. A request sent to Imperial Chemical to develop a compound that would bridge the gap between mescaline and adrenaline ended up in failure. Molecular diagrams of mescaline and adrenaline may have looked similar in book illustrations but they were worlds apart under a microscope. Undeterred, Osmond focused his attention on the chemical structures of amenochromes—metabolites that are produced through the corrosion of adrenaline. Of the amenochromes, adrenochrome seemed the most likely candidate as an endogenous psychosis-producing chemical, due to its similarities with mescaline. Perhaps it would succeed where adrenaline had failed? In 1952, Osmond injected himself with homemade adrenochrome, the results confirming what many researchers believed at the time to be model psychosis. Osmond "felt hostile" toward the doctors who supervised his trial run with adrenochrome. "I didn't want to talk to them . . . [i]t was a feeling of being intruded upon," he explained. The following morning, he felt "extremely lively and active and interested, in fact, rather hyperactive."[32] This initial harsh reaction coupled with later feelings of hyperactivity drew close parallels to some hypomanic schizophrenic patients under observation at Saskatchewan Mental Hospital, Weyburne. Jane Osmond (1924–2009), Humphry's wife, grew worried. "I sometimes dream that Humphry's taken the ultimate drug—the one that makes him permanently schizophrenic."[33] Nonetheless, his "streamlined hyperactive mind" forced him to keep exploring the furthest reaches of his psyche though weird chemicals, both natural and synthetic.[34]

Intrigued by adrenochrome's performance, Osmond gave it to Hoffer, who, in turn, gave it to his wife, Rose. For several days thereafter Rose felt trapped "in what was clearly a clinical depression. She had lost insight . . . [and] everything seemed so hopeless and she didn't have any energy."[35] Although the symptoms wore off after a few days, these initial reactions in both Osmond and Mrs. Hoffer fascinated and troubled the Canadian psychiatrists. They felt that further examination of adrenochrome was necessary if they were to understand how that drug affected the mind. Unfortunately for Osmond and Smythies, adreno-chrome proved highly unstable and their supply deteriorated shortly after Mrs. Hoffer's adrenochrome depression.

Impressed with Osmond and Mrs. Hoffer's reactions, Rinkel, who was still busily working in Boston with Delysid, also tried to obtain adrenochrome. However, none was available, and Rinkel decided to use a more stable derivative of adrenochrome, which was then widely employed during surgery as a hemostatic (a bleeding or hemorrhage suppressant). This little change made a large difference. Rinkel noted, "our experiments had a completely negative result. No mental alterations were experienced or observed, and no mental symptoms had been reported."[36]

Rinkel determined that Osmond and Hoffer's experiences with adrenochrome had to do with it having been homemade. He hypothesized that adrenoxine, a byproduct of deteriorating adrenochrome, may have been what caused the psychosis in the Canadians. Rinkel concluded, "Adrenoxine, in addition to its LSD-like physiological effects, also may have mental effects similar to those obtained by LSD interference with the adrenaline cycle. If this assumption proves to be correct," he reasoned, still pursuing his negative logic, "the conclusion will become inevitable that adrenoxine, a natural metabolite of the decomposition of adrenalin, may well be operative in psychosis."[37] Adrenoxine seemed to confirm the M-factor theory for the time, but researchers nonetheless continued to remain fascinated by LSD.

Back in Saskatchewan Mental Hospital, Weyburn, Hoffer experimented with another psychoactive chemical, nicotinic acid, and postulated that it "would modify the LSD psychosis." It did, although not as expected. Instead of accelerating LSD's effects, Hoffer found that an injection of nicotinic acid "given at the height of the LSD experience resulted in a striking reduction in all LSD-induced disturbances."[38] In a "reverse type of experiment," Hoffer gave nicotinic acid to patients for three consecutive days before giving them LSD. Psychotomimetic phenomena were not as apparent on the fourth day when LSD was administered, and took longer to reveal themselves in the patients.

Hoffer concluded that consistent administration of nicotinic acid prior to LSD ingestion "split the changes into the neurological and psychiatric . . . [nicotinic acid] prevents most of the neurological changes, the automatic changes; yet permits many of the psychiatric changes to run their course."[39] Hoffer felt that if he could find a chemical similarity between LSD and schizophrenia, nicotinic acid might be the cure Rinkel had so long sought. Unfortunately, as testing continued, the doctors soon discovered that the LSD state was very different from the schizophrenic state, and thus the very premise of Rinkel's theory became a dead issue.

LYSERGIZED

Still there remained a plethora of areas to explore. Doctors began to note changes in hostility, spurred on by Hyde's initial experience with Delysid. He wrote both a follow-up report of his experience (now lost) and a paper that dealt with "hostility in the lysergic psychosis." Hyde studied ten "lysergized subjects" who received an unreported amount of LSD in order to measure the "relationship between their affective interplay with other persons and the degree and quality of their distortion of these other persons." The results, which may seem self-evident to us today, were not yet properly understood in those days. When the subject's "interplay attitude" remained congenial under Delysid, they spoke in "soft and warm" tones, "glowing with youth and health." Hostile attitudes devalued the object in question. For example, a face would turn diabolical or flat. Of the 233 "important relationships" examined, Hyde concluded that the "thoughts and feelings about other persons and objects gained reality through visual distortion."[40]

In other words, Delysid can briefly manifest one's thoughts into visual realities.

Working alongside Hyde in these aggression studies was Harvard sociologist Kiyo Morimoto (1918–2004). Only Morimoto took the concept a step further, developing a study that gauged "the sociopsychological behavior" of the lysergized. Morimoto outlined four human reactions to interpersonal relationships: *away,* which dealt with "avoidance, withdrawal, denial" of the individual; *against,* which dealt with "hostile, punitive, competitive" behavior; *toward,* or "seeking of nurturance, support, reassurance"; and *with,* which included "brotherly, friendly, reciprocal, equalitarian" behavior. Forty-three volunteers participated in Morimoto's study, the majority exhibiting the more antisocial behaviors (*away, against*) instead of the more positive and social (*toward, with*).[41] One sixty-five-year-old woman who had been hospitalized for around twenty-five years for "agitated depression" underwent a lobotomy, after which she "became calm, and no outward sign of fear or anxiety could be detected." Six weeks later, she received an unknown amount of Delysid. She immediately fell back into her "original state of agitated depression, asking for help, saying that everything was lost, and expressing feelings of guilt."[42]

But not everyone responded in such a way. One young man "who ha[d] been usually aggressive, occasionally assault[ing] aides and doctors, spit[ting] in the doctor's face" suddenly "began to laugh hilariously" a half-hour after taking Delysid. He had no explanation for his giddiness beyond feeling "so happy." In fact, during his entire trial with LSD (which may have been a few weeks or months), he never once had a single "aggressive outburst."[43] Another patient "who was commonly assaultive," so much so that she was often secluded from the other patients, "became calm, friendly and laughed" once she took Delysid. She even tried to kiss one of the female aides.

When she seemed safe to approach, the doctors asked how she was feeling.

"Crazy."[44]

◎

LSD was so clearly *different.* So much of the experience depended on the doctor. And the patient. And the setting. *All* of it. Delysid made the subtlest feeling—the most infinitesimal emotional vibration—as palpable as an earthquake. The wrong motion at an inopportune moment could send the lysergized individual spiraling into hell. It was like mescaline . . . *but not really*—there was simply no other medicine with which to compare this remarkable new wonder child. How did the volunteer feel? What did the volunteer expect? Even knowing the answers to these questions held no guarantee that the lysergized volunteers would behave according to clinical protocols, best guesses, and theories.

But there was hope. Early on, doctors noticed that their behavior had an *enormous* effect on their lysergized patients. Some shrinks ignored the dynamics of this phenomenon, while others paid special attention to it. Dr. Juliana Day (1919–2013), medical officer and psychiatrist working at the National Institute of Mental Health in Bethesda, Maryland, fell into the latter category, "adjusting the venetian blinds" in the experiment room to cut "the painful brightness" experienced by some of her volunteers. If a patient started to cry, she "reached for the Kleenex more swiftly than usual."[45] As Day saw it, therapists administering LSD had two obstacles to overcome: first, they needed to suppress their own feelings of helplessness, anxiety, and distance in the face of a patient having a harsh reaction to Delysid. This was no easy task, as giving *anyone* Delysid "sets in motion certain processes . . . which are out of the therapists' and the patient's control." Stoicism was key. This point fed directly into her second observed obstacle regarding the therapists' role in an LSD session: never interrupt the patient or volunteer—especially if they are about to pontificate "marvelous sensations." Day had watched a film titled *The Schizophrenic Model Psychosis Induced by LSD,* and couldn't believe how many times the doctors would interrupt their patients when the latter abreacted. The irony was not lost on her, "Here was just the experience [the doctor] wished to record—a subject with an impressive reaction to the drug effect. Yet, he attempted to interrupt the drug effect."[46]

Further tests supported the abreaction potential of Delysid—sometimes without even trying. In Ypsilanti State Hospital in Michigan, Drs. Gordon Forrer (1922–2015) and Richard Goldner (1924–2018) had begun their ventures testing not the mental effects of LSD but rather the physiological effects. These studies included blood pressure readings, pulse and respiration rates, pupillary dilation monitoring, and urinalysis. The doctors measured these physiological functions while consistently increasing doses of LSD. Except for a boost in the heart rate and dilated pupils, Forrer and Goldner didn't note any major aberrations in their write-up regarding their patients' physiology. In fact, they felt that LSD was both "an extremely safe and relatively nontoxic drug."[47]

Despite the nature of their physiological studies, they nonetheless noticed "definite psychotic changes" in their patients' mentalities that included "increased spontaneous verbal productivity and alteration from [a] surly antagonistic attitude toward the physician to amiability, talkativeness, euphoria, and outbursts of laughter." One of these patients recalled while on LSD "a homosexual episode which he had as a youth and which had not previously been accessible."[48]

In a few short years, from 1949 to 1952, LSD went from showing promise as a way to mimic madness to leaving researchers even more confused. The model psychosis hypotheses aimed to contribute to two major areas of schizophrenia. Some doctors hoped to gain insight into their patients' mental health issues by "experiencing" said issues. Others, like Rinkel, hoped to create psychosis and then carefully unweave it. When the researchers finally determined that LSD was nothing like schizophrenia (or any form of mental illness), they were left with little more than the abreaction theory of Delysid to investigate.

But theirs is not the only clinical LSD story born of the 1950s. Indeed, across the pond in Great Britain, a handful of doctors would not only embrace the abreaction potential of LSD, but, in their enthusiasm, invent what we today call "psychedelic psychotherapy."

5

The Great Lips

An Intentional Approach to Set and Setting

Some of these patients (treated with LSD) equate forgiveness of sins with healing.

CHARLES SAVAGE

THE LIFE-GIVING SPIRIT

~ *December 1952* ~

Deputy Medical Superintendent at Powick Hospital in Worchester, England, Dr. Ronald Sandison (1916–2010) understood the odd predicament in which he found himself. He had just returned home from Sandoz with a box of Delysid that December. While LSD held no negative connotations back then, many therapists nonetheless still frowned upon the use of medicine—any medicine—as an adjunct in psychotherapy. Sandison knew that substances like LSD stood "in relation to orthodox psychiatry, rather as alchemy in the time of Galen stood to medical treatment."[1] Even the great Carl Jung, as just one example, frowned upon LSD therapy.[2]

Powick Hospital seemed an odd location for LSD experiments. Built in 1852 with a two-hundred-patient capacity, the hospital housed a thousand people by the time Sandison arrived that September 1951 to take his new position as consultant psychiatrist. A "grey and dismal" institution, Powick had the feel of "all the schools, orphanages, and prisons of Charlotte Brontë and Dickens wrapped into one."[3] Even Sandison himself remarked how the hospital was "bleak in the extreme."[4] But it had its charms as well. Over 550 acres of "ancient farmland" called White Chimneys supplied Powick's backdrop. The grounds featured a chapel that the residents refigured into a store and a barn that they refigured into a chapel. Up until the Edwardian Age, Powick was "a self-sufficient village . . . many patients were employed in its departments."[5] All head nurses were required to know how to play at least one musical instrument.

Sandison went right to work updating the facilities, hiring additional staff, creating outpatient treatment centers, and more. He also introduced a new form of evaluation for those who came to reside at Powick—psychotherapy. It took him an entire calendar year to get the place up to snuff, but by September 1952, Powick had been transformed (at least bureaucratically—it was still a drab, Dickensian nightmare). By December, the hospital could function soundly from its own well-oiled inertia, granting Sandison the freedom to accept an invitation from Dr. Isobel Wilson (1895–1982), senior commissioner of the Board of Control,* to tour mental hospitals in Switzerland. At the beginning of their tour they made two visits—not to a hospital, but to a laboratory, Sandoz Pharmaceuticals. On their first visit, Sandison and Wilson met with Cerletti, the pharmacologist who had been experimenting with LSD on fish and arachnids, and his colleague Rudolph Bircher (1914–1966). On their second visit, they met with Albert Hofmann. Hofmann noticed Sandison's excitement with LSD and was receptive, gifting him copies of the few published papers regarding the strange new chemical. Most importantly, Hofmann also entrusted Sandison with a box filled with one hundred ampoules of pure Sandoz LSD.

---

*In 1960 the Board of Control was replaced with the now more familiar Ministry of Health, of which Wilson took position as the principal medical officer.

Returning to Powick Hospital, Sandison began clinical experiments with LSD. Working only with two others—Drs. Arthur Spencer and John Whitelaw—Sandison had no overseer and could therefore test Delysid for Sandoz's two stated purposes: to plumb the subconscious mind for materials that he could then discuss in therapeutic settings, and give doctors insight into madness. Sandison was game for both— only his natural introversion led him to ingest Delysid just three times.

Based on the Sandoz recommendations, Sandison, Spencer, and Whitelaw quickly set about developing a protocol for administering Delysid to patients. The first step seemed self-evident: use a less-powerful drug to introduce each patient to the concept of medication-assisted therapy. Pentothal, an anti-anxiety drug, would serve this purpose. Once the patient graduated from Pentothal, they received a starter dose of 25 micrograms of Delysid, which would be increased two or three times a week; under careful observation, each patient would up their dose until either the correct amount was individually gauged or the test was terminated— this process usually taking from two to four weeks. Once the doctors deemed Delysid safe for further treatment, a patient might take their "active" dose upward of forty times. They even allowed one to take LSD at home; another was administered a whopping 400 micrograms!

The first major study at Powick Hospital involved thirty-six hospitalized "psychoneurotic" patients who took LSD over the course of one year.* The program yielded some initial insights. Firstly, the doctors found no correlation "between the duration of the illness and the number of treatments required." In other words, whereas a couple of LSD sessions might cure a severe case of psychoneurosis, more mild cases might take months of intensive psychedelic psychotherapy. There was no way of telling what particular circumstances would lead to a fast recovery or a deeper descent into despair. Sandison also determined that "material of value" only started to come through in their patients after four or five LSD sessions—whether severe or mild.[6]

---

*Of the thirty-six volunteers, only one dropped out of the study.

At some moments, Sandison could sound downright mystical. Take his description of a woman who, after ingesting Delysid, seems to have tripped something inside her that burned for something beyond material existence. Sandison writes that she developed "a great hunger and thirst, a craving from something she knew not what." Eventually this manifested in desires for "mother-love and the need for the life-giving spirit." Delysid caused her to "come alive . . . she had a great sense of mind and spirit."[7] Another patient, who "was tortured with all sorts of obsessions regarding water," had finally found relief from her compulsion. Driven to perform lengthy "washing rituals" that could take up to eight hours to complete, she had been free of such habits for at least two years after her LSD treatment.[8]

The original thirty-six patients eventually grew into ninety, with "most encouraging" results: 55 percent recovered and stayed well, 12 percent showed no improvement at all, and the remaining 33 percent showed "various degrees of adjustment compatible with a reasonable life outside the hospital."[9] Sandison and the team noticed "early in the LSD studies . . . three types of LSD experiences." One type included "[g]eneralized nonspecific images . . . coloured patterns and other hallucinatory experiences of the non-personal kind." Another was typified by "the experiencing of archaic, impersonal images . . . of the collective unconscious." But the experience that intrigued the doctors the most was the way the majority of their patients relived or recalled birth trauma.[10] For some women, this form of trauma manifested in birth pangs, as if they were delivering an invisible child into the world. For others (both women and men), this included re-experiencing birth.

One man in particular was especially descriptive in his report of this phenomenon:

> I'm going to make the effort of being born now. I am pulling back great walls of thick slime to find an opening, but I have not found an opening yet . . . I have found the vaginal passage, and I have found the great lips of the vagina sealed. . . . I am pressing against them

with my feet and hands and the seals are giving way. . . . I feel I must grow away from the womb, I feel I have left it, but not quite. I have been returning to the womb and seeing myself as a sperm swimming about, and others dying, clinging to the wall of the womb and then falling away.

It all reminded Sandison of "the recognition by many religions of the importance of re-birth."[11] Psychenauts* today are all too familiar with the "death/rebirth" experience, but things were not so obvious in the early 1950s, as the doctors were still working in a "model psychosis" paradigm. Some psychologists raised concerns about whether these rebirth experiences represented authentic or fabricated memories, arguing that "memory cannot go back as far as birth." In these doctors' estimations, the cortex had not sufficiently developed enough to store memories yet. Other researchers begged to differ. A certain Professor Elkes, who worked closely with Delysid, showed that the drug had "selective action on certain parts of the mid-brain and medulla, which are present even in the embryo" making it possible that "restimulation of these cells could be translated into the original experience through the adult brain with its later cortical development."[12]

In other words, the extent of the authenticity of these abreacted, early childhood experiences was far from a finished discussion. As we will see, some of those who abreacted particularly early memories had family members who served as eyewitnesses for (and later confirmed) some of the traumatic events they described during their Delysid sessions.

News spread about the success of LSD, inspiring others to work with this strange chemical. The deputy chief male nurse at Powick Hospital, E. Ball, conducted studies on "nursing and care of mentally-ill patients"

---

*To further distance these substances from the term *psychotomimetic,* I prefer "psychenaut" to "psychonaut."

with LSD. Ball's approach differed from Sandison's in one fundamental way: he didn't feel it necessary to ease a patient into the study with a warm-up drug like Pentothal. He felt that the nurse's value for the patient presented itself at the height of the LSD experience, "the reaction," as he called it, when "[f]ears of insanity and suicidal tendencies" could manifest.[13]

Ball also seemed keen on a concept that is very popular among psychenauts today, but was virtually unheard of in the early 1950s: *integration*. Patients were "encouraged a few days after treatment to write, paint, or draw an account of their experience when under LSD 25." Additionally, he set up a special center "where patients of both sexes meet to discuss their LSD experience."[14] But it seems as if integration flowed throughout Powick Hospital. Sandison, too, spoke of Delysid eliciting a "[s]econd, inner self; the neglected side of the personality, which must be integrated into consciousness if the personality is to be developed."[15] For Sandison, LSD offered keen insight into the Jungian shadow.

Perhaps this focus on integration is what sowed the seeds of the need for a special place within Powick Hospital that could be dedicated to LSD entirely. In 1955, Sandison requested (and gained) approval from the Regional Hospital Board to expand their work and create a space dedicated to LSD. This new "LSD Block" came equipped with eight rooms: five rooms for patients that consisted of a couch, a chalkboard, and a chair; two rooms for nurses; and a post-LSD session meeting area.[16]

That same year the Jungian analyst Margot Cutner (1905–1987) joined the staff at Powick Hospital. Like Sandison, Cutner was a rarity in the field—a fellow Jungian harboring a desire to work with LSD, even in the face of Jung's disapproval. She didn't care much for biochemistry and/or LSD's potential as a key to unlock the secrets of schizophrenia. Instead Cutner's fascination with LSD rested "solely . . . with the psychotherapeutic aspect of the work with the drug and the way in which it can be integrated into general analytical procedure."[17] It was Cutner who first demonstrated that the subconscious material that bubbled up from the strangest depths of the psyche when invoked by LSD "far from being chaotic, reveals, on the contrary, a definite relationship to the psychological needs of the patient."[18] Rinkel had been wrong. Indeed, everyone had been wrong. Through the Jungian frame, those lysergized "babbles" were really "archetypes." It was all in knowing how to decipher them. For Cutner, LSD provided a decoder-ring for trauma. The Jungian collective unconscious, and all its undiagnosed pains and forgotten disturbances, could now be brought to the fore for dissection.

Her influence would have a major impact on the hospital.

Within three years the LSD Block at Powick was revamped into "an environment in which traumatic childhood experiences could be relived in the emotional security of a family-like group." Sandison's research partner Spencer spearheaded the project, eventually designing the new wing with rooms that included toys, a sandbox, a piano, a record player, and even a small petting zoo. Sometimes patients would tape record their experiences, although many grew uncomfortable when they listened back after the session. One woman commented that listening to the recording "was like hearing her soul speaking." And the patients were no longer confined to the inside walls of the wing. Merrily under the spell of Delysid, they might walk among the grounds, "pick flowers, and even swim naked in a nearby brook."[19]

However, this lenient approach might not have been the best strategy for everyone, as two of Sandison's patients attempted to drown themselves. One even spoke of developing "drowning fantasies."[20] Needless to say, access to the brook shrunk to a privileged few.

~ May 1955 ~

While this might not jive with modern sensibilities, it is nonetheless true: during the 1950s, both homosexuality and forms of sexual fetishism were seen as mental disorders. In fact, Whitelaw developed an interest in working specifically with the rebirth experience (under the wider gaze of abreaction) and funneling it down into a specific study that would explore LSD's potential to uncover the psychological origins of fetishism and/or homosexuality. Whitelaw reports on a thirty-three-year-old man—let's call him "Mac" for ease—who first entered Powick Hospital that spring. Mac had been married a year earlier and still had not yet consummated the courtship. Since a young age, Mac had fetishized both raincoats and golf trousers—something about the feel (and sound) of rubber rubbing against itself excited him. Through a series of thirty-two LSD sessions that ended in March 1956, Mac clawed his way deeper into the abysses of childhood trauma. During one sitting, he recalled receiving a "white rubber doll" at age one that he cuddled at night—this fact later confirmed by his mother. As he grew older, he came to associate a special importance with people who wore raincoats, dubbing them "rubber people." Rubber equaled comfort—a shield against bogeymen and monsters under his bed. It wasn't long after that (around age eight to ten) when he was donning his own mackintosh living the life of a bona fide "rubber person."[21] By the time he hit puberty Mac would wait for the safe solitude of nightfall; he would then put on a raincoat and tie himself up while he lay in bed.[22]

And then, *of course,* he masturbated.

Now in his adult life, Mac felt his compulsion had "sapped his confidence," which, in turn, manifested in an unhappy marriage. He turned to the study of language as a defense against suicidal depression.[23]

Thankfully, Mac would eventually have a rebirth experience with LSD—or maybe it was more a rebirth insight? While in session, he found himself "in his mother's womb and had a barrier to penetrate to enter a new world where his fetish did not exist." In another session, he held dialogue with a "wise and kind old man," who Mac took to be the "father . . . of us all." This holy father tried to "make [Mac] fit" for his wife.[24] And yet, even this awe-inspiring experience could not override decades of conditioned behavior.

But this is where the rubber meets the . . . *skin.* Now that Mac had broken through to the other side, he could at last explore the terrain of repressed emotion. In September 1955, while in session, a vision of a hand emerging from a biker's black, rubber sleeve appeared before him.

He decided to go with it, and followed the revelation back to "a stage in early childhood when pleasant emotion was aroused when he was deprived of comfort by being tied up or locked in an uncomfortable place."[25] Numerous sessions brought more abundant insights, and by January 1956, Mac "felt loathing for the fetish for the first time and 'wished to destroy the person who worshiped it.'" His final session occurred two months later. After ingesting the Delysid, Mac reached a place in his subconscious mind so ecstatic that he "imagin[ed] himself tied to something." The experience proved so rapturous that he erupted in his loins in front of the doctors.[26]

Whitelaw noted, "The pleasure seemed to arise from feeling himself utterly at the mercy of someone or something. Sometimes the thought consisted of imagining himself being confined hopelessly in a very small space into which he could just fit."[27] And so, with LSD, that which was once hidden became illuminated: beneath it all—white dolls, linguistic studies, raincoats, biker threads, suicidal thoughts, rubber people, and feelings of inadequacy—Mac was just a sexual masochist, the byproduct of feeling alone and unloved as a child. Any attention—even negative attention—he viewed as exhilarating.

~ *On an otherwise quiet night, September 1956* ~

Mac finally banged his very patient wife. A calendar year later, he was reporting "regular and successful relations," which eventually resulted in a pregnancy.

He discontinued treatment soon thereafter.

NERO PATHOLOGY

A two-and-a-half-hour drive west from Powick Hospital used to bring motorists to the Marlborough Day Hospital in London,* where other tests into sexual "deviance"—at least by 1950s standards—took place.

---

*Today known as the Marlborough Family Day Unit.

Indeed, in those days, doctors did not just label fetishism as a pathological condition; homosexuality, too, they considered a psychotic disorder that warranted medical attention. In fact, one of Sandison's original thirty-six patients was homosexual. But Sandison never considered a full-scale study on whether or not LSD could be used as a form of gay conversion therapy.

But one doctor at Marlborough did.

Heading up the studies, Dr. Joyce Martin (1905–1969) treated twelve gay men using LSD—well, *almost*. While they are all labeled "homosexual," there is evidence that two of them weren't so much gay as they were pedophiles; one of whom found "[i]nterest in older men" after LSD treatment. The other comes with the eerie note, "Compulsion for boys less. Sublimation in politics."[28]

In the mid-1950s, most psychiatrists who felt that homosexuality constituted a kind of mental disorder fell into one of three schools of thought on the subject. *The Congenital School* held that homosexuality was hereditary and nothing could be done about it. *The Complex Adaptation School* did not think homosexuality was an inborn trait, but rather a behavior picked up over time and experience. *The Arrested Development School*—of which Martin considered herself a student—based its philosophies on those of Freud. The famed Austrian shrink believed that homosexuality represented a stage in early childhood development that every person went through. While most moved through this phase and grew into heterosexual adults, some experienced traumatic incidents during this stage that kept their sexual minds locked in that time. Since Delysid already had a reputation for abreaction, Martin wanted to see if she could use it to uncover the precise moment a person became "stuck" in homosexuality. Then, once the roots had been identified, transference could take place. Deciding she'd rather work with outpatients than inpatients, Martin set up her criteria for selecting suitable candidates for the test; such things like "[n]o history of any previous psychotic episodes," "high intelligence," "good ego development," and "a strong desire to get well" fit her profile.[29]

Of her twelve selected subjects, Martin reported seven as "[h]eterosexually oriented" after LSD treatment, three of whom were married; two of whom, she noted, were "happily" married. An eighth man had a "[m]ore responsible job" and was "[m]eeting girls socially."[30]

Like Whitelaw's study at Powick Hospital, the true insights into the phantastic '50s come not from numbers, tables, and statistics, but instead from the individual stories of those treated with LSD. One tale concerns a thirty-two-year-old Jewish man, Ben, who came to Marlborough Day Hospital after jumping from one clinic to the next "receiv[ing] every possible form of treatment."[31]

None of it worked. By the time Ben reached Powick Hospital, he was "extremely miserable and desperate." His backstory is sad, but all too common for queers of all kinds living in the 1950s. His homosexuality (which he "despised") left him "feeling antisocial and completely unable to get on with people at work or in private." He couldn't hold down a job for more than a few weeks, as he would always come to believe that his coworkers secretly hated him.

Ben had grown suicidal; LSD was his "last hope."[32]

He didn't even pass Martin's criteria for Delysid treatment. Something about him made her uncomfortable. He was so "weak and unstable" that—*forget abreaction*—Martin feared LSD might inspire in him "a paranoid psychosis . . . a more deranged and unstable personality." Not easily deterred, Martin decided to "take this risk anyway."[33] Beginning with 50 micrograms of Delysid, Ben realized that his suspicions of his neighbors and coworkers were unfounded. No one was out to get him. For the first time, Martin saw not a distressed Ben, but a "more co-operative" Ben.[34] She decided to up the dose to 75 micrograms at the next session.

This time, he abreacted.

His body temperature dropped drastically and he started screaming at Martin for "neglecting him." The more blankets Martin piled on his shivering body, the more Ben berated her for the chilliness he felt. Keep in mind this session took place on a "hot July day." He cried out that he was "lying in a pool of blood" and again insulted Martin for not tending to him.[35]

Here's what was happening:

In Ben's mind, he had just been born and was sitting in the after-birth. No one cared; everyone was busy tending to his mother, who had been sick the days leading up to the delivery. Ben was reliving his birth right before Martin. When the session ended, Martin asked Ben to follow-up with a family member about his mother's health at the time he was born. His aunt confirmed that Ben's mother was indeed ill—possibly suffering a hemorrhage—during her labor with him. After the experience—and because of it—Ben would later tell Martin that blood no longer made him squeamish.[36]

He had passed through the great lips.

Upping the dose to 100 micrograms of Delysid at the next treatment sent Ben back to his early childhood when he would spend days in a bar looked over by prostitutes while his mother worked. They would often taunt him by telling him licentious stories and "be amused because he had a big penis, and they told him what to do with it." Sadly, the impressionable Ben took the sex workers' advice and "went around exposing himself to girls," which obviously earned him a bad reputation. He grew angry during the session and started shouting obscenities at the nurses and nuns. By the next treatment, which saw Ben taking 125 micrograms, "rape desires developed very quickly" toward any woman on staff, but most specifically toward Martin, who fluctuated between being the object of Ben's abuse one moment and then being courted for sex in the next. But this allowed him to work through some very difficult recollections—for example a sexual assault perpetrated against his mother at age ten. As difficult as reliving that experience must have been, it "liberated a tremendous amount of guilt and shame."[37]

By 150 micrograms, no one was safe from Ben. He manifested within himself "a great feeling of omnipotence, and that he was the Emperor Nero." He began to devilishly outline his gruesome plans for the innocent masses—torture, murder, genocide, all fair game to this ruthless demagogue; Martin even noted the "great pleasure" Nero felt from reveling in his sadistic fantasies. When the Delysid had waned, Ben—not surprisingly—wanted to uncover the origins of such heinous and barbaric visions. He concluded that he "had never forgiven his mother for deserting him by going to work . . . and had killed off his father and taken on his role herself." At this point Ben admitted that he had initially feared Martin in much the same way, but that he no longer did.[38] Ben relived childhood fantasies about killing his mother, and realized "these were the feelings that put him off to women, and made him afraid to approach them."[39]

Ben only received a few more treatments after that (in the 200 microgram range) that allowed him to both abreact and "continue working through the transference situation."[40] He finally understood "the feelings he had as a child for his mother . . . [and] his grandmother and grandfather, all of which he in turn projected onto [Martin] and was able now to make them conscious, and assimilate them into his conscious personality."[41]

Putting aside our contemporary thoughts on the matter of treating homosexuality as a form of psychosis, this method appears to have worked for Ben. A year after he stopped seeing Martin, he not only found a job and stuck with it, but also wed one of the nurses who oversaw his LSD sessions (whether he was one of the two "happily married" gents of the study remains unclear). A follow-up interview five years later revealed that they were still married.

BEHIND THE UNIVERSE

Two years after her initial study with homosexuality, Martin started another one—this time with fifty "chronic psychoneurotic" patients. The fifty were funneled into four groups: nineteen "obsessionals," six "psychopaths," three "sexual neurotics," and twenty-two in states of "chronic tension." Of the nineteen obsessionals, only one "recovered" totally, while six "greatly improved," ten "slightly improved," and two did not improve at all. Of the six "psychopaths," three recovered, two greatly improved, and one "slightly improved." Those dealing with "sexual neurosis" (which probably meant anything other than straight, vanilla sex) ended with one greatly improved and one slightly improved. Of the twenty-two patients dealing with chronic tension, one recovered, five improved greatly, fourteen improved slightly, and two had not improved at all.[42]

One of these fifty patients was a thirty-year-old married mother of three children. She was sexually immature "on an exhibitionist level." An alcoholic for a decade, she had also attempted suicide three times and spent a few months behind bars (during which time her husband cheated on her) before reaching Marlborough Day Hospital. During her first Delysid session she relived a memory of her husband strangling her, which was later confirmed. Additional treatments stirred memories of abuse by a matron at an orphanage where she ended up after her mother passed away. As the Delysid pulled her mind deeper into these unpleasant reminiscences, she vomited and writhed around screaming on the floor. Visions and memories rushed through her head like a waterfall: she recalled the sadness of her mother's death, that awful matron at the orphanage, the feelings of loneliness, her abusive husband—all of which resulted in "exaggerated exhibitionist response to the opposite sex."[43]

She eventually overcame her sexual immaturity through the mysterious power of Delysid. At the Second International Congress for Psychiatry held in 1957, Martin revealed something to the audience that she felt worth mentioning: "disintegration of the ego under LSD leads to a beneficial effect deriving from the experience of belonging to and being accepted by a higher mind behind the universe. This appears to cause stabilisation and integration of the personality."[44]

At both Powick and Marlborough Day Hospitals, we see the beginnings of "dose, set, and setting" and even "integration." Additionally, while the tests at Powick Hospital indicated that "tense, driving obsessional patients" did well with LSD in ways that, say, "shallow, affectionless hysterics" did not, the team found that "successes in treatment [were] not confined to any one class of neurosis."[45] While LSD held no promises of curing *everyone,* it did seem in those days like it could cure *anything.*

A MEETING OF THE MINDS

Sandison's calendar filled up more and more as he received one speaking offer after the next. In 1955, the American Psychiatric Association (APA) requested his presence at their annual meeting. The APA conference organizers sought to include a "round table" discussion about LSD and by that time Sandison's experiments were well on the psychiatric community's radar. Instead of taking an airplane to the United States, Sandison fulfilled a lifelong dream: on April 30, 1955, he set sail on the *Parthia,* a cargo ship outfitted to accommodate seventy passengers. As the *Parthia* took to the horizon on that foggy spring morning, Sandison couldn't help but notice how LSD shared much in common with the deep blue sea. "The sea requires that those who sail on her do so with knowledge, respect and true love," he reflected. "LSD, like the sea, was prepared to destroy those who used it without full knowledge, or without respect and love."[46]

The conference took place in New Jersey, courtesy of a large sponsorship from one of Sandoz's offices in Hanover, a small township in that state. There, Sandison would join an impressive roster in the first ever "Round Table Discussion on the uses of LSD and Mescaline" in history. But the conference was important for two other reasons, if only symbolically. In the first instance, as we will see in the next few chapters, by 1955 the CIA had infiltrated the medical community working with LSD. Second, among the doctors and psychiatrists at the round table sat a most surprising gent, the literary giant Aldous Huxley.

How CIA-funded scientists, independent researchers, and a fiction writer ended up at the same conference will be the subject of the next few chapters.

6
Mind Fields
Weaponizing LSD

I have used narcotic hypnosis successfully as a means of eliciting confessions of guilt of all degrees.

J. STEPHEN HORSLEY

A NEW LOOK

~ *May 8, 1945* ~

The war was over.

Hitler was dead.

Led by General Dwight D. Eisenhower, American forces had joined England and France (and in the end, Russia), ultimately winning the Second World War; he had also won the admiration of his homeland as evidenced by his overwhelming victory in the '52 presidential election. Eisenhower had seen the horrors of battle firsthand; when he took office, he initiated a New Look program to avoid a third World War. The New Look sought to create a manageable balance between domestic and foreign problems under the auspices of the National Security Council (formed in 1947). To achieve this goal, the New Look not only emphasized nuclear deterrence but also prized imaginative chemical weaponry tactics over conventional warfare. Eisenhower's scientific advisor, George Kistiakowsky, best exemplified imaginative chemical weaponry when he created "Aunt Jemima," a gooey pancake-like mix that was perfect for baking homemade cookies, but that could also be used as an explosive.[1] The timing was convenient. Like most intelligence operations, the CIA's drug tests were secretly underway before they were officially authorized. Allen Dulles (1893–1969), brother of Secretary of State John Foster Dulles, became the director of the CIA's Clandestine Services Department twenty-six days after the latter took position as Eisenhower's right-hand man.

◎

The Cold War was an odd period for many Americans. New and disconcerting phrases had entered the lexicon—*atomic weapons, arms race, bloc countries*—making it seem as if, despite the victory over the Axis Powers, the world might still fall apart. By 1953, even popular publications like *Newsweek* ran stories about "some drug or 'lie serum'" donning headlines like "Washed Brains of POWs: Can They be Rewashed?"[2] Out of the still-settling ashes of the Second Great War, an apocalyptic rivalry between the United States and the Soviet Union arose, both countries harboring antithetical visions of the postwar world.

And the Soviets had backup. The People's Republic of China and communist uprisings in several other countries caused quite the stir among many Americans, especially those in the Pentagon. Most troubling, intelligence reports had claimed that Josef Stalin (1878–1953) busily stockpiled as much raw material as possible to create massive amounts of LSD. All this led Sidney Gottlieb (1918–1999), the head of the CIA's infamous mind-control project, MKUltra, to recall:

> To mention just a few examples, there was concern about the apparent manipulated conversations of Americans interned in Red China for a short time; there was also concern about apparently irrational remarks made by a senior American diplomat returning from the Soviet Union; perhaps most immediate and urgent in our minds

was the apparent buying up of the world supply of that little-known new psychogenic material LSD; lastly, there was a growing library of documented instances of routine use by the Soviet Security Services to covertly administer drugs.[3]

The extent of the Soviet Union's fascination with LSD and mind control in general remained unclear. But American intelligence looked to the 1949 trial of Hungarian Archbishop of Esztergom, József Cardinal Mindszenty (1892–1975), for answers. The communists had come to power in 1945 after the Soviet Red Army had expelled the Germans from Hungary. That same year, the ruling communists seized the lands of the Catholic Church (along with the churches of other denominations), their schools, and assorted properties. In 1948, authorities arrested Mindszenty, an ardent antagonist of the land grabs (and communism altogether), on charges of treason. During a sensational trial, Mindszenty admitted to perpetrating crimes that many believed he did not commit. This baffled the CIA; one particular memorandum claimed that some "unknown force" had rendered Mindszenty "zombie-like."[4] Incidentally, Mindszenty's confession came after five weeks of torture. But in times of war—even a cold war—nothing can be taken lightly. At the time of Mindszenty's trial, the CIA did not know about the torture. They believed the Hungarian authorities had used psychoactive substances with which to draw the bogus confessions. As such, they justified MKUltra.

And so the CIA, the Bureau of Narcotics (BON), and the U.S. Navy began a two-decade long search for the ultimate mind-control drug as the newest means of unconventional warfare.

TWILIGHT SLEEP

The unfortunate man made his final pleas for mercy as the hands around his neck choked the last breaths of his life away. He was a lynching victim, only the noose had not killed him. One of those in the crowd decided to take the matter into his own hands—strangling the poor man to death. Among the ghoulish cheers from the mob as they celebrated the gruesome spectacle before them, Dr. Robert Ernest House (1875–1930) had a thought—a thought that might have well served this barbarically executed individual not but five minutes earlier: *What if he wasn't guilty? What if this unruly mob just murdered a man who did nothing wrong?* As it turned out, evidence eventually surfaced proving his innocence.[5]

House was a religious man who, despite his participation in a lynching, felt motivated by "a higher order of duty."[6] Such a calling gave him an uncanny ability to ignore critics later in life. Born and raised in Farmer's Branch, Texas (fifteen miles northwest of Dallas), House received his medical degree from Tulane University in 1899, later settling in Ferris (twenty miles southeast of Dallas) with his wife Mary Alma Orr and two sons.

House is largely remembered as "the father of truth serum."[7] His serum of choice was scopolamine. Scopolamine is the active alkaloid found in henbane, mandrake, and belladonna—the so-called "hexing herbs" employed by medieval and early modern wise-women. Indeed, these plants would be mixed in the "flying ointments" that carried them away to "witch dances" on mountaintops like the Heuberg and Blocksberg.[8]

Around the time that House settled in Ferris, German doctors, notably Richard von Steinbuchel (1865–1952) in Freiburg, busily experimented with mixing scopolamine and morphine as an aid in childbirth. The concoction had two effects: the morphine "dulled labor pains without materially interfering with the muscular contractions of labor"; the scopolamine induced amnesia of the experience.[9] Von Steinbuchel had been trying to reduce pain, not cause a narcotic stupor; though, as time went on, his focus shifted to the latter. He eventually started using the mixture to induce a "hypnotic condition," called *dämmerschalf* or "twilight sleep." And this twilight sleep was causing quite a stir—both in Europe and America. The euphoria experienced under twilight sleep

was apparently very enticing. One medicine company invested in scopolamine pills advertised that women would "cancel their engagements
with their old physicians to secure the attendance of those who employ
the Hyoscin-Morphin-Cactin tablet." Another writer, with a fair degree
of humor, remarked how twilight sleep was so desirable it was "enough
to make a man break down and weep because he [c]ould not have
a baby."[10]

Problems quickly mounted, mostly in the form of overdoses. Soon
many obstetricians rejected such a powerful combination of substances.
By 1915 twilight sleep had fallen completely out of their favor.[11]

But something else besides women's health and euphoric pills had
piqued the interest of criminologists. As a person drifted out of twilight
sleep (and anesthesia in general), they were "prone to make extremely
naïve remarks about personal matters, which, in their normal state,
would never have revealed."[12] And most enthusiastic about these prospects was House. House first discovered twilight sleep while in New
York. Floored by the combined power of morphine and scopolamine,
he quickly brought the mix back to Texas and began experimenting.
He gave the blend to some five hundred of his own patients, as well as
inmates of federal penitentiaries. While testing his methods on prisoners at San Quentin, House injected one veteran with scopolamine. This
particular inmate had had no memory of life before the Meuse–*Argonne*
offensive of World War I (September 26, 1918–November 11, 1918),
when a grenade exploded near his head. To House's surprise, this veteran abreacted! Memories from his earlier life came flooding through
his consciousness.

House was enthralled. He shot off a series of letters to various mental hospitals encouraging them to give scopolamine a chance as an aid in
therapy. By the end of his career, House had a reverence for scopolamine
as a panacea unmatched by anyone else of his day. In the *Diagnosis and
Treatment of Insanity by the Detection of Delusion* (1929), House almost

sounds like he has descended from Mount Sinai with baskets full of scopolamine as he justifies why he wrote the paper in the first place:

1) In respect to the Creator who gave to mankind scopolamine; 2) it is the most useful drug for the control of the insane; 3) it ranks supreme in the humane treatment of addicts; 4) in my opinion, it is God's greatest gift to the parturient woman; 5) it will serve more medical requirements than any one drug to be found in the U.S. Pharmacopeia; 6) it is the most abused and least understood drug which should be regarded as a friend to the physician.[13]

Others, like Dr. William F. Lorenz (1882–1958) at the University of Wisconsin's Psychiatric Institute, who had conducted similar trials with sodium amytal in the 1930s, did not agree with House at all (although, he does not seem to have been privy to the man's work). In his own reports, Lorenz wrote that the term "truth serum" was largely baseless. Due to scopolamine's ability to cause amnesia, Lorenz classified it as a delirifacient—a maker of delirium. He also felt that sodium amytal worked better—and didn't require the addition of morphine.[14] In fact, he administered sodium amytal to Harold Best, who stood trial for murder in Crawford County, Wisconsin. The judge ordered Lorenz to "make whatever examinations . . . advisable and necessary" to pull the truth from Best. Lorenz injected Best with sodium amytal and questioned him. Despite an objection from the plaintiff's counsel, the drug-induced testimony was admitted into court.[15]

This, more or less, represents the extent of American studies into the question of whether a skilled interrogator could administer a chemical substance to an obstinate criminal, traitor, enemy, or otherwise for the sake of gaining information.

That was, until, the Office of Strategic Services (OSS)—the fore-runner of the CIA—decided to study the mind's ability to endure highly psychoactive substances (like mescaline) in the late 1940s. OSS examinations ranged from testing the resilience of captured

U.S. soldiers enduring an enemy's brainwashing efforts to the dosing of unknowing citizens to see how they would react to a possible Soviet mind-drug attack.

~ *Sometime in 1945* ~

Intelligence officials turned their eyes to mescaline after an OSS-directed mission called "Project Paperclip"* brought it back to America from Germany. Under Paperclip, scientists, engineers, and military commanders combed Germany for "every scrap of industrial material and scientific data that could be gathered from the fallen Reich."[16] Along with knowledge of V-Weapons (*Vergeltungswaffen* or "Vengeance Weapons") the team also returned with evidence of mescaline-based Nazi brainwashing experiments at Dachau, a concentration camp for political prisoners directed by Hubertus Strughold (1898– 1986). Walter Neff, a former prisoner of Dachau that later testified at Nuremberg, spoke of how mescaline made the unfortunate prisoners divulge all kinds of secrets from sexual habits to anti-Nazism. Hitler had considered the possibilities of psychological warfare; to win the Cold War, American intelligence needed to pursue every possible angle.

The Dachau mescaline discovery opened the door to concepts that the OSS had overlooked in the past. As a result of Paperclip's findings, some six hundred Nazi scientists, who otherwise should have been tried at Nuremburg, ended up employed by the U.S. government in a variety of scientific positions. Some, like Strughold, found work at NASA, where he is remembered as the "father of space medicine." The Aeromedical Library at the U.S. Air Force School of Aerospace Medicine was named for him in 1977. Strughold's prized brainwashing tool, mescaline, eventually proved useless as a truth serum. But the newly formed CIA (1947) had no plans of giving up the search.

---

*The Office of Strategic Services was the forerunner of the CIA. The name "Project Paperclip" was rumored "to have originated because scientific recruits' papers were paperclipped [*sic*] with regular immigration forms." See "Recruitment of Germans: Project Paperclip."

Mescaline, it was felt, appeared to work some of the time; it was all in how the questions were asked. Straightforward demands were met with fear and confusion; circuitous, open-ended questions sometimes led to usable intelligence. Thus, mescaline stayed on the scene, often mixed with other sedatives or mood enhancers.

But not everyone was excited about Paperclip. General Leslie Groves (1896–1970) sent a memorandum to the War Department in 1946 stating clearly his objection to the program. At the time, Groves had directed the notorious Manhattan Project and feared foreign influence infiltrating that program:

> [I do] not desire to utilize the services of foreign scientists in the United States, either directly with the [Manhattan] Project or any other affiliated organization. This has consistently been my views [*sic*]. . . . I strongly recommend against foreign physicists coming in contact with our atomic energy program in any way. If they are allowed to see or discuss the work of the Project, the security of our information would get out of control.[17]

Capturing Nazi scientists for Allied gain actually preceded Project Paperclip. Even as American infantry stormed the beaches of Normandy, scores of intelligence agents (called T-Forces) followed in tow. The T-Forces' mission was straightforward: apprehend technicians, scientists, munitions specialists, and anyone and anything else they could collect that dealt in the war sciences. Predating Groves as a critic for these measures, President Franklin Delano Roosevelt (1882–1945) dismissed the idea of bringing Nazi scientists onto American soil before the Second Great War had even ended. He had been approached by both Allen Dulles (then head of intelligence operations for the OSS) and William "Wild Bill" Donovan (1883–1959, head of the OSS) to authorize such capture-the-flag tactics in 1944. Roosevelt rejected the proposal with sober pragmatism: "we can expect that the number of Germans who are anxious to save their skins and property will rapidly increase. Among them may be some who should properly be tried for war crimes, or at least arrested for active participation in Nazi activities. . . . I am not prepared to authorize the giving of guarantees."[18]

The president lost this debate. Many believed that staffing Nazi war criminals "was justified as necessary to the continuing war against Japan." A secret agenda, Operation Overcast, successfully immigrated Nazi scientists like Wernher von Braun (1912–1977) to America. Von Braun had worked the Dora concentration camp near the southern Harz Mountains, where slave labor in the Mittelwerk complex was *de rigueur*. There, von Braun often ordered the Gestapo to club weaker children to death, seen as they were as nothing more than "useless mouths."[19]

~ *August 1952* ~

The four travelers waited patiently and silently at Andrews Air Force Base. Three of the four we can account for: there was Navy commander and pharmacologist Samuel Thompson; University of Rochester chair of the psychology department who did side work for the Navy, Richard Wendt (1906–1977); and Wendt's assistant, a young woman whose mere presence irked the other three. We know neither her name nor that of the fourth person. Thompson oversaw the Navy's mind-control venture, dubbed Project CHATTER (established in 1947), which independently contracted Wendt to work with that program. They would soon board a plane that would take them to Frankfurt, Germany, where they would meet with a CIA agent.

Then, CHATTER's drug experiments would commence.

Project CHATTER used a smorgasbord of substances like mescaline, caffeine, heroin, and cannabis on human subjects "in interrogations and recruitments of agents."[20] Thompson justified the project: "[If] someone planted an A-Bomb in one of our cities and we had twelve hours to find out from a person where it was. . . . What could we do to make him talk?"[21] At times, mind torture occurred while the subjects were under the influence. Mind torture included such disgraceful acts like dosing unsuspecting subjects and threatening to keep them in semi-psychotic states indefinitely. CHATTER grew significantly during the Korean War but ended shortly thereafter.

While the U.S Navy ran CHATTER, the CIA adopted its own program, Project Bluebird, which unwaveringly "look[ed] into brainwashing."[22] With Colonel Sheffield Edwards (1902–1975) acting as director, Bluebird took flight as the first major systematic attempt by the CIA to succeed in "readjusting" the brains of POWs, possible double agents, informers, and others.

Edwards took two overseas trips: first to Japan where three Bluebird operatives tried to use mescaline, sodium amytal (a depressant), and Benzedrine (a stimulant) in hopes of inducing amnesia in four Japanese subjects. The second trip found Edwards in North Korea, where he tried similar drug combinations on twenty-five POWs. The reports from both trips read vaguely, meaning that the missions produced no clear results. For six years, military personnel, volunteers, and others tested a variety of psychoactive substances to see if they could find a secret trigger into the human psyche that would turn an obstinate POW into a stool pigeon.

But no trigger emerged.

No door unlocked.

Far from beaten, the CIA again sent scientific teams all over the world to find, seize, and bring back to America stronger mind drugs—preferably ones that could remain undetected. Indeed, one of the problems with the assessments (besides the palpable immorality of it all) was that substances like mescaline "had such a bitter taste that it was not possible to keep the human subjects from knowing about the tests."[23] The moment someone tasted something weird in their coffee or soft drink, they knew they were the target that day.

Then, late in 1951, a most troubling report reached the CIA claiming that the Politburo had received a hefty supply of LSD from Sandoz—enough for fifty million doses![24] Two years later, while speaking at Princeton University's National Alumni Conference, Allen Dulles remarked about "how sinister the battle for men's minds had become in Soviet hands."[25] That same year (1953), MKUltra officially formed. The intelligence turned out to be mistaken; Sandoz had made no such deal with the Politburo. But no one in 1951—or '53 for that matter—knew that yet. Two CIA scientists quickly boarded a plane bound for Switzerland with $240,000 cash—not one drop of LSD should be left at Sandoz; they were to buy it *all*. Once arrived, they met with the heads of Sandoz and struck a deal. Sandoz would send the Agency 100 grams per week and keep the agents abreast of any requests for Delysid from the Eastern bloc.[26]

LSD had joined the arms race.

7

Academic Espionage

Lucy in Disguise with Doctors

Should the course of recent history have been slightly different from what it was, I can easily imagine a congressional meeting being extremely critical of the agency for not having done investigations of this nature.

SIDNEY GOTTLIEB

Thank God there is something decent coming out of our bag of dirty tricks. We are delighted.

ALLEN DULLES

TRUTH SERUM

MKUltra led a most surreptitious life.

While it saw much potential in LSD, the program dealt with a variety of chemicals and compounds. But it was LSD that dazzled Agency personnel the most. Multiple subprojects under MKUltra quickly developed. Such tactics like dosing unsuspecting government officials with LSD at the office and during countryside work retreats, slipping LSD to regular civilians in CIA safe-houses and asylum patients, and giving various chemicals to children at undisclosed laboratories all fill out those opaque years.

It gets . . . *messy.*

In *Poisoner in Chief* (2019) journalist Stephen Kinzer suggested that the CIA sought "a way to control the human mind [with] nothing less than global mastery" in sight.[1] However, there is little evidence to support his claim. The surviving MKUltra source materials strike this historian as more paranoid than bold, reading closer to a bizarrely histrionic fear of communism than anything like a plan for global hegemony. Might MKUltra have evolved into a totally dominating force over the planet if it survived?

Perhaps.

But that doesn't seem to have been the agency's motive. At no point do we find documents mentioning "global mastery," or anything of that sort.

The first CIA tests occurred as in-house dosings of LSD. MKUltra head, Gottlieb, while being grilled by Senator Robert Kennedy in 1977, later remarked on "that period when there was an extensive amount of self-experimentation for the reason that we felt that a first-hand knowledge of the subjective effects of these drugs were [*sic*] important to those of us who were involved in the program."[2] Remarkably, most dosings were taken in stride. But every now and then someone had a harsh reaction. The number of agents and lower-level office employees dosed will remain unknown, though a few anecdotes survive. For example, one dude descended into agony when he realized the ultimate truth about automobiles—they had been invented to turn into monsters and eat him! By the end of the day, he was relieved to be perfectly fine, although somewhat embarrassed by his behavior.[3]

Perhaps these adolescent pranks were not the best methods for unlocking the secrets of Delysid. Some Agency officials started to wonder if they could use some help from researchers who had already been experimenting with mind drugs—ideally doctors already employed by a government body. One of the first tapped by the CIA was Dr. Charles Savage (1918–2007).

Savage had considerable experience working with mescaline during the latter half of the 1940s. His extensive inquiries made him question psychoactive-drug therapy. One alcoholic whom he assisted in 1949 was "so guarded that he would not even admit to drinking." However, after a few sessions, the drinker finally opened up to Savage, admitting that what he had been revealing to the doctor over the past three months was "a mass of ingeniously constructed fabrications, many even lies."[4] Savage's conclusion regarding this particular volunteer was that the mescaline caused the doctor-patient relationship to progress too quickly for him. The patient eventually stopped seeing Savage altogether.

Although Savage ended his mescaline studies ultimately indecisive regarding psychoactive treatment, he pounced on the opportunity to work with a new mind drug, a wonder child that supposedly trumped the mescaline experience, and only necessitated microscopic doses. The State Department, CIA, and U.S. Navy, of course, heavily monitored the LSD imports coming from Sandoz, and in 1952 Savage received his very own supply. But Savage might not have been the best doctor with which to start. He was a true intellectual—infinitely curious and little concerned with the opinions of his overseers. He graciously accepted government paychecks and support, all the while continuing along with his own research interests. For Delysid fascinated him beyond any covert motive. "The opinions and assertions contained herein," declared Savage in his first report on the use of LSD in 1952, "are the private ones of the writer and are not to be construed as official or reflecting the views of the naval service at large." Savage sought a different approach to Delysid—one self-evident today, but novel in his day. Focusing on a vague possibility that had come up during Stoll's first descriptions of his tests with Delysid, Savage decided to study the euphoric nature of the drug—specifically, "if such a euphoria might be of value in the treatment of depression."[5]

However, this strategy seemed to rely *heavily* on how responsive a person was to the "ego-death" experience. As many seasoned psychenauts will concur, "bad trips" usually arise as a result of a person fighting the experience. Their ego is dissolving and they do not want to let it go. And while Savage never used the term "ego death," we can certainly feel that sentiment in his following description: "Some individuals find the distortion of reality too threatening, and instead of euphoria there is a heightened anxiety, a desperate holding on and an effort to maintain control of the situation, together with a heightened suspicion of the motives of others and hypochondriacal concern over the above symptoms." Various forms of mental hell awaited those who simply would not surrender their ego to the experience: "One person complained it was like being caught in a burning building; another thought that it was like going under ether; a third that it was like hanging off a cliff."[6]

But deeper than these surface reports of physiological vacillations and various manias bubbled up some truly bizarre episodes. Take Miss B, who had been hospitalized for fifteen years. A hebephrenic schizophrenic, Miss B usually spent her spring days "giggling and laughing about the birds and the flowers."[7] After ingesting 100 micrograms of Savage's LSD, all joy fell from her face. She grew emotionally cold— distant. Her mutters became more and more disjointed.

The next morning Miss B still felt distraught from the experience— still serious, still aloof. When "Dr. X"* asked her about the previous day, Miss B replied with a cold glare, "This is serious business—we are pathetic people—don't play with us."[8] Fascinated by the fluctuations in Miss B, the doctors gave her another 100 micrograms of LSD.

At one point while sitting with her psychiatrist, Miss B "looked off into space and talked to someone out there." Later that afternoon, she soiled herself, stripped nude, attacked the hospital staff, and made "sexual overtures" to the head nurse. Miss B ended her second LSD session by climbing on top of a projector screen in the common area and hanging nude.[9]

Allen Dulles, ever firm in his convictions, addressed a hearty crowd at Princeton University in 1953. Speaking on the "brain perversion tech-

---

*The doctor is not named in the write-up.

niques" employed by the Soviets, Dulles warned, "The minds of selected individuals who are subjected to such treatment . . . are deprived of their ability to state their own thought. Parrot-like, the individuals so conditioned can merely repeat the thoughts which have been implanted in their minds by suggestion from outside. In effect the brain . . . becomes a phonograph playing a disc put on its spindle by an outside genius over which it has control."[10] If we are to go by what Dulles thought about using mind-drugs to control a person, then Savage did inadvertently create a kind of "Manchurian Candidate." His particular patient (we are left wondering what he suffered from, if anything) took Delysid. And while it did not turn him into a phonograph, the patient nonetheless "complained . . . that the LSD turned him into a television set and that someone was controlling him by sending him impulses. . . . Not only could that someone control him but could even read his mind and everything the individual was seeing. The someone else was conceived to be the doctor who by using LSD may have gained this ascendancy over the subject. . . . It seemed to him that whoever could control the supply of LSD could control the rest of the world."[11] By this time, Savage seems to have left the agency's graces, his studies now financed directly through Sandoz Chemical Works, located in New York.[12]

Savage was a bit of a vanguard, actually setting up a one-month "course of LSD," wherein volunteers were schooled in all the available information on how the drug operated and what to expect.[13] He was also quite candid about detailing the various effects Delysid had on a variety of patients. Whereas those like Rinkel and Hyde remained conservative in their descriptions of Delysid, Savage offers detailed examples of what early tests with LSD look like (as we saw with Miss B).

Another early researcher cashing CIA checks was Dr. Nicholas Bercel, who had a private psychiatric practice in Los Angeles. Bercel had already sampled LSD back in 1949 while visiting Europe, and he now looked to expand his portfolio. The CIA offered just such an opportunity. They wanted him to look into "the possible consequences if the Russians were to put LSD in the water supply of a large

American city."[14] They left Bercel to calculate how much LSD such an attack would require. Bercel dropped the LSD powder into a glass of chlorinated water, which effectively deactivated the chemical's potency. Despite the failure of the experiment, the very idea lit a fire under the agency's ass, and they set about chemically redesigning LSD and rethinking the logistics of such an operation.

One internal CIA memo read:

> If the concept of contaminating a city's water supply seems, or in actual fact, is found to be far-fetched (this is by no means certain), there is still the possibility of contaminating, say, the water supply of a bomber base or, more easily still, that of a battleship. . . . Our current work contains the strong suggestion that LSD-25 will produce hysteria (unaccountable laughing, anxiety, terror). . . . It requires little imagination to realize what the consequences might be if a battleship's crew were so affected.[15]

Back at Boston Psychopathic Hospital, Robert Hyde also found grant money through the CIA, as evidenced by his name attached to several subproject documents.[16] Granted, like many of those in the academic espionage camp, Hyde courted no affiliation with the Agency when he had his first LSD experience. But that soon changed when, in 1952, the CIA added his name to the payroll, to the tune of $40,000 annually (that's over $370,000 today). His task was to study the effects of Delysid on patients, nurses, volunteers, CIA agents, and himself—*just keep it quiet.* Only Hyde and his colleague Herbert DeShon had any idea of the CIA's hand in later tests. Hyde oversaw Delysid experiments in both hospital patients and CIA agents. One agent to whom Hyde had administered Delysid later spoke fondly of the doctor, noting his classical approach to studying LSD "[a]s a sharp M.D. in the old school sense, he would look at things in ways that a lot of recent light brights couldn't get. . . . He had a good sense of make-do."[17]

Others received grant money as well. In New York, the physician

Harold Abramson (1899–1980) worked with LSD at both Mount Sinai Hospital in Manhattan and the Biological Laboratory in Cold Spring Harbor on Long Island. He could at times have a rather cavalier attitude toward the chemical's effects on himself. One time he accidentally ingested LSD and reportedly brushed it off saying, "Oh, it's nothing serious. . . . It's just an LSD psychosis. I'll just go to bed and sleep it off."[18] Abramson "got a real kick" out of giving LSD to his friends and colleagues at his home in Brookhaven, Suffolk County, in far east Long Island.[19] He would pay his volunteers twenty-five dollars and invite them to dinner. But word soon spread quickly through Suffolk County. "It was all I could do to prevent all of Brookhaven, people in the school system, friends, and so on, to come to dinner with us on Friday evenings to take LSD."[20] One of his colleagues, Frank Fremont-Smith (1895–1974)—a regular at Abramson's Friday night LSD dinner parties—was so taken by the experience that he helped funnel enough CIA money to host two conferences on LSD through the Josiah Macy Jr. Foundation, of which he served as director.

Abramson was used to screening the mentally compromised, not the mentally healthy. One person who made it through Abramson's dragnet was a forty-year-old woman, married with children, who had begun to feel that she had latent homosexual desires spurred by a dream about two sexually engaged dogs. Additionally, she had reoccurring psychosomatic tendencies. As it turned out, LSD enabled the distraught woman to recall key aspects of her youth. Abramson recorded the session and after reviewing the tape he determined that "the patient's psycho-sexual development . . . led to her confusing her childhood manner of relieving anxiety through masturbatory channels with later aspects of psychosexual development which in the pre-analytic and analytic frame of reference led to the patient's believing she was a lesbian." Abramson concluded this LSD report quite optimistically, stating, "A study of the psychoanalytic material of this patient after the LSD interview revealed consistently that the LSD experience gave the patient much more confidence in re-constructing and re-evaluating data for a longer period than had previously been possible without LSD."[21]

⊚

Paul Hoch (1902–1964) and James Cattell (d. 1994) of the New York State Psychiatric Institute also worked with mescaline and LSD prior to any intelligence agencies tapping their shoulder. Unlike most researchers (both those involved with government branches and those who were not), Hoch stood apart from the rest: he absolutely *refused* to take LSD.[22*] He also seems to have been the first person to apply the term "psychotomimetic" to both mescaline and Hofmann's wonder child.[23] His and Cattell's tests focused on giving schizophrenics the chemicals in combination with hypnosis, which proved "very difficult," and electroshock therapy given "at the height of mescaline psychosis."[24]

Perhaps most interesting, we can gauge how CIA involvement affected LSD research through reviewing Hoch and Cattell's publications on the topic. Early in 1952, Hoch and Cattell candidly reported, "One patient talked about his penis being wet, small, or absent and that he had breasts like a little girl. . . . [A]nother female patient went into a state of sexual ecstasy with memories and fantasies illustrative of practically all heterosexual and homosexual activity. She also expressed the desire to become a man, of swallowing the doctor's penis, and of its transformation into a baby." Hoch and Cattell concluded that "normal" subjects spoke of "elation," whereas schizophrenic patients spoke of "sexual content."[25] A patient or volunteer might exhibit the usual symptoms based on set and setting, namely, "euphoria, depression, or anxiety."[26] Some of the volunteers thought the experience garnered profound and deep personal insight; others, not so much.

So far, it was all fairly typical stuff.

However, after government funds started to appear, Hoch and Cattell ramped up the experiments. Where they once capped off their volunteer capacity at fifty-nine, they were now giving LSD to one hundred patients at the Psychiatric Institute. These later, intelligence-directed experiments left all one hundred volunteers reeling from the

---

*Which, odd as it may sound to us today, was a breach of medical protocol at the time.

Delysid: "None of [Hoch's patients] had a pleasant experience. None of them wanted to take it again."[27] It should therefore come as no surprise that the first death of an LSD volunteer happened on Hoch's watch. Harold Blauer (1910–1953), a professional tennis player, entered the Psychiatric Institute after a harsh divorce caused "severe depression."[28] From December 5, 1952, through January 8, 1953, Blauer received a series of five injections for the purposes of finding a "potential discombobulater of enemy populations."[29] He, of course, wasn't told any of this. The four earlier syringes contained various mescaline modifications. But the fifth—that's anyone's guess, including Hoch and Cattell. "We didn't know whether it was dog piss or what it was we were giving him," remembers Cattell.[30] Our shadowy government immediately began a cover-up "to avoid embarrassment and adverse publicity."[31] Harold's widow, Amy Blauer, received a paltry $18,000 from the state of New York (though, like the funding for the test itself, the money came from the Army and was nothing more than hush money). In the late 1980s, she received a second round of money to the tune of over $700,000. This time, it wasn't hush money; it was mea culpa money.

As more and more doctors signed on to accept money from the CIA, more questions were raised about LSD. They overwhelmed the small cadre of inner-circle CIA scientists. Early on, Gottlieb and Richard Helms (1913–2002), the deputy director of the CIA, channeled some of MKUltra's budget money into research grants via three fronts: the Geschickter Fund for Medical Research, the Society for the Investigation of Human Ecology, and the Josiah Macy Jr. Foundation (mentioned earlier). This latter organization held two conferences, one in 1956 and the other in 1959. The Geschickter Fund received a cumulative sum of two million dollars from the CIA over a period of twenty years. The Society for the Investigation of Human Ecology funded research that tested drugs and radiation on children. And perhaps that original McCurdy grant that Rinkel received for his initial

LSD research had some kind of line back to Wendt (chairperson of the Psychology Department at the University of Rochester with ties to the CIA), who was contracted to work on the U.S. Navy's mind-control initiative, Project CHATTER. Not to entertain conspiracy theories—although when we consider the very real practice of the CIA using dummy-fronts to funnel money to researchers, it is not so outlandish—but perhaps Wendt and someone from the McCurdy company kicked it in Rochester. After all, Gilbert McCurdy (1895–1978) sat on the Board of Trustees at the University of Rochester.[32] It just seems odd, in retrospect, that some random family-owned department store company in Rochester, New York, would care to sponsor—or had even heard of—LSD research in 1951.

The academic world, sometimes knowingly, sometimes not, helped "provide badly needed answers to some pressing national security problems, in the shortest possible time, without altering potential enemies to the U.S. government's interest in these matters. . . . [T]he amount of available reliable data on LSD and similar materials was essentially nil."[33] Feelings within the academic community split between those who cooperated with the CIA and those who avoided what felt like an unholy alliance. Some, like National Institutes of Health (NIH) researcher Dr. John Lilly (1915–2001) outright refused to participate.[34] Others, like DeShon at Boston Psychopathic Hospital, felt differently: "I don't see any objection to this. We never gave [LSD] to anyone without his consent and without explaining it in detail."[35] It really boils down to who followed the proscriptions that DeShon would recommend, and who administered LSD in far more irresponsible ways.

If we are to believe Gottlieb:

MKUltra took place in academic and other research settings. These projects have always represented the work that the individual investigators would have been doing in any case. . . . The degree of wittingness [sic] of the principal investigators on these projects varied depending on whether we judged his knowledge of our specific interest to be necessary in providing useful results to us. Thus, many projects were established in which the principal investigator was fully knowledgeable of who we were and exactly what our interests in the research were. Others were simply provided funds through a covert organization and had no idea of ultimate CIA sponsorship.

Gottlieb also chose investigators that he believed would ensure "adequate safeguards" for the volunteers.[36] Most doctors who received grants from the CIA did in fact follow highly strict guidelines when testing human subjects. However, some CIA-funded doctors exhibited unethical practices. Under the auspices of the MKUltra group, these doctors broke numerous laws concerning medical malpractice.

◎

Dr. William Henry Wall (1902–1967) frantically phoned his concerned wife Hallie Anne (1903–2003). He had been locked away at the Lexington, Kentucky, Addiction Center for over a month now. Some days he would drink his water or eat his lunch and suddenly the walls would start to "undulate around [him] . . . the air hum[med] with unearthly vibrations, and the faces of those around . . . constantly shift[ed] from human to animal to gargoyles and back to human again. Wall started to "sweat profusely [and experience] 'goose bump' skin and a racing heart. . . . [H]e would feel himself grow huge, then imagine he had shrunk to the size of his own thumb."[37]

The doctors, he whispered frantically to Hallie Anne, were poisoning him—but how, and with what? He hadn't tasted anything in his food or drink . . .

Wall, once a respected physician and two-time Georgia senator, had taken a fall that had all the makings of a Shakespearean tragedy. After a minor oral procedure, his dentist prescribed the opioid Demerol to help with the pain. As sometimes happens in these situations, Wall developed an unhealthy addiction to the narcotic that eventually landed him in prison. Due to the nature of his "crime" (drug dependency), authorities granted Wall the opportunity to take residence at a so-called "narcotic farm" (or "narco")—a low-security rehab house that had been set up in the 1920s and 1930s. The main agenda of the Lexington, Kentucky, Addiction Center was "the confinement and treatment of persons addicted to the use of habit-forming drugs."[38] However, there was another, more ominous side to the center. Human experimentation with LSD at this particular narco received funds from the Josiah Macy Jr. Foundation, which funneled money to Dr. Harris Isbell (1910–1994).

Inmates at the narco became guinea pigs for MKUltra.

Wall had expected a four-month stretch at the Addiction Center in Lexington. But his mind was needed by the researchers. And so he stayed a resident at the center for an additional four months with no explanation as to why. Wall's son believed the unprecedented extension was so the doctors could "observe and record his behavior following the drug assault."[39]

In their article "The Lexington Narcotic Farm," Drs. Thomas R. Kosten and David A. Gorelick list several names among the "leadership" of the farm's doctoral members, including Drs. Lawrence C. Kolb Sr., Clifton K. Himmelsbach, and George E. Vaillant.[40] One name not listed among the leadership is that of Isbell, despite the infamy he earned during his tenure at the Addiction Center. Highlights (or lowlights—depending on one's perspective) of Isbell's career included giving seven recovering heroin addicts LSD for eighty-five days straight.[41] However, LSD is a very adaptable drug; one quickly develops a tolerance to it. In response, Isbell increased the dosages as necessary with each passing day, filling those unfortunate addicts with merciless amounts of LSD. In the end, "Isbell found no evidence that his volunteers suffered any damage from their multiple-dose LSD experience."[42] At least this is what James Ketchum, a CIA physician who worked at Edgewood Arsenal in Maryland, wrote in his apologist *Chemical Warfare: Secrets Almost*

Forgotten (2006). There has never been a follow-up study on those poor drug-addicted subjects, therefore Ketchum's words cannot be confirmed. However, Isbell wrote in a personal memo that the volunteers "tended to be afraid of the doctors and were not as open in describing their experiences as the experimenters would have wished."[43]

At the Lexington Addiction Center, rumors circulated among the patients that signing on as a test subject came with an added bonus: as a reward for volunteering, each addict received either a small supply of the narcotic of their choice or a reduced sentence. Most took the narcotics. Wall was one of the inpatients who had refused the barter, but he was unique; nonetheless, Isbell dosed him with LSD against his will.

Other inpatients jumped at the chance to score *pure* dope and safely shoot-up with the staff's blessings. One young man was so eager to participate in the barter system that he lied about his age. Nineteen-year-old Eddie Flowers had been at the Addiction Center for a year, but claimed he was twenty-one so he could participate in the project. Those in charge clearly practiced a lackadaisical approach at this narco, as simply pulling Flowers's file would have revealed his true age. He would soon regret the ruse. Entering the examination room, doctors gave him a small graham cracker. No one told Flowers about the LSD that soaked the small wafer. The experience terrified him. He later recalled: "It was the worst shit I ever had. . . . I was frightened. I wouldn't take it again."[44]

Isbell ran a very tight protocol: "Pulse rate, systolic and diastolic blood pressures, respiratory rate, and rectal temperature were determined at hourly intervals, after 10 minutes rest in bed, and 2 hours before and 8 hours after administration of the drug." But he also demonstrated a willingness to lie in his published works with LSD. In one of his earlier papers outlining how LSD affected recovering morphine and heroin users, he not only neglected to mention the barter system but even went so far as to claim that the volunteers "had been abstinent from opiates for three months or more when these studies were carried out."[45] This is most certainly not true—he was quite literally trading heroin for volunteer cooperation at that time.

Isbell felt the tests (and bartering system) perfectly ethical, having no regrets. Even later in life, after many other MKUltra researchers apologized for their reckless actions, Isbell told a Senate subcommittee in 1975 that the "barter" practices were "custom[ary] in those days," claiming he and his team did a "very excellent job."[46] He further defended himself by asserting a "lack of high development in ethical codes" at the time, a defense that does not withstand scrutiny. The American Medical Association (AMA) had debated domestic human experiment considerations as early as 1946. The AMA statutes clearly state: "subjects must give voluntary consent, that animal experimentation must precede human experimentation, and that human experiments should be 'performed under proper medical protection and management.'"[47] Isbell only followed these statutes if bribery can be considered consent. In April 1950, the Department of Defense's Joint Panel on the Medical Aspects of Atomic Warfare championed the selection of inmates of "true volunteer status," whose use met "the requirements of accepted American standards for the use of human subjects for research purposes." One military official felt that earlier standards and practices were "not cruel and unusual," to which former medical director of the Manhattan Project, Shields Warren (1898–1980), replied, "It's not very long since we got through trying Germans for doing exactly the same thing."[48]

8
Enlightened Operatives
The Blood of Patriots

I do not contend that driving people crazy even for a few hours is a pleasant prospect. But warfare is never pleasant . . . would you rather be temporarily deranged . . . by a chemical agent, or burned alive . . . ?

MAJOR GENERAL WILLIAM CREASY

They [in] the Agency think I'm a god.

WILSON GREENE

When discussing the personnel who worked with LSD for MKUltra we might want to consider two distinct groups. The first group comprises those like Hyde, Hoch, and Abramson—independent researchers whom the CIA tapped for one reason or another. These researchers had already been working with LSD and/or mescaline and graciously accepted large funds from the CIA to continue their work. Then there was a second group that we have not met yet. These folks worked with LSD and had direct employment with a government office.

In D.C. MKUltra researchers had begun to guard everything they ate and drank as if their lives (and minds) depended on it. LSD appeared most advantageous when the person receiving it remained

99

unsuspecting. After all, that was one of the reasons LSD undermined all the other experimental substances—it remained undetectable until only after the effects manifested. Giving LSD to knowing participants (many of them mentally unwell) provided interesting anecdotes, but not much else. *Unsuspecting* people made the best subjects. This would mean testing LSD "without proximate safeguards [or] consideration of the rights of the individual."[1]

It would only be a matter of time before something terrible happened.

◎

It was at this point that MKUltra took, perhaps, its darkest turn. Gottlieb and Helms decided that there was only one way to move forward; they had to find unsuspecting *citizens* to dose. But not just anyone—they needed people who wouldn't be believed when they returned to their regular lives telling horrific stories of kidnapping and mind-control experiments. Gottlieb and Helms felt that three kinds of people fit this profile: Mafiosi, barflies, and sex workers. Dealing with the Mafia did not tickle the fancy of the MKUltra group. So Gottlieb focused on the more vulnerable of the remaining two groups.

As it turned out, someone already had that same idea . . .

FUN, FUN, FUN

~ May 1, 1953 ~
Morgan Hall rented an apartment at 81 Bedford Street in New York's Greenwich Village. He immediately began redecorating: double-glass windows, cameras, microphones, sound recording equipment, a stockpile of illegal drugs, and a bounteous supply of booze. Hall was really George Hunter White (1908–1975), a towering, intimidating figure who "made that fruitcake [J. Edgar] Hoover look like Nancy Drew."[2] His resume was telling: he had made a name for himself

training American spies in espionage tactics during the Second Great War; kept a picture on his wall of the Japanese agent he had killed with his bare hands; arrested Billie Holiday in 1949 on bogus opium charges; once used his .22 automatic (with silencer) to shoot his initials into the wall of a room at the Roosevelt Hotel during a drinking binge; attempted to send a Cuban sex worker to Fidel Castro with LSD-laced cigars; and, finally, as a member of the Federal Bureau of Narcotics, often sampled many of the substances he arrested people for possessing.[3]

White had received clearance to open the safehouse from his boss Harry Anslinger, the notorious anti-cannabis crusader and fraud. The idea behind the apartment at 81 Bedford was for White, posing as Hall, to lure both alcoholics and sex workers back to the pad, and dose them with LSD. By the summer of 1953, code name "Operation Midnight Climax" was fully operational.

Given the nature of this most foul environment, the "tests" that took place at the apartment proved unpredictable. Some people experienced horrific visions and cried in the corner; others experienced euphoria and danced the night away. In a letter to Gottlieb about his time in the apartment, White commented that it was "fun, fun, fun. Where else could a red-blooded American lie, cheat, rape and pillage with the sanction of the all-highest?"[4]

~ November 18, 1953 ~

A team of biological warfare scientists arrived late at night to a cabin in Deep Creek Lake, Maryland. Camouflaged as a "winter meeting of script writers, editors, authors, and lecturers" in liquor-free Swanton County, the scientists were actually unwitting guinea pigs for a MKUltra subproject experiment.[5] They settled in and went to sleep.

The next day around noon, Gottlieb spiked a small amount of LSD into everyone's Cointreau (notwithstanding two men; one had a stomachache and the other was a recovering alcoholic). Roughly twenty minutes after the guests finished their drinks, Gottlieb informed them of the dosing. Once the LSD kicked in, most of the participants, like Robert Lashbrook (1918–2002), laughed incessantly; others argued philosophy all day and night. Still others grew frightened—Frank Olson (1910–1953) and his boss, Colonel Vincent Ruwet (1916–1996), noticeably so. Olson yelled at his cohorts and wandered aimlessly around the cabin muttering to himself. Afterward, feeling he had "messed up the experiment," he delivered his resignation to Ruwet the following week.[6]

Although somewhat secretive due to the nature of his work, Olson was a "very warm, family-loving man," according to his wife.[7] Employed at Fort Dietrich, he helped establish the Special Operations Division (SOD) of the Army Chemical Corps, a highly covert research division that prohibited anyone from documenting anything in writing.[8] SOD projects included the "development of assassination materials, collaboration with former Nazi scientists, LSD mind-control research, and the use of biological weapons during the Korean War."[9] Olson's direct employer was actually the CIA.[10]

Returning from the retreat, Olson appeared aloof; a different man than the husband his wife had kissed good-bye a few days earlier. His colleagues put him under the care of Lashbrook, and the two flew to New York and checked into the Statler Hotel on 7th Avenue in Manhattan. Olson was supposedly "ashamed to see his family," fearing he might become violent.[11] What took place in New York remains shrouded in mystery. Some say that Olson became erratic, throwing away his wallet and claiming that he just wanted to disappear. But he also phoned his wife at one point, saying he felt fine and looked forward to coming home. In some versions, Lashbrook, Ruwet, and Gottlieb attended Olson; in others, Gottlieb never arrived in New York at all. The story I believe is that Olson met up with sleight-of-hand magician John Mulholland (1898–1970). Gottlieb had employed Mulholland to teach undercover operatives how to "apply the magician's art to covert activities, such as slipping drugs into drinks" to dose or poison enemies.* His book *The Art of Illusion* (1944) had even been downsized to fit into the shirt pockets of service members during the Second Great War. Mulholland harbored no direct affiliation with the CIA; the full extent of his relations with Gottlieb were likewise opaque. He took on these kinds of assignments "because his government asked him to."[12]

Olson took several trips with Lashbrook and Ruwet (and possibly Gottlieb) out to Long Island to see Harold Abramson, the LSD researcher we met in the previous chapter who invited folks from around Brookhaven to his home for LSD dinner parties. Despite Abramson's qualifications to discuss the LSD experience with Olson, he wasn't a psychiatrist or psychologist, but an allergist. Abramson later claimed that Olson confided that he believed the CIA continually drugged him to cause sleeplessness. Back in New York, only Lashbrook remained with Olson.

~ November 23, 1953 ~

Olson plunged to his death from the thirteenth-floor window of his and Lashbrook's hotel room, 1018A. A cursory investigation resulted in police declaring the death a suicide. The official story: Olson simply went crazy and killed himself.

After Olson's death, all LSD testing (including White's apartment) momentarily froze while the CIA decided how to clean up the mess. Several months later, CIA Deputy Director Helms† pleaded with CIA Director of Intelligence, Dulles, to reopen these shady, deplorable apartments. The only "operationally realistic" way of continuing LSD research, Helms explained, was by monitoring the unwary.[13] The apartment tactics recommenced, but not in New York. Reluctant to have White operating in the same city where Olson had

---

*It was not uncommon for the magician's arts to be used by Europeans to deceive enemies. To name a few examples, Robert-Houdin went to Algeria in 1856 on behalf of Napoleon III to help quell the Marabout-led uprising; likewise, Jasper Maskelyne worked with the Royal Engineers in Britain during the First World War on camouflage techniques. Gottlieb commissioned Mulholland the same day Allen Dulles approved MKUltra.

†Helms would become director of Central Intelligence for the CIA from 1966 to 1973.

perished, Gottlieb rented another apartment in Telegraph Hill, San Francisco. This time, White wouldn't run the apartment alone. He hired John Gittinger (1917–2003) and Ira "Ike" Feldman to nest in the San Francisco house.

Feldman recalled those days:

> As George White once told me, "Ike, your best information outside comes from the whores and the junkies. If you treat a whore nice, she'll treat you nice. If you treat a junkie nice, he'll treat you nice." But sometimes, when people had information, there was only one way you could get it: if it was a girl, you put her tits in the drawer and slammed the drawer. If it was a guy, you took his cock and hit it with a hammer. And they would talk to you. Now, with these drugs, you could get information without having to abuse people.[14]

U.S. tax dollars at work.

White, Feldman, and Gittinger arrived in the Bay Area and immediately began frequenting the local bars. They would gain the trust of the locals and lure them back to the apartment where they would test the effectiveness of an aerosol delivery of LSD. Gittinger would mist them with the spray, while White and Feldman busily took notes behind a double-mirror. On their first night they ran into problems. Lacking an air conditioner, they had to leave the windows open. Gittinger didn't want to spray it into the common area for fear that it would sail out into the streets. Frustrated, Gittinger ended the party, locked himself in the bathroom, and sprayed himself with the aerosol can. Much to his surprise, nothing happened—LSD cannot be inhaled from the air.[15]

White may be called an equal-opportunity bastard. He didn't relegate his LSD experiments solely to sex workers and barflies—even police officers and high-ranking government personnel were not safe from his chicanery.

~ *December 20, 1957* ~

Deputy U.S. Marshal Wayne Ritchie (1927–2012) started to feel uneasy. Not but a half-hour earlier he had been enjoying a few bourbon and sodas at a Christmas party held at the James R. Browning U.S. Courthouse, not far from the Marshal's office. He had returned to the office to start his rounds and relieve his boss. Now alone in the office, Ritchie's thoughts began to run away from him. Paranoia quickly crept through his nerves. Despite his stellar reputation around the department, Ritchie now felt "disliked and secretly laughed at by his fellow officers." He grew suspicious, then alarmed. His coworkers must be conspiring against him! He needed to get out of there—*fast*. Violating proper protocol, he closed the office early and walked home to find comfort with his girlfriend. Only she wasn't very comforting. She was whiny, lamenting how she wanted to leave the Bay Area for New York.

The conspiracy had been even bigger than Ritchie thought—even his girlfriend wanted him gone! Growing evermore distraught, he left his house and walked to the Vagabond Bar, owned and operated by his friend Tony. Perhaps Tony had something on his mind, or the bar was busy due to the holidays, but he was not as attentive to Ritchie as Ritchie would have preferred. His whole life had been a lie—even Tony had turned his back on him. The cosmic loneliness was crushing!

It was time to make things right. And so Ritchie hatched a plan. His experience with guns had landed him a most coveted position at the department: he was a firearms instructor and, as such, had the keys to the gun locker. He would grab a gun and then rob a bar. This would have a twofold effect: he would use the money to buy his girlfriend a plane ticket home; and, now a criminal, he would be fired from the force. Problems solved.

He returned to the office, grabbed two pistols from the locker, and walked to the Shady Grove Bar. He ordered one last bourbon and soda, drank it down, and then pulled a pistol on the bartender. When a waitress startled Ritchie from behind, an unknown individual grabbed his pistol, and clocked him over the noggin, knocking him out cold. He awoke, was arrested and processed, and confessed to everything. The courts fined him $500 and sentenced him to five years of probation. The Marshal's Office did not fire him, so he resigned.[16]

As it turned out, Ritchie's boss at the Marshal's Office had been complicit with White's clandestine LSD tests. Over time, their relationship failed and great disdain developed between the two men. Ritchie believes, in fact, that his boss was White's primary target. But since he couldn't make the party, Ritchie became White's mark. In fact, White's own diary entry for the evening indicates that he stayed at home, sick with the flu. However, it also reads "xmas party Fed bldg press room." *Someone* under White's direction—either Gittinger or Feldman—was at that party.[17]

Years later, when Ritchie tried to sue the U.S. government for surreptitiously dosing him with LSD, he was surprised to find out that the Marshal's Office had no record of him ever working there . . . he didn't exist. Ritchie called a lawyer, Sidney Bender, who had experience with these kinds of matters. The case eventually went to court, but it was too late. Too much time had passed—there was no one to interview, or call to the stand, expose for malfeasance, or anything. The court ruled that while it was "possible that Ritchie's apparent lapse of judgment was exactly what it appears to be . . . [t]o take this [inference] to its logical conclusion" would open a floodgate, obliging the court "to find that LSD intoxication is the likely cause of almost any unexplained and superficially inexplicable behavior."[18]

Ritchie would receive no justice.*

---

*Ritchie would not be the only person denied due compensation for unlawful participation in LSD experiments. In 1982, retired soldier Calvin Sweet lost his 3.9 million dollar lawsuit against the United States Army for exposure to LSD at Edgewood Arsenal in September 1957. Sadly, the statute of limitations had expired by the time Sweet brought the suit. Federal District Judge Donald Porter also noted that Sweet "failed to prove that the drug experiments . . . ha[d] caused his mental illness." See Levine, "Former Soldier," 7.

Confused by the unpredictable nature of LSD (but unwilling to abandon it completely), some figureheads in the CIA proposed a flipside to the notion of using the chemical as a means of interrogation. What if LSD's true purpose rested elsewhere—not as a way to make an enemy talk, but rather as a way to prevent one of our POWs from talking? LSD took on a new role within the Agency—as an anti-interrogation serum. Since the reactions that testers observed in their subjects often fluctuated between anxiety, debilitating fear, euphoria, non-sequitur babbling, and uncontrollable laughter, MKUltra researchers felt that American POWs might use LSD much like a non-lethal cyanide capsule and "offer an operative temporary protection against interrogation."[19] This radical change from LSD's perceived potential as a truth drug to a lie serum reinforces the simple fact that the CIA's top scientists still had very little understanding of the chemical they busily tried to control.

But the awesome power of LSD could not be contained. In one particular early test, an agent was briefed "fake" secrets and administered LSD. His superiors instructed him not to divulge any information when interrogated by his "captors."

He sang like a canary.

After the fact, he claimed he did not recall spilling the beans to his interrogators. But he was clearly lying. LSD has zero effect on the short-term memory.[20] Indeed, one of the aspects the CIA puzzled over was the remarkable way LSD took the mind across the limits of human cognition all while leaving it unscathed in its wake. Either the agent told tall tales or this is the only case on record (of thousands) where a person experienced amnesia from LSD.

◎

Still, the most sinister aspects of these mind-control projects had yet to be seen. At an undisclosed location in Arizona, tests performed by Dr. Wilson Greene involved teaching one little girl, Christine deNicola, not only how to pick locks but also how "to kill dolls that looked like real children." DeNicola recalls, "I stabbed a doll with a spear once after being severely traumatized." As she got older, deNicola "resisted more and more" against her "training" and eventually became so uncooperative that she was put in a cage between tests.[21]

Another woman, Claudia Mullen, testified alongside deNicola at the Presidential Advisory Committee on Human Radiation Experiments (PACHRE). The Deep Creek Lake cabin where Olson had his disastrous encounter with LSD was used several other times for far more disreputable purposes: training children as assassins, of which Mullen recalls her involvement. In 1995, Mullen spoke before the PACHRE and detailed some of what she remembers of the tests. Not yet a teenager when "the sexual humiliation began," Mullen recalls a doctor, Greene, telling another doctor that "'children were used as subjects because they were more fun to work with and cheaper too.' They needed lower profile subjects than soldiers and government people so only young girls would do. 'Besides . . . I like scaring them. They and the Agency think I'm a god, creating subjects in experiments for whatever deviant purposes Sid [Gottlieb] and James [Hamilton]* could think up.'" During her testimony, Mullen describes her experience at Deep Creek Lake:

> I was sent to a lodge in Maryland called Deep Creek Cabins to learn how to sexually please men. I was taught how to coerce them into talking about themselves. It was Richard Helms, who was Deputy Director of the CIA, Dr. Gottlieb, Capt. George White, Morris Allan who all planned on filling as many high government agency officials and heads of academic institutions and foundations as possible so that later when the funding for mind control and radiation started to dwindle, projects would continue.[22]

Mullen was ten years old at the time.

---

*Friend and colleague of George Hunter White. Hamilton tested "truth drugs" for the OSS. See Marks, *The Search for the Manchurian Candidate*, 98.

◎

Despite many years of testing LSD on MKUltra agents, civilians, inmates, and children, U.S. intelligence agencies still had no insights into the nature of the drug they prized so highly. Outside the CIA, Major General William Creasy (1905–1987), who served as chief officer of the U.S. Army Chemical Corps, saw in LSD a facet that had been overlooked by the Agency. Creasy believed that LSD showed promise as a chemical warfare agent because it could possibly induce madness on an entire city populace overrun with insurgents. Chemical Corps researchers at Edgewood Arsenal and Fort Detrick immediately began working out the details for a new kind of chemical agent. This was the first concentrated effort by top military officials in history to "use chemical weapons to spare lives, rather than extinguish them."[23]

WAR WITHOUT DEATH?

In the late 1950s, Creasy "promoted the psychochemical cause with eccentric and visionary zeal" and believed that drugs like LSD could serve a purpose as a "safe" (relatively speaking) wartime inebriant, used to usher in a new era of warfare.[24] In 1959, he began campaigning across America, proselytizing for the use of LSD not as a covert operational agent but as a spectacular addition to America's arsenal—much like the atomic bomb. After almost a decade of both respectable and haphazard tests, LSD had failed to show usable results in the clandestine world; Creasy therefore believed it was time to take LSD out of interrogation rooms and onto the battlefields. "I think the future lies in psychochemicals," said Creasy to the House Committee on Science and Astronautics in 1959.[25] One idea was to use the drug to corrupt an unfriendly city's water supply. Creasy felt that instead of killing people by blanketing an area with bombs, the military could simply put whole cities under an LSD trance for a few hours while the infantry rounded up the troublemakers. Medics would tend to innocent civilians and military personnel would easily apprehend insurgents. He rationalized that this tactic avoided pulverizing whole cities just to kill a few bad actors. This would also spare the lives of regular citizens and allied soldiers who might otherwise perish in urban warfare crossfire. He proposed to the House Committee on Science and Astronautics that bombing an American subway with LSD was worth a try to see how it affected ordinary people during their everyday business. Though the committee rejected the subway LSD bomb idea, they still voted to increase the Chemical Corps' budget in hopes of discovering a "non-lethal incapacitant that could subdue a foe without inflicting permanent injury."[26] Having complete support from President Eisenhower (and later John F. Kennedy who promoted a "Blue Sky" strategy that approved incapacitating agents), Creasy set out realizing his dream.

After Creasy testified to the Biological and Radiological Warfare Agents hearings before the Committee on Science and Aeronautics in June 1959, the Army Chemical Corps was awarded additional funding to carry out their research. Unfortunately for Creasy, many new problems joined the older ones. For one thing, as Gittinger had already established, LSD could not be successfully sprayed out of an aerosol can. As far as contaminating water supplies was concerned, there were other problems with this idea as well. One researcher commented that "[m]uch depends on the quantity released and the success of dissemination . . . assuming that . . . only 10 per cent of the inhabitants became directly involved, a large number of fatalities would result. The devastating effects of LSD on people unaware that a chemical is the cause of their mental distortions is enormous and hardly calculable . . . they will be prone to lose emotional control and behave aggressively."[27]

Unwilling to give up his dream of war without death, Creasy ordered the Army Chemical Corps to develop a stronger mind drug that could succeed where LSD had failed. The Chemical Corps soon introduced quinuclidinyl benzilate, or "BZ"—a "superhallucinogen," as they called it. The drug was first synthesized as a possible ulcer alleviant; it had as much success as an ulcer alleviant as LSD had as a cure for migraines. After the Chemical Corps scientists realized its psychological effects, they cautioned that Communists may already "have it in their arsenal."[28] But BZ had problems, too: One was that its effects were *too* strong—infinitely more maniacal than those of LSD. A BZ stupor also lasted for days, and in some cases, weeks at a time. Additionally, while it had been confirmed that LSD had benign, if any, aftereffects, no one was sure what the long-term effects of BZ would be, as the drug was too new. To the researchers who never wavered from testing these chemicals on themselves, LSD intoxication seemed like a glass of champagne compared to BZ intoxication. Bill Richards (1942–2014), a researcher working with BZ, remembered how the drug "zonked [him] for three days."[29] Also unlike LSD, a BZ overdose of an uncertain amount could be deadly. Finally, there was the problem of wind change during urban combat; a redirection in the breeze could send the drug back to its point of origin. However, BZ's promises outweighed its uncertainties, and it became the focal point of military intelligence chemical testing well into the 1960s. Unlike LSD, BZ could be released from an aerosol can, it was cheaper to produce, and it was far more powerful, causing "burning of the eyes, irritation of the throat and lungs, incoordination [*sic*], headache, nausea and vomiting, and general debility lasting for many hours or days after contact."[30] LSD was the stepping-stone to BZ.

One of the final LSD projects conducted during the 1950s involved military tests to ascertain whether soldiers could still display the "right stuff" under the drug's influence. By this time, the U.S. Army had been courting Hofmann, paying a visit to Sandoz biyearly. Their only concern rested in hoping that Hofmann might find "a way to mass-produce large quantities" of Delysid. Hofmann was never successful,* and once other laboratories cracked the secret to producing "many kilos" of LSD, all contact with Hofmann ceased.[31]

---

*Although, given his negative attitude toward military and intelligence agencies, it is also possible that Hofmann discovered a way to mass-produce Delysid but kept quiet about it.

Some tests that took place at Fort Bragg, North Carolina, were intended to serve as a war games "aid." The report of these tests, only released in 1975, cited the soldiers "show[ing] performance ranging 'from total incapacity to marked decrease in proficiency.'"[32] Other tests conducted at Edgewood Arsenal ended up with soldiers looting laboratories for their LSD supplies and using them recreationally, an act that prefigured the use of LSD as a recreational inebriant that would emerge in the coming decade.

During the 1950s, LSD was given to roughly fifteen hundred assorted military doctors, intelligence agents, soldiers, secretaries, and others. LSD may also have been used on Viet Cong POWs, one letter from an Army Inspector General reveals.[33] In one odd incident, a MKUltra test subject began to cry over the sheer beauty of what he felt to be a spiritually moving experience. His observers mistakenly felt that he was having a bad trip and wrote in their report that he had "experienced depression," reinforcing the fact that even the CIA's brightest scientists, whether using the drug to manipulate or stupefy, had no real handle on the substance they desperately sought to understand.[34]

MKUltra finally ended in 1973, leaving behind a trail of ruined lives and at least two deaths. Despite the program's survival throughout the sixties and into the early 1970s, we will have to move on for the time being. That story will be told one day, for sure. But for now, we must leave the espionage world behind and explore other aspects to find what was truly phantastic about the fifties.

9
The World Where Everything Is Known
María Sabina's Gift

We ate the mushrooms and I had a vision. . . . I spoke to God who each time I felt to be more familiar. Closer to me. I felt as if everything that surrounded me was God.

MARÍA SABINA

FLESH OF THE FLOWERS

~ *c. 1910* ~

"Bless us. . . . Teach us the way, the truth, the cure. . . . I will take your blood. I will take your heart. Because my conscience is pure, it is clean like yours. Give me truth. May Saint Peter and Saint Paul be with me," the young medicine woman, María Sabina Magdalena García (1894– 1985), prayed over the sacred mushrooms, sometimes called the *Little Ones Who Spring Forth.* She then dressed the *Little Ones* with incense. The altar was decorated in the traditional ways of the ancient Mazatec medicine workers: three candles of pure wax (*no substitutes!*), white lily and gladiola flowers, a small brazier burning copal, and a small San Pedro cactus.[1]

María Sabina's sister, María Ana (c. 1900–1980), had succumbed to a strange illness. Her legs would give out and she would fall over, her skin would darken in some areas, and she would lie limp. Several *curanderos* (medicine workers) tried to help Ana by using "herbs and magic rites" and burying eggs in strategic places under the dirt floor of Ana's room. Still, Ana's health continued to decline.[2]

⊚

Ana was not the first patient of her sister, the *curandera* María Sabina. Neither would she be the last. For María Sabina had learned the songs of the Little Ones Who Spring Forth since childhood, sometime around age five or six. Residing in the Mazatec mountain village of Huautla de Jiménez, the sisters' chores included far more exotic duties than cleaning the dishes and mowing the lawn. Instead, they worked for their grandparents raising silkworms, which is more difficult than it sounds. María Sabina and Ana fed the worms mora leaves until they grew roughly the size of a pointer-finger, ensuring the worms had a very specific amount of food each day to guarantee a bountiful harvest. Having tended the silkworms, the sisters next herded the chickens and goats (fighting off the hawks and foxes that tried to eat them) and planted and reaped corn and beans.

~ c. 1902 ~

At the age of six or seven (or five or eight) María Sabina watched her uncle, Emilio Cristino, fall terribly ill. The Wise Man Juan Manuel came to Cristino's hut. His curandero arsenal included a wrap of banana leaves that he handled with much intention and care. María Sabina's curiosity got the best of her. *What lay hidden in those banana leaves?* As she approached the curandero, the Wise Man snapped at her.

"Nobody can look at what I have here. It isn't good: a curious look could decompose what I have here," he scolded.[3]

María Sabina continued to look on, but with adolescent caution. One by one, the Wise Man unwrapped the banana leaves to reveal a cache of mushrooms, the Little Ones Who Spring Forth.

But the Wise Man had been wrong about young María Sabina. She was quite familiar with those mushrooms. She had spent many days out in the grazing fields of Huautla de Jiménez. The way their deep brown hue freckled the verdant symphonies meant that such Saint Children, or Little Saints (as they were also called), were instantly recognizable to her, and to Ana as well. In fact, their father Santo Feliciano and grandfather Juan Feliciano had also been *curanderos,* and had always spoken of the Little Saints "with great respect."[4]

The Wise Man ate the Little Saints and sang the songs of stars, animals, and other mysteries of human existence. He held Cristino's arms out and rubbed San Pedro on them. He burned incense. When the Wise Man ended the healing ceremony, Cristino found himself able to stand on his own two feet, a feat he hadn't done in days. Within a couple weeks after the vigil, he fully recovered.*

Such magic sparked a curiosity in little María Sabina and her sister Ana. Not long after the Wise Man healed Cristino, they found themselves out in the pastures herding goats and chickens. This time, they took special note of the decorative mushrooms that sprinkled the landscape. María Sabina's curiosity got the best of her. She found a small, solitary mushroom and pulled it from the ground. Then another.

And another.

Holding the Little Ones Who Spring Forth in her hand she said, "If I eat you . . . I know that you will make me sing beautifully."[5] The Little Saints tasted of earth, of roots, of deep connection to something beyond. Nonetheless, the mushrooms did not initiate her gently. She and Ana felt dizzy and drunk, and cried for their mistake of having eaten the Little Saints. Though, once the dizziness passed, the two girls felt rather well and agreeable within the space of the Little Saints. They felt their souls leave their bodies and enter a new world, a strange world, a "world where everything is known."[6] Palaces and bejeweled temples

---

*There are two different accounts of this event. In Munn's translation of Estrada's *María Sabina: Her Life and Chants* (39), the Wise Man heals Cristino. In a retelling of the story found in Joan Halifax's *Shamanic Voices* (131–32), it is María Sabina who heals her uncle.

spun out of corners and foregrounds of this enchanted space. What's more, the sisters occupied that *same space*—like two sleeping people sharing the same dream. The Little Saints presented themselves as dwarves and children playing trumpets, singing, and dancing—these beings as gentle and inviting as the "flesh of flowers."[7] María Sabina and Ana suddenly felt a presence. These mushrooms were *conscious*. An intelligence every bit as real as their own. *This* was surely how the Wise Man cured Cristino. María Sabina decided to plead with this intelligence.

"We are so poor. How are we going to live? What will happen to us?"[8]

The girls heard voices. The same voices. *We shall protect you. Whenever you should want for anything, come to us and we shall bestow.*

SEÑORA SIN MANCHA

They continued to eat the mushrooms day after day, going deeper and deeper into the world where everything is known. On one occasion a "well dressed man" appeared before María Sabina and told her, "[K]neel down. Kneel and pray." María Sabina kneeled and prayed. She "spoke to God," who grew more and more familiar to her the more she ate the Little Ones Who Spring Forth. Eventually, she realized that the mushrooms "gave wisdom . . . cured illnesses . . . they were the blood of Christ."[9] Sometimes the girls would be caught eating mushrooms in the pastures by their grandfather or their mother, who would scoop them into their arms and delicately carry them home, but never reprimand them, not even once, for eating the mushrooms.

The years went by and María Sabina honed her skills as a curandera. Later writers would remember her as *La Señora Sin Mancha,* a "woman without sin."[10] Ana also tried to sharpen her shamanic powers. Alas, it was not meant to be. As María Sabina explained: "The mushroom is similar to your soul. . . . And not all souls are the same. . . . Ana María, my sister . . . talked to the mushrooms, but the mushrooms did not reveal all their secrets."[11]

~ *c. 1910* ~

One day Ana fell ill. Her family called for the local curanderos, who applied their usual medical techniques of rubbing herbs on her body and burying eggs beneath the dirt floor of her home. María Sabina had a different approach. She rounded up some Little Saints, asked for their blessings, and pleaded that they teach her how to find the cure. She fed her sister three of the Little Saints and ate an exorbitant amount herself, "thirty plus thirty."[12] She loved her sister, and would journey to the farthest reaches of the world where everything is known to find a cure. Far into the depths of that space, surrounded by music played by a trumpet, dulcimer, and violin, she found herself before a table where about seven of the "Principal Ones" sat. The Principal Ones, the mushrooms anthropomorphized, epitomized goodness, healing, wisdom, and charity. They knew all that could be known in the world where everything is known. They guarded epiphany from the unworthy and understood the beginning and end of all the mysteries of existence.

"But what do you want to become, you, María Sabina?" one of the Ones asked.

"I wish to become a saint."

A large book—the *Book of Wisdom*—manifested on the table where sat the Principal Ones. The tome kept expanding larger until it grew to the size of a human.

"María Sabina, this is the book of wisdom," a Principal One said. "It is the Book of Language. Everything that is written in it is for you. The Book is yours, take it so that you can work."

"This is for me. I receive it."[13]

María Sabina took the *Book of Wisdom* and flipped through the pages. Despite her lack of formal education (including literacy) in the regular world, in *this* world she could read every word, every sentence, on every page. And in that glorious moment, María Sabina went from an apprentice to a curandera. "I . . . understood all that was written in the Book and . . . became as though richer, wiser, and that in one moment I learned millions of things."[14]

One of those learned things was how to cure Ana. First, she had to undo all that the previous curanderos had done. She disinterred the eggs that they had buried and rubbed an herbal ointment on her sister's belly. She then blew out the three candles, the darkness providing a perfect backdrop for the revelations. The visions shifted away from medical cures, the *Book of Wisdom,* and the Principal Ones toward another entity, Chicon Nindó, the Supreme Lord of the Mountains who had the "power to enchant spirits."[15] He rode up to María Sabina on a white horse, wearing a white sombrero, surrounded by a giant halo that embossed his whole body. But as he approached the young medicine woman, she could see that his face was merely a shadow. He said nothing. She said nothing. The horseman continued on his way home, to the Mountain of Adoration. María Sabina went back inside her hut and began to chant and dance, clap and cry. The reveries within her grew so powerful that she even knocked one of the walls of the hut down through her dancing and gyrations!

By cockcrow, María Sabina finally fell into a light sleep. Over the next few days, she watched with delight as Ana slowly crawled back from her illness. She was cured.

News of María Sabina's powers traveled throughout Huautla de Jiménez. The people brought their tired, sick, and poor, yearning to breathe the air of the world where everything is known. Soon, word spread beyond the village. From as far away as Tenango (fifteen miles to the east) and San Juan Coatzospan (thirteen miles to the south), the people came, desperate for cures. With each new case, no matter how puzzling the cause and cure of sickness, María Sabina was able to look up the proper remedies from the *Book of Wisdom.* Other times, she would simply sit with the Principal Ones, drink beers with them, and discuss treatments for the infirm.

THE FOREIGNERS

María Sabina and some others ate the Little Saints that night.

Something was off though. She did not meet and sit with the

Principal Ones, nor did she encounter Nindó. "I don't know what's happening. I see strange people," she told her friend Guadalupe García. Acting quickly, García "prayed to God the Christ."[16]

~ June 29, 1955 ~

Four strange looking people (two women and two men) sat before María Sabina. She had never seen anything quite like their white skin and light-colored hair. Her friend Cayetano García (Guadalupe's husband) had brought the visitors to her home, assuring that they were of good nature. The foreigners consisted of pediatrician and amateur-mycologist Valentina Wasson (1901–1958), her husband, Wall Street banker and amateur-mycologist Robert Gordon Wasson (1898–1986), their daughter Mary (who they called "Masha"), and a photographer friend, Allan Richardson (1889–1990). Both Valentina and Gordon viewed María Sabina as the last living relic of an unbroken line of shamans—a pedigree, a keeper of wisdom passed down since ancient times when medicine priestesses guided the infirm seeking spiritual cures through the byways of the world where everything is known. They had been searching for her for about two decades—*La Señora Sin Mancha*! Mr. Wasson had surprised García the day before by perfectly pronouncing *'nti sheeto,* the local name for the Little Saints. Against her better judgment, María Sabina agreed to hold a *velada,* or all-night vigil, for the two strangers. Around 10:00 p.m., as cups of ceremonial chocolate passed among the congregants (numbering around twenty), María Sabina lit some incense that sat in a pile on the floor. One by one, she passed the sacred mushrooms through the smoke, cleansing them, preparing them, and respecting them; giving due reverence to the sacred fungi. Keeping twenty-six pairs of mushrooms (divided evenly) for herself and for her daughter, Polonia, María Sabina passed the rest out to the others. Mr. Wasson and Richardson received six pairs of mushrooms. Mrs. Wasson and Masha ate five pairs each. Just before midnight, María Sabina pulled a flower from the vase on her altar and doused the candles.

Darkness.

Across the room, she could hear the foreigners whispering to each other in their strange tongue, but had no idea what they said. It mattered not. She began a low hum that slowly grew into "articulate syllables . . . cutting the darkness sharply."[17] Polonia joined her in song. They sang beautifully. Not forcefully—but with authority. She stood up and started to clap and slap her body, which "had pitch, the rhythm at times was complex, and the speed and volume varied subtly."[18] The others who partook in the velada also "were playing a part in the vocal activity. In the moments of tension they would utter exclamations of wonder and adoration, not loud, responsive to the singers and harmonizing with them, spontaneously yet with art."[19]

Her experience was unlike any she'd had before. Not to say that it was bad or that the *velada* felt empty (it wasn't and it didn't), just that instead of the familiar landscapes in the world where everything is known, María Sabina had visions of big cities, "the place the foreigners came from."[20] Perhaps her thoughts were cross-pollinating with those of Mrs. Wasson? Indeed, she had hoped to experience visions of Russia, her homeland, which she had not seen in almost forty years. Instead, she found herself in eighteenth century Versailles, at the court of Louis XV attending a lavish dance party fueled by the music of Mozart. From there, she found herself in a Spanish church, and then the Metropolitan Opera house, first watching a production of "Les Sylphides" and then flying into the air with some of the ballerinas.[21]* The vigil ended around 4:00 a.m. When María Sabina and the others woke later that morning (around 6:00 a.m.), she fixed them some bread and coffee. And just as suddenly as these four pale-faced, light-haired strange visitors had come into María Sabina's life, they were gone.

---

*Interestingly, even after the Wassons joined Sabina in ceremony, Valentina still jostled between calling the mushrooms "sacred" and thinking of them in "model psychosis" terms, writing that the fungi caused "a self-induced bout of schizophrenia." See Wasson, "The Sacred Mushroom," 8.

~ *1956* ~

The two male pale-faced, light-haired foreigners returned.

This time, three more pale-faced foreigners accompanied them.

María Sabina did not know who these people were, but we do. The company consisted of Mr. Wasson, the one who could so flawlessly pronounce the Mazatec name for the mushroom, and Richardson, camera in hand. The three unfamiliar gents were French botanist Roger Heim (1900–1979), French anthropologist Guy Stresser-Péan (1913–2009), and James Moore (born c. 1926), a chemist at Parke-Davis and Co., the very company that had taken an interest in peyote a little over a half century earlier. And Moore came with a bonus: an all-expenses paid grant from the Geschickter Fund for Medical Research (recall that the Geschickter Fund was a CIA front that secretly funneled money into possible mind-control projects for the Agency). While Wasson, Heim, Richardson, and Stresser-Péan didn't know it at the time, the twenty-nine-year-old Moore (the youngest of the company) had only accompanied them on the trip to see María Sabina as part of a clandestine MKUltra subproject. He was there to bring the sacred mushroom back to the United States to see if the CIA could turn it into a mind-control weapon.

Moore hadn't been the first CIA agent to travel to Mexico in search of the Little Saints. Early in 1953, an anonymous operative arrived in Huautla de Jiménez, hoping to find the prized (though at this point still legendary) mushrooms. And while he procured a number of exotic specimens culled from the rich countryside (including piule, the highly psychoactive Mexican red bean), his aggressive way of trying to locate the mushrooms did not jive well with the locals. He returned to the United States without any mushroom samples.[22] He had been sent by then head of Operation ARTICHOKE, Morse Allen, who had hoped first to determine whether such mushrooms even existed; and second, if they did, to produce synthetic versions in a lab, so that ARTICHOKE would not be held up by growing seasons and lack of supply. And so Allen tapped the one man who knew more about strange mind chemicals than anyone else in the United States—Sidney Gottlieb, head of MKUltra. And just as the Agency had done with many other pharmaceutical companies, Parke-Davis and Co. joined the roster. One day, Moore's boss called him into his office and just asked outright, "How would you like to work inside the company on a CIA project?"[23] And just like that, the unnamed agent's exotic samples passed from Allen to Gottlieb and finally to Moore.

Still, while the unnamed agent's score of various medicinal and psychoactive plants proved useful, Gottlieb focused his attention on the fabled Mexican mushroom. In fact, that no one even knew if such a mushroom existed tells us how obsessed the CIA was with the possibilities. And Moore seemed the perfect candidate. He was a quiet, unassuming, scrawny professor employed at the University of Delaware, who looked exactly like the kind of person no one would expect to dabble in the cloak and dagger trade—a nerd. Gottlieb appreciated this in the young scientist, commenting, "[Moore] maintains the fiction that the botanical specimens he collects are for his own use."[24] Nonetheless, this nerd took up the task of traveling to the most remote parts of Mexico searching for the mushroom—penetrating parts of the world that even the cockiest jock wouldn't tread. But just as the unnamed ARTICHOKE agent's fact-finding methods proved too aggressive to the remote villagers of Central America, Moore's proved too passive. He could penetrate the thick overgrowths, but not the "atmosphere of secrecy about the mushrooms."[25] Moore, too, returned to the United States empty-handed. The Little Saints proved evasive—they wanted nothing to do with the CIA.

Even in remote regions gossip can travel far and wide. From the secluded village of Huautla de Jiménez nestled high in the mountains of Oaxaca, news of the pale-faced, light-haired strangers made the three-hundred-mile trek to Mexico City, specifically to the University of Mexico. There, a botanist, one of the CIA's informal associates, heard news of the foreigners' visit to María Sabina and sent the Agency a report. Gottlieb relayed this message to Moore, and Moore sent Wasson a friendly letter, asking to accompany the banker on his next journey. Moore even had financial backing and would bankroll the whole expedition.

~ *March 1956* ~

María Sabina was not aware of any of this. She welcomed them all to participate in the velada when they unexpectedly showed up in Huautla de Jiménez again that spring.

The Little Saints, however, *knew.* First, they tried to crash the Cessna that Moore rode into Huautla de Jiménez—the pilot acting quickly and landing the small plane on the side of a mountain. Moore was left stranded in a nearby, isolated mountain village for a day—the kind of place one only finds due to emergency landings. Whatever happened that day, we don't know, but he appeared utterly miserable by the time the Cessna returned to pick him up. Once Moore arrived in Huautla de Jiménez, the Little Saints hit him hard with explosive diarrhea. And then . . . then that excruciating itching began. The local insects seemed to have a special taste for Moore's skin. No one else on the team suffered such harsh bodily purges or felt so dined upon by the insects. He complained throughout the expedition. When it came time for the velada, Moore's four companions experienced a fantastic night of visions. He felt only "distorted."[26] They had sat with the Little Saints "to find God."[27] Moore had sought a weapon. By the time they all left, Moore was fully ostracized from the group. Richardson recalled, "all we knew was that we didn't like Jim."[28]

The Little Saints knew too.

They didn't like Jim either.

◎

Both Moore and Heim brought samples back with them. And while Moore's efforts resulted in nothing, Heim successfully grew the Little Saints in his Parisian lab from a spore print he had taken while in Huautla de Jiménez. Dubbed *Psilocybe mexicana,* the mushroom adapted to the laboratory setting quite smoothly. Now that he could create a steady supply, he sought a chemist to isolate the active principle. He wrote a letter to Yves Dunant (1912–1994), who was the director of the Paris division of Sandoz Pharmaceuticals. Dunant passed the request on to the best research chemist he knew . . .

◎

Albert Hofmann was reading the daily paper when an article caught his attention. A small group of French and American researchers had penetrated the deep forests of Central America, discovering mushrooms that not only produced fantastic visions but were also intimately tied to the spiritual sensibilities of the locals who ate them. Oh, how he'd love to get his hands on those mushrooms! But the newspaper did not include any names or professional affiliations that might help locate and start correspondence with these researchers.

Fate once again smiled upon Hofmann. With much excitement, he read the letter from Heim, delivered to him via Dunant. Others at Sandoz, though, were less excited. LSD was already a handful. Should they really be releasing another psychosis-producing chemical into the world? Hofmann thought so and instantly responded to Heim that he was happy to take the problem to task and unlock the secret of the curandera's mushroom. Heim sent Hofmann around 100 grams of the dried mushroom. Initial tests with mice and dogs revealed no outward symptoms. Had the Little Saints spoiled by drying them? Hofmann realized that the only way to answer that question was to eat the Little Ones Who Spring Forth himself.

~ *July 1957* ~

That afternoon, Hofmann found himself in the highlands of Central America . . . all in the privacy of his own home in Zurich.

He had eaten 2.5 grams of the Little Saints, the standard dose of the curandera, according to Heim. And now, for the second time in his life, Hofmann had to be escorted home by his assistant, this time Hans Tscherter, for possibly overdosing on a laboratory-created psychochemical (although this time, the war over, Tscherter drove Hofmann home). And of his home—Hofmann explained that it had taken on a "Mexican character," though he had expected this kind of reaction: "I was perfectly well aware that my knowledge of the Mexican origin of the mushroom would lead me to imagine only Mexican scenery." However, try as he might to stave off the Central American imagery, all efforts "proved ineffective. . . . Whether my eyes were closed or open, I saw only Mexican motifs and colors." When Hans leaned over to check Hofmann's pulse, he transformed into an "Aztec priest."[29]

Hofmann offers us a most intriguing proposition. In this moment he is claiming to be able to *direct* his experience (if even involuntarily). But could this kind of "direct set" be used for other purposes? Sure, the CIA, Navy, and Army wanted a mind-control chemical. But where LSD and mescaline continually failed, might this new synthetic, based on the sacred mushrooms of Central America, prove successful? Only time would tell.

Hofmann eventually isolated the active alkaloids in the Little Saints. Like LSD-25, this new, synthetic active principle, culled from a natural original, received a name equal parts letters and numbers: PS 39. Hofmann called this new chemical "psilocybin."* Sandoz would market it as *Indocybin*.

Heim had hoped to publish his findings first. In homage to his New York banker friend, Gordon Wasson, he would name the mushroom

---

*From the Greek *psilos* ("bald") and *kubē* ("head").

after him, *Psilocybe wassonii*. However, one of his students, the National University of Tucumán (in Argentina) mycologist Rolf Singer (1906–1994), beat him to the punch. Singer was so enthused about the prospects that he formed his own expedition team to traverse and circumvent the thick Oaxacan underbrush and seemingly impenetrable forests. The team scored big, and Singer quickly published his findings, calling the would-be Wasson-named mushroom by a more authentic name: *Psilocybe muliercula,* or "psilocybin of the little woman."

Once Hofmann synthesized psilocybin, the CIA was all over it. Isbell—the same Harris Isbell that veritably tortured people like William Henry Wall with psychedelics at the Lexington, Kentucky, Addiction Center—received some of the Little Saints shortly thereafter. Nine "negro males who were former drug addicts," and had already participated in prior LSD studies at the Addiction Center, received the psilocybin. The general reaction was an otherworldly state, as real as this one. They were entering the world where everything is known. But since they did not know how to approach the experience, they did not encounter the Principal Ones. Instead, they felt "fear that something evil was going to happen, fear of insanity, or of death." This feeling usually slowly descended into the pits of hell; though sometimes it grew into feelings of elation "expressed by almost continuous gales of laughter."[30] Some reported "trips to the moon." At least two subjects had worthwhile reactions for the CIA's purposes: they thought "their experiences were caused by the experimenters controlling their minds."[31]

And of María Sabina . . . she suffered a most tragic misfortune. The Little Saints stopped talking to her. Their purity faded. And try as María Sabina might, she could do nothing about it. Before the foreigners had showed up the Little Saints "elevated" María Sabina. "The force has diminished," she lamented. "If Cayetano hadn't brought

the foreigners . . . the saint children would have kept their power."[32]
Additionally, by the early and mid-1960s, a swarm of hippie tourists
descended on Huautla de Jiménez, seeking the woman without sin,
desiring her Little Saints. Some trashed the small mountain village; others trashed María Sabina's home. One sacred mushroom–seeker with
a particularly undesirable personality rather rudely remarked, "Look,
man. You can go for that curandero shit if you like but it's not my bag.
I don't need an old hag mumbling in Mazatecan to turn me on. . . . You
just score the mushrooms . . . we'll do the rest."[33]

Back in the United States, and outside the CIA's oversight, a new
paradigm crept into clinical consciousness. It was a paradigm that
Western culture had certainly seen in the past, but had long since lost
the thread of tradition. The Little Saints represented a novel approach
to understanding other synthetics like LSD and mescaline, one not
of psychotomimeticism or chemical warfare agents, but rather one of
supernatural connections with forces beyond those available through
normal consciousness.

And as it turned out, the United States in the middle 1950s was
just ripe for such a paradigm shift.

10
Voices from Behind the Veil
ESP and LSD

No settled conclusion has followed the exploratory inquiries on . . . drugs in connection with ESP tests.

J. B. RHINE AND J. G. PRATT

ORDERS

Dr. Wilhelm Mayer-Gross (1889–1961) only cared about one question: Could parapsychologist Rosalind Heywood (1895–1980) see the connections between two usually unrelated objects while under the influence of mescaline?*

Was everything truly *all one*?

"It's quite simple," Heywood replied from across the universe. "They are the same thing. It's seeing from the *middle,* you see."

She spoke from the perspective of infinite connections, endless possibilities. From the vista point of a life of science and the supernatural, all mixed like tiny tiles creating a church mosaic.

Unlike other doctors working with mescaline and/or LSD at the time, Mayer-Gross, a German-born psychiatrist who fled the Third

---

*Heywood does not personally name Mayer-Gross as the facilitator of her first mescaline journey. However, he was the only doctor working with mescaline in England in 1952, so I surmise that it is him of whom she speaks.

128

Reich for England, had a deep interest in uncommon states of consciousness, stemming back at least to his doctorate dissertation, which explored "ecstasy and abnormal happiness."[1]

And in the very least, Heywood qualified as "abnormal."

◎

We might best summarize Heywood's childhood with a single word: *hell*. But that hell came with an unforeseen byproduct. Her unique demeanor (and perceived supernatural gifts) left her ostracized from other people, inculcating in her a "longing for 'real communication.'"[2] Anything would do—other weird children, or weirder adults, or even ghosts. Heywood was a very vocal child, which sometimes resulted in a silk cloth fastening her mouth shut courtesy of her nanny. *Little girls must not ask "Why,"* her overbearing parents insisted. How dare a mere girl express her feelings while living in Edwardian England? It was an existence that encouraged a very black-and-white view of the world.

Raised in such an atmosphere, Heywood nonetheless developed a natural curiosity and a scientific mind—despite what material reductionists might decry about her parapsychological leanings. A couple examples shall suffice. Once, around age eight, Heywood stood on a staircase that featured a collection of Zulu spears adorning the wall above the banister. The arrows had poisoned tips to kill their target quicker, an adult who was present told her. The temptation to prick her finger on the arrow—"Why not, I thought, do what's not done, just to see what would happen?"—to test the claim might have resulted in her death. Although the young Heywood had not yet fully developed her psychic abilities, she nonetheless (thankfully) had the wherewithal to leave the arrow alone.[3]

A second experiment involved a doll. One Sunday morning, as per her usual, she found herself bored at church. The priest droned on and on about God knows what, and someone in the choir was singing off-key, the sour notes piercing little Heywood down to her very soul. During the sermon, the priest had mentioned that worms feast upon the bodies of the deceased. Heywood thought about those awful corsets made of whalebone that were all the Edwardian vogue at the time. Dolls, too, were made of such bone. Heywood decided to put the priest's claim to task by burying her doll. She had no use for it anyway, and a sacrifice on the altar of science appealed to her more than did brushing its hair. A week later, the uneaten doll disinterred, Heywood looked upon it and realized "that a statement made in Church could be inaccurate."[4]

Later in life, she heard "Voices from behind the Veil," which she referred to as "Orders."[5] She made no premature decision as to where Orders originated, only that they came from a place beyond her everyday consciousness. Sometimes she followed Orders to her detriment—they steered her down the wrong path. Other times, she wouldn't follow Orders and would lose out. Take that time in July 1949, when she and her husband busily readied their house to leave on holiday. Orders told Heywood to turn off the water, lest the pipes burst. She took this as a false order—"more like fussing than ESP." After all, water pipes do not burst in the summertime (as both her husband and their maintenance worker confirmed). However, she made a compromise with herself: she would leave the water on and give the maintenance man a key to their home (just in case the pipe should burst). The pipes did burst; the maintenance man charged them twenty quid for repairs.[6]

On another occasion, Heywood found herself sitting at home writing, while her husband with whom she felt a "subconscious linkage" worked upstairs in the study with his new secretary. Despite having nothing to say to him, Heywood nonetheless felt the need to go upstairs. She entered the study—her husband had a look of satisfaction, while the secretary had a look of shock.

"I told you so," he said to his secretary.

"Told her what?" asked Heywood.

"That you'd come if I called you mentally," he said laughing.[7]

None of this shocked Heywood anymore (though she feared the incident caused the new secretary to believe that Aleister Crowley had just hired her). How could she best explain that her unique union with her husband was not Thelemic magick, but instead what Cambridge psychical philosopher Charlie Dunbar Broad (1887–1971) considered an underlying telepathic connection present in all humans—a bond that strengthened through cultivation of relationships: friends, romantic partners, family members, and the like.

For our own protection, our minds act as pressure-reducers, cutting off the constant flow of information that would "overwhelm [the mind] if unshielded." Some called this natural valve, which drastically reduces the endless amounts of information in the universe to a digestible form, the "Freudian censor."[8] Others, like Broad, called this phenomenon "Mind at Large." Mind at Large represented all the thoughts, all the information, of every entity (human or otherwise) that had ever existed since the Big Bang. As Broad surmised: "Each person is at each moment capable of remembering all that has ever happened to [them] and of perceiving everything that is happening everywhere in the universe. . . . [B]y shutting out most of what we should otherwise perceive or remember at any moment, [we are left with] only that very small and special selection which is likely to be practically useful."[9] Even poets like W. B. Yeats felt that "the borders of our minds are ever shifting and that many minds can flow into one another, as it were, and create or reveal a single mind, a single energy."[10]

Westerners—at least those who stood outside the world of the artist and poet—for all practical purposes, had cut themselves off fully from Mind at Large. That's why stories of paranormal activity tended to hold more weight among Eastern peoples. As Heywood observed, "the consciousness of *I* being separate from *you* is far less strong [in the East] than in the West"[11]—a lesson she would later learn while in the presence of a Grand Madame who headed a cult "based on Oriental philosophy."[12] Through the Madame, Heywood met Mary, a member of the cult who apparently had very finely tuned psychic powers herself. One day Heywood noticed that Mary's petticoat was showing beneath her short skirt and wondered if she knew Mary well enough to say something about it. Well, she needn't say anything at all. Mary turned to Heywood and remarked, "I'll hitch it up." This, and other encounters with Mary's psychic abilities, only "caused ESP to become a more vivid reality" for Heywood.[13]

◎

We may sum up the cultural atmosphere of ESP and other aspects of parapsychology among the scientific class in the 1950s by eavesdropping on a conversation between two scientists, sitting at a dinner party, enjoying exquisite food and strong drinks. One of the scientists at the table had responded to Heywood's reluctant confession that her main interest of study was ESP. Her tipsy courage inspired audacity in others, leaving another dinner guest to admit that he had once encountered "a visionary figure" that gave him very specific instructions (these instructions he did not disclose to the rest of the diners).

"Why didn't you tell me this before?" the host of the party inquired.

"How could I?" he replied. "You were a scientist."

"But I am very interested in these experiences," the host answered.

"Then why didn't you tell me so?"

"How could I? You were a scientist."[14]

◎

Heywood didn't even like the term ESP. But the abbreviated form of "extrasensory perception" had entered modern parlance; so, to avoid confusion, she used it anyway. For she was well-acquainted with popular resistance to new ideas. We all learned in high school of the scorn and mockery endured by Nicolaus Copernicus (1473–1543) for foolishly claiming that we lived not in a geocentric universe but rather in a heliocentric universe. And was not Wilhelm Röntgen (1845–1923) ridiculed for having the audacity to claim that doctors could take pictures of the inside of the body? His detractors sheepishly ate their criticisms once he discovered the magic of the X-ray. And who could forget the way other scientists derided electrical engineer Guglielmo Marconi

(1874–1937) for stupidly thinking that invisible pulses could be sent, unfelt and undetected, through the air? "The earth is round," claimed the experts, "and radio waves go straight."[15] However, as we may surmise with hindsight in our favor, only Marconi was laughing after accepting his Nobel Prize for sending a wireless signal over a mile away from its point of origin. We today call this once discredited magic "wifi."

But this raised a very interesting question. If we could transmit radio waves through the air, could we not also send thoughts and intentions similarly? The paranormal was real. It just hadn't been discovered, dissected, and classified by science—*yet*. And one day, the parapsychologists would be laughing as they accepted their own Nobel Prizes. At least, that's how Heywood justified her experiments with LSD and ESP. Perhaps somewhere in the outer regions, through the space dust of what we oft call today "cosmic consciousness," there was a path that could lead anyone into the world of psychic abilities, contacting entities, and various sorts of preternatural activities.

THE DANCE

~ *Sometime in 1952* ~

Such experiences led Heywood to want to test the powers of ESP in various altered states. Well aware that doctors at the time believed that LSD and mescaline caused "a temporary condition of schizophrenia," Heywood rejected such interpretations.[16] Instead, she felt that the psychic state of awareness "resemble[d] those induced by mescaline and other hallucinogens."[17] And so she found herself in Mayer-Gross's office, having taken an amount of mescaline that is lost to us, which plunged her into the depths of her subconscious, trying to find the oddest areas of esoteric awareness available to the human mind.

We can imagine a rather drab, clinical *setting* in 1952. But Heywood's *set* had been primed for a mystical experience since her childhood. So much so that it overrode the uninspired setting, which her own thoughts had transformed into an array of majestic patterns.

Mayer-Gross's questions felt inane at this point of the journey. Any words she tried to use to describe the patterns would "be so misleading that it is almost better to say nothing," she replied to Mayer-Gross.

"Why misleading?" he probed.

"Because if I said they were solid you would think I meant they were solid. . . . I can't see them. . . . It is the awareness of pattern. . . . Now you are trying to make me divide them up into one or another and you can't do that. . . . You can't say a great mass of pattern. It is PATTERN."

Soon after this exchange, Heywood sunk even deeper into the experience, into the "hinterland of essence."

The hinterland of essence? Mayer-Gross thought. "What is the most pleasant of the images you have just seen?"

"The pure light at the top of the mountain," Heywood replied.

She closed her eyes and drifted deeper and deeper into herself. Further into the "symbols of universal interrelatedness [of] mystics, artists, saints, and sensitives."[18]

In answer to Mayer-Gross's question, she continued:

[T]he inter-relatedness was symbolized by a delicate spidery web . . . which linked everything to everything from atom to nebula. . . . Nothing was static. The entire Universe was in constant fluid movement. Gradually I became aware of that movement as a crucial fact: it was *The Dance,* the inter-weaving eternal impersonal relentless inevitable Cosmic Dance—the Dance of Beingness. I saw the God, the Krishna, dancing . . . I cried out in extreme delight. . . . [T]here appeared a supreme Figure, motionless, Buddha-like, eternally at peace.[19]

This entity was "the Divine Mother."[20] She spoke: "You are being shown the universe before the principle of communication, which is love, has been injected into it."[21]

The cognitive dissonance set in. This place was beautiful, not scary.

The Divine Mother was kind, not cruel. Nothing like what *madness* probably felt like. Heywood turned to Mayer-Gross. "What exactly are you trying to figure out through me?"

"What goes on in the mind of a schizophrenic," he answered.[22]

Heywood decided to use her exceptional powers of perception to find that place; find that corner of the universe that sends mixed signals into the human mind—the land deep in the recesses of black holes, where schizophrenia lies. She focused her mind and landed in an arid desert. A cold lifeless landscape . . . *almost.* Clustered beyond the rocks and barren dirt, Heywood could see "grey veiled figures." These were the Lost. Heywood wanted to help them; wanted to give them all the love they never felt, but she couldn't. She simply wasn't "perfectly Good"—and only the perfectly Good could help the Lost, she realized. Only the perfectly Good could "sink in sacrifice, even below [the Lost], to become the objects of their pity and compassion."[23]

A couple of days after the experience, while cooking lunch, Heywood experienced the first recorded "flashback" in history. Granted, the term (as least with regards to reliving psychedelic experiences) didn't exist yet, so instead, she termed the occurrence a "throw-back." The Divine Mother appeared in her kitchen, not visually, but as a *presence.* Nonetheless, Her Presence spoke: "the Universe could not become conscious of its unity until the principle of communication, which was the kind of love she had made me aware of, had been injected into it."[24] And it was Heywood's job to bring that love into the world, for the benefit of all humankind.

The visit invigorated her! Now simple tasks like cooking lunch seemed so much more important, less like a chore and more like "an ecstatic act of service." She appreciated her "model psychosis," which had "tweaked my eyes open," as she reflects: "Now at least I know that [my eyes] are shut, that my senses are merely parochial and that to take my yapping little ego at all seriously is quite ridiculous."[25]

And, of course, *everyone* had an opinion about her experience.

The Freudians went right to work. "It's obvious," they said, "Your Divine Mother was a construct of your own. You were doubtless brought up in an Edwardian nursery and saw too little of your own mother." The Jungians tripped over themselves to label the Divine Mother "an archetype," while the eyes of Catholics would light up with reverence, and interpret Heywood's retelling of her encounter to blurt out "Our Lady!"[26] The most egregious interpretation came from a psychiatrist who explained to Heywood that the Divine Mother was her own mental projection of herself.

These misunderstandings and somewhat arrogant analyses at first bothered Heywood. But only for a moment. Then she realized how silly the whole idea of judgment really was in the grander scheme of things.

Pretentious claims from the scientific class meant nothing to her anymore.

Heywood felt "unified."[27] Flying higher than she ever had before.

Soaring angelic.

11

To Soar Angelic

Birth of the Psychedelic Renaissance

Nature develops . . . up to a certain point and then leaves [us] to develop further. . . . Evolution . . . in this case will mean the development of certain inner qualities and features which usually remain undeveloped.

PYOTR OUSPENSKY

ISTIGKEIT

~ *March 1953* ~

Facial hair almost ruined everything.

Maria Huxley (1899–1955), a rather conservative woman, sat at the breakfast table in her home at 740 North King's Road—not far from Santa Monica Boulevard in West Hollywood. Her husband, the famed writer Aldous Huxley, had just returned from a visit to their mailbox. He took his seat across from Maria, and looked over the assortment of letters in his hands. Another pleasant morning in sunny Los Angeles.

The two had settled in Hollywood during the height of Aldous's illustrious literary career. That year the APA would hold their conference in Los Angeles. This gave Aldous a most inspired idea as he flipped through his mail. A recent article he had read in the *Hibbert*

137

Journal had mentioned a new use for mescaline. This most intrigued him. He desired a conversation with the authors of the paper, who were none other than John Smythies and Humphry Osmond, the two researchers at Saskatchewan Mental Hospital, Weyburn, previously discussed. Most people had not heard of mescaline or its natural parent medicine, peyote, in 1953.

Aldous Huxley wasn't most people.

He'd heard of both.

Huxley had been looking for "a new pleasure . . . derived from the invention of a new drug" since as early as 1931.[1] After scouring the literature on "sacramental intoxicants" in various societies, he chanced upon a "dusty and neglected . . . ponderous work by a German pharmacologist."[2] The German pharmacologist was Louis Lewin, the "neglected" volume, his drug lexicon *Phantastica* (1924).* Lewin's research had led to his discovery that many "Phantastica are said to bestow a like gift of divination" to various tribal peoples the world over.[3] Fascinated by such ideas, Huxley sought his own visionary experience. He felt that it wasn't the tribal cultures that lacked religiosity, but rather that it was "the rich and highly educated whites who have left ourselves bare behind."[4] But he had already tried Eastern techniques. A bout with insomnia in his late twenties led him to mix sleeping aids with "breathing exercises of the Yoga sort." Only he found that this method was not only a dreadful bore but also that it called for a "careful regulation of diet and sexual habits."[5] Huxley desired a much quicker and less instructional way into the subconscious realms.

His next step was locating a *phantastikum* to ingest and a doctor to help navigate his journey to that outlandish place in his mind that he would later name "The Other World."

Aldous looked up from the mail, "Let's ask this fellow Osmond to stay."

---

*Recall that Lewin published the first paper on peyote's alkaloids (p. 7 of this book)

Maria could not believe her ears. Aldous, who ever-enjoyed the quiet solitude writers notoriously seek, *never* invited guests for a visit. Maria was undoubtedly curious. Who exactly was this Osmond fellow, she inquired?

"He's a Canadian psychiatrist who works with mescaline," Aldous replied.

"But he may have a beard and we may not like him," Maria protested.[6]

Aldous struck up a bargain. They would allow Osmond to stay and if they felt they were not jiving with him they could always use Aldous's busy schedule as an excuse to stay out late. Funnily enough, two-thousand miles north (and a week or so later) in Saskatchewan, Amy "Jane" Osmond had a similar idea. Her husband Humphry had been vacillating between excitement and "apprehensi[on]" about possibly staying with the Huxleys after receiving Aldous's invitation. After all, Humphry was a longtime fan of Aldous's work—he even kept a copy of *Texts and Pretexts* (1933) handy during the London blitz (September 1940–May 1941). But this also worried him. What if Aldous was "disillusioned, cynical or even savage?"[7] Jane told Humphry not to worry. If he did not jive with the Huxleys he could always pretend to "be kept late at an A.P.A. session," she said craftily.[8]

Osmond responded that he would indeed take up the Huxleys on their offer. Aldous was delighted. Although he hadn't mentioned it to Osmond in his first letter, Huxley desired a mescaline experience. So that he would *just so happen* to have some mescaline lying around when Osmond showed up on his doorstep, he set about obtaining some, asking a "young doctor friend" of his if he might acquire the chemical from pharmaceutical giant, Hoffmann-La Roche. The company could get Huxley's friend the mescaline, but they would have to first write-off to Sandoz Pharmaceuticals, as they had none on hand. Delivery of the mescaline would take at least a week—maybe longer. The timing was too close for Huxley's liking. He quickly penned a flattering, follow-up letter to Osmond: "do you have any [mescaline] on hand? If so I hope you can bring a little; for I am eager to make the experiment and would feel particularly happy to do so under the supervision of an experienced investigator like yourself."[9]*

Osmond was not sure of the laws concerning bringing mescaline over the U.S.–Canadian border. But it also didn't faze him enough to even check. He packed his bags—shirt, ties, socks, *mescaline*—and took a flight to Los Angeles. Once arrived, he boarded the airline bus to the Hollywood Roosevelt Hotel, where Maria met him.

That weekend, Aldous joined Osmond at the APA conference, where he busied himself chatting it up with other Freudians—the famed Viennese doctor another of a seemingly endless number of topics of which Huxley was familiar. The one, foremost topic on both Huxley's and Osmond's mind, mescaline, however, did not come up once. After the conference, Maria (tired of waiting for the two reserved English gents to just *say it already!*) broached the subject with Osmond.[10]

~ *May 5, 1953* ~

Osmond had a restless night. On the one paw, he savored the idea of giving mescaline not to a schizophrenic patient, but instead to "the most sane man he knew."[11] On the other paw, Osmond "did not relish the possibility, however remote, of being the man who drove Aldous Huxley mad."[12] Nonetheless, late that morning he proceeded with the experiment joined by Maria, personal assistant and friend Onnie

---

*Journalist Michael Pollan claims in his book *How to Change Your Mind* that Osmond sought out Huxley to try the mescaline (and not the other way around). He writes, "[Osmond] gave [Huxley] mescaline in the explicit hope that a great writer's descriptions and metaphors would help him and his colleagues make sense of an experience they were struggling to interpret" (114). However, as the above letter indicates, Huxley, not Osmond, broached the topic. Additionally, Huxley had no plans to write about the experience at the time of the experiment.

Wesley, and a very excited Aldous Huxley.* The day had rolled off the morning perfectly, greeting the city with spring-blue skies; the setting, as exquisite as a man of Huxley's caliber demanded. Osmond dropped the silver mescaline crystals into a glass of water and gently began to stir. At 11 a.m., Huxley drank the potion and waited . . . and waited . . . and waited some more. Nothing happened. What he had expected, "visions of many-colored geometries, of animated architectures . . . landscapes with heroic figures, of symbolic dramas trembling perpetually on the verge of the ultimate revelation," did not occur. What did occur was a wrestling "with the idiosyncrasies of [his] mental makeup, the facts of [his] temperament, training and habits."[13]

Frustrated, Huxley retired to his study. A small vase containing three flowers caught his attention. The mescaline was starting to break through. The flower petals, "in their living light," began to appear as if breathing. *No—not breathing*—more of a "repeated flow from beauty to heightened beauty, from deeper to ever deeper meaning."[14] This same ever-tuning beatific effect moved from the flowers to the walls, brushing across his impressive book collection that lined the shelves of his study. Sitting beside Victor White's *God and the Unconscious*—a book he had borrowed from his cousin Renee and still had not read—sat a large tome about Italian Renaissance painter Sandro Botticelli. As Aldous flipped through the pictures in the Botticelli book, he started to notice details within them that he had never seen before. "My attention was arrested and I gazed in fascination," he recalled while looking at Botticelli's *Judith,* "not at the pale, neurotic heroine or her attendant . . . not at the . . . vernal landscape in the background, but at the purplish silk of Judith's pleated

---

*Aldous's personal assistant and Maria's friend, a black woman named Onnie Wesley, was present during Aldous's first mescaline experience. He does not mention her anywhere in *The Doors of Perception* (1954), his famous essay on mescaline; however, in a letter to Humphry Osmond dated February 21, 1955, he references "Onnie . . . who was with us at the time of [Osmond's] first visit" (see Smith, *Letters of Aldous Huxley,* 734).

bodice and long wind-blown skirts." Huxley turned his head "down by chance," and noticed his legs: "Those folds in the trousers—what a labyrinth of endlessly significant complexity! And the texture of the gray flannel*—how rich, how deeply, mysteriously sumptuous!"[15]

At long last, Huxley was tripping!

Osmond quickly jumped in. "What about spatial relationships?" he asked from the other side of the veil.

They didn't really matter, thought Huxley. Spatial relations? What a fantastically boring question, considering the waves of beauty overtaking the book spines. *Spatial relations?* How pedestrian!

Osmond decided to try a different question. One perhaps not so boring. What were Huxley's thoughts on time?

"There seems to be plenty of it," Huxley replied. He thought briefly of looking at his watch and giving a less cheeky answer. Then he realized his watch was "in another universe" and the effort to look at it much too great.[16] In fact, any ordinary task seemed so inconsequential when compared with this new sense of perception. Why would anyone waste time looking at a watch ever again? And anyway, weren't we all part of the watch anyway? All part of . . . *oh, what was that word Meister Eckhart used?*

Ahh, yes, "'Istgkeit.' . . . 'Is-ness.' The Being of Platonic Philosophy."[17]

The two men occupied two very different worlds at that time. Huxley, mesmerized by the folds in his jeans; Osmond frantically following him around the house, asking questions, recording answers. What most busied Osmond's mind? Huxley's thoughts on madness, of course. After all, Osmond still saw mescaline as a psychotomimetic. So did Huxley. And so Osmond asked Huxley if he was indeed experiencing a model psychosis; if he knew what "madness" meant;

---

*Aldous wore blue jeans that day, not gray flannel trousers. During Aldous's writing of *The Doors of Perception,* Maria had urged him to be "better dressed for [his] readers." Taking Maria's advice, he changed his attire for his audience (see Dunaway, *Aldous Huxley Recollected,* 96).

if he could control that place in his mind that felt like a model psychosis.

"If you started in the wrong way," Huxley responded, "everything that happened would be proof of the conspiracy against you. It would all be self-validating. You couldn't draw a breath without knowing it was part of the plot."

Osmond grew evermore intrigued. "So you think you know where madness lies?" he asked.

"Yes."

"And you couldn't control it?"

"No. . . . If one began with fear and hate as the major premise, one would have to go on to [that] conclusion."[18]

Maria grew bored of these bland parlays between her husband and the Canadian doctor. There was something much deeper to the mescaline experience, which had nothing to do with evaluating how "psychotic" her husband felt from moment to moment. But how to get their minds away from psychology (after all, Aldous was quite mentally healthy) and onto something beyond the clinical approach? She decided to steer the conversation toward the metaphysical. "Would you be able . . . to fix your attention on what *The Tibetan Book of the Dead* calls the Clear Light?"* she asked.[19]

The Clear Light: that place of cosmic perfection where all is whole and whole is all. Our final resting place, whence we merge with everything—from every wrinkle of every crater on every moon from our local one to those past Pluto, to the smallest ant struggling for life in a spider's web.

This is important. While Osmond and Huxley thought in terms of mimicking madness, Maria recognized the *transcendent* value of the mescaline experience. But even Maria's suggestion couldn't shake the medical model from Aldous's mind. He didn't think he could see—let

---

*Recall that Heywood spoke of the "pure light," p. 134 of this book.

alone hold on to—the Clear Light. The problem, as Aldous saw it, was that such feats required a guide, a shaman; someone who had been to the other world, mapped it, and could direct his experience through the byways of eternity.

But this was 1953. Most Americans—at least those not located at 740 North Kings Road—had never even heard of a shaman. Osmond and Huxley decided to take a drive to the World's Biggest Drugstore, while Maria and Onnie stayed behind. Huxley laughed at the "Red Sea of traffic" in which he and Osmond found themselves.[20] He found American drugstores fascinating (as opposed to those found in England). Months earlier he had visited the World's Biggest with a friend, Peggy Kiskadden, who noted how Aldous, despite his poor vision, would "wander around and see these really absurd things that you can get." Even without the mescaline, Kiskadden noticed an "enchanted" look in his eye.[21] Imagine what it must have been like for Aldous on that fine May afternoon! Aisle after aisle, absurd product after absurd product, Huxley gazed upon the shelves until almost an hour had passed. Not long after, the two arrived back at 740 North Kings Road where Huxley—much to his dissatisfaction—had almost completely returned to baseline.

His journey was over.

Or perhaps it was just beginning . . .

Following the experiment, both Osmond and Huxley began formulating ideas for respective projects. Osmond wanted to give mescaline to between fifty and one hundred people "of outstanding abilities in various fields" and record their experience—essentially what he did with Huxley but on a much grander scale. Huxley couldn't control his enthusiasm. He wanted Osmond's experiment to happen; he had so many questions—*Is there any marked difference between the average reactions of extreme cerebrotonics, viscerotonics, and somatotonics? Do people with a profound musical gift get auditory counterparts of the*

visions and transfigurations of the external world experienced by others?
How are pure mathematicians and professional philosophers affected?—
only a much larger sample size could answer these and countless other
queries.[22] Osmond started looking for investors for future psychedelic research. Huxley had the connections. He sent a friendly letter
to one of his correspondents, Robert Hutchins, director of the Ford
Foundation. Perhaps Ford would be interested in sponsoring this bold,
new research?[23]

Huxley also had his own project in mind as well—a long essay
that would detail the profound nuances of his mescaline experience. He wrote to Harold Raymond (his literary editor at Chatto
and Windus), where he describes "set." He does not use that term,
of course, but rather juxtaposes the psychotomimetic model with
the spiritual model: "The schizophrenic gets this kind of consciousness sometimes," wrote Huxley. "[B]ut since he starts with fear and
since the fact of not knowing when and how he is to emerge from
this condition of changed consciousness tends to increase that fear,
his commonest experiences are of an Other World, not heavenly but
infernal and purgatorial." He ends the letter quoting the now famous
line from poet William Blake from whence he would title his essay,
"If the doors of perception were cleansed, everything will appear as it
is, infinite and holy."[24]

Huxley also fostered a lifelong friendship with Osmond. Perhaps
they bonded over a fascination with the paranormal. Osmond proved
every bit as interested in clairvoyance and other forms of medium-
ship. "Many people have unusual powers," he held. "There is a need
to investigate them scientifically." Huxley even introduced Osmond
to a psychic friend of his who told him details that he could not
possibly have known. The specifics were striking: Osmond would
publish a book within the following year; he would almost drown
while swimming in Malta; and someone in his family would die
in a plane crash. "These things all actually happened," Osmond
remembers.[25]

~ *June 18, 1953* ~

The carpets had started to morph into a "heaving mass of living matter, part vegetable, part animal." Familiar faces took on the forms of "menacing witches, pigs, and weasels." Time meant nothing. *What the hell is time anyway?*

Journalist Sidney Katz was going insane: "I was repeatedly held in the grip of a terrifying hallucination in which I could feel and see my body convulse and shrink. . . . The room I was in changed with every breath I drew. . . . Pictures, chairs, curtains and lamps flew endlessly about, like planets in their orbits." Katz also gives us an early description of synesthesia,* though he does not seem to have been familiar with the term: "My senses of feeling, smelling and hearing ran amuck. It was as though someone had rooted out the nerve nets in my brain, which control the senses, then joined them together again without thought of their proper placings [*sic*]."[26]

It wasn't all hell though. Eventually, Katz broke through. He recalls, "At times I beheld visions of dazzling beauty—visions so rapturous, so unearthly. . . . I lived in a paradise where the sky was a mass of jewels . . . the air was filled with . . . sheaths of rainbow light—all constantly changing in color, design, texture and dimension so that each scene was more lovely than the one which preceded it."[27]

Almost two months after that most mystical afternoon at the Huxleys' home in Los Angeles, Osmond continued his studies with mescaline and LSD, hoping to give it to between fifty and one hundred "persons with special gifts and high abilities."[28] One of his volunteers, Katz, wrote that vacillating account of mescaline. New doors—*new possibilities*—slowly opened. Leaving the psychological gestalt and seeing the experience through a mystical lens, obvious questions quickly arose: do substances like LSD and mescaline

---

*Synesthesia, or "cross-overs of sensation from one sense modality to another." People experiencing this phenomenon "will say that [they] can hear colors . . . or speak of the scent of music." See Cohen, *The Beyond Within*, 51.

produce beauty or terror, ecstasy or torment, Heaven or Hell?

Huxley spent part of this time pondering these questions as he and Maria toured the Pacific Northwest early that June. As they drove through the evergreens, his gifted mind started ruminating on the "philosophical, aesthetic, and religious implications" of his mescaline experience.[29] Keen on answering these questions, Huxley wrote frantically upon their return. Within a month, he had a working draft of *The Doors of Perception**(1954)—arguably the most famous essay ever written on the subject of mescaline. By New Year, the publisher Chatto and Windus was sending Huxley galley proofs of the essay, one of which he sent to his good friend Joseph Banks Rhine (1895–1980), the so-called father of parapsychology. Rhine had also founded the parapsychology department at Duke University, but certainly achieved his height of fame by coining the term "extrasensory perception" or ESP. On this latter point, Huxley grew more and more enthusiastic, not only because of his recent experiment with mescaline (and its mind-manifesting implications), but also due to a rather odd experience Maria had earlier that summer. She had sat with a hypnotist and entered a visionary state. Fully entranced, she saw a book, the pages of which not only used the Hebrew alphabet but also used Roman numerals for page numbers (instead of the usual Arabic numerals). When asked what kind of book it was, Maria replied "alchemy," with only a fair amount of certainty. The next day at an art show, "a young surrealist artist" presented the Huxleys with a large book on alchemy, complete with Hebraic lettering and Roman numeral page numbers! Huxley called this, "A rather good case of spontaneous prevision under hypnosis."[30] And now, like Heywood in the previous chapter, he sought to merge the psychedelic state with the sensitive state.

While Aldous had favored hypnotism and trance states as authentic for a while, *The Doors* represented a sharp depart from Huxley's

---

*Hereafter referred to as *The Doors* for ease.

earlier thoughts on substance use. Only two years prior to his mescaline journey, he had written in the epilogue to his nonfiction novel, *The Devils of Loudun* (1952), of three different kinds of transcendence: downward, horizontal, and upward. To define in reverse order: upward transcendence dealt with natural abilities of the human body, namely song and dance. "Music is a powerful drug," Huxley wrote, "partly stimulant, partly narcotic, but wholly alternative." Now, to be clear, music could also lead to what Huxley called "herd intoxication," which belongs in the sphere of downward transcendence. The antidote to the manifestation of herd intoxication via music was *mantra;* Huxley considered mantra a form of upward transcendence. In this space, such rhythmic vocalizations can "produce their quasi-hypnotic effects."[31]

"Horizontal transcendence" struck Huxley as "too obvious to require analysis," but he still kindly unpacked the concept for us mere humans. In short, horizontal transcendence occurs when a person engages in an activity larger than the self—anything from playing on a sports team to full-blown community and global activism. In other words, an "escape from the horrors of insulated selfhood" allowed a form of transcendence.[32]

Finally, downward transcendence was that achieved through avenues like sex and chemicals, and the latter's byproduct, herd intoxication. Huxley harbored a rather dismissive tone about this form of transcendence. "[T]here are probably moments in the course of intoxication by almost any drug, when awareness of a not-self superior to the disintegrated ego becomes briefly possible. But these occasional flashes of revelation are brought about at an enormous price." And that price included "subhuman stupor, frenzy or hallucinations . . . [and] permanent and fatal impairment of bodily health and mental power."[33]

What a fantastic reversal when Huxley wrote Osmond post-mescaline that such substances "can be used to raise the horizontal self-transcendence which goes on with purposive groups . . . so that it becomes an upward transcendence."[34]

◎

~ *May 12, 1955* ~

There were two conferences held that month.

The APA's annual meeting featuring the first roundtable discussion on LSD and mescaline convened in Atlantic City, New Jersey. The conference hosted a motley group of researchers—some funded directly by the CIA, like Harold Abramson and Paul Hoch; some surreptitiously monitored by the CIA, like Max Rinkel; and some who had nothing to do with the Agency at all, like Ronald Sandison. And then there was Huxley, the lone literary nerd. Huxley had been touring the lecture circuit harboring fervor unmatched by any of the earlier American researchers. Using his famed intellectual precision, Huxley had refined his speech so well that he scored a spot as the only non-scientist to speak at the APA conference.

Huxley shocked the crowd by announcing a very different interpretation of chemicals like LSD and mescaline than most of the medical professionals in attendance were used to hearing. He panned the other speakers' talks as "colored by fear and anxiety," and instead pontificated on the "classic mescaline experience" that had been revered by those like Ellis and Mitchell:

> [which does not include] consciously or unconsciously remembered events, does not concern itself with early traumas, and is not, in most cases tinged with anxiety and fear. It is as though those who were going through it had been transported by mescaline to some remote, non-personal region of the mind.

But there existed a problem, as Huxley diagnosed:

> The mental climate of our age is not favorable to visionaries. Those who have such spontaneous experiences, and are unwise enough to talk about them, are looked on with suspicion and told that they

ought to see a psychiatrist. This is one of the reasons (though not perhaps the only reason) why there were more visionaries in earlier centuries than there are today.[35]

NAME GAMES

~ *May 25, 1955* ~

Huxley's paradigm resurrected a debate that was as old as LSD itself, namely what to call it. Sure, *Delysid,* but what *kind* of drug was Delysid? Certainly not a sedative or an antibiotic. The conversation would come to a head at the second conference that May, a CIA-funded* gathering called the *Second Conference on Neuropharmacology.*

The discussion had begun at Sandoz between Stoll and Becker. Becker had worked with none other than Otto Kauders (the researcher who introduced Max Rinkel to LSD) in the Clinic of Neurology and Psychiatry at the University of Vienna. In one early report on the effects of LSD, Kauders and Becker indicate, "Whereas Becker refers to LSD as a 'psychosis agent,' Stoll . . . calls it a 'fantasy agent.'"[36] While at the conference, Rinkel ran off a couple of possible names for substances like LSD and mescaline: "Dr. [Ralph W.] Gerard speaks of 'psychosomimetic'† drugs. Dr. Osmond and Dr. Hoffer coined the word 'hallucinogens.'"

"I think we would probably like to withdraw that one," Osmond quickly piped up.[37] Perhaps it is no coincidence that earlier that year Huxley had written to Osmond addressing the need to reconceptualize the other-worldly state away from a psychotomimetic paradigm: "People [under the influence of LSD or mescaline] will think they are going mad, when in fact they are beginning, when they take it, to go sane— or at least to understand what going sane must be like."[38] Osmond agreed, feeling that "psychotomimetic" was too negatively charged: "If

---

*Through its Josiah Macy Jr. Foundation front.
†Synonymous with psychotomimetic.

mimicking mental illness were the main characteristic of these agents, 'psychotomimetics' would indeed be a suitable and generic term," he claimed. "Why are we always preoccupied with the pathological, the negative? Is health only the lack of sickness?"[39] Osmond went on to list a battery of possible new names for mind chemicals, among them: *psychephoric* ("mind-moving"), *psychelytic* ("mind-releasing"), *psycheroxic* ("mind-sharpening"), and, his personal choice, *psychedelic* ("mind-manifesting").[40] He quickly scrawled these hopefuls on some letterhead and sent then off to Huxley for review.

But Osmond's handwriting was somewhat illegible, leading Huxley to believe that he wanted to call substances like LSD and mescaline *psychodetics*. "I don't quite get the hang of [psychodetic]," Huxley wrote back. Was Osmond referring to "geodetic?" he asked. "If so, it would mean 'mind-dividing.'" Huxley didn't care for the name and opted for a word that was "euphonious and easy to pronounce . . . [and] has relatives in the jargon of psychology." So he marshaled his own possibilities, based around the ancient Greek "phanerein" meaning, "that which makes itself available to human perception":[41] *psychophans* or *phaneropsychic* (both more or less meaning "mind-revealing") would do nicely. But the word he felt best fit this description was *phanerothyme,* a mix of the verb "phaneroein" and "thymos," the Greek word for "soul." Perhaps a short poem might solidify this latter option.

And so Huxley wrote back to Osmond:

> *To make this trivial world sublime*
> *Take half a gramme of phanerothyme*

But here's what Huxley didn't know: Osmond was philosophically moving further away from the medical model—more so than Huxley had anticipated. Osmond, too, wanted a term "uncontaminated by other associates."[42] For this same reason, "psychodetic" would have presented a problem for him anyway. Something about the prefix "psycho"—it just steered too close to terms like "psychotomimetic." Osmond opted instead for "psyche," an infinitely more neutral adjunct. And since Huxley's misreading of "psychodetic" was only muddying the waters more, Osmond decided to untangle his legibility problem by placing his term of choice in a small poem—just like Huxley had done for him.

> *To fathom Hell or soar angelic*
> *Just take a pinch of psychedelic*[43]

And just like that, a new term was born that changed the conversation about these medicines forever.

12

The Vitalist Heretic

Critics of Chemical Mysticism

> *Nothing could be more repugnant to this cultural tradition*
> *than the notion of spiritual or psychological growth through*
> *the use of drugs.*

ALAN WATTS

CHOIRS OF SERAPHS

In memoriam for our next historical guest, Eastern religions scholar
Robert Charles Zaehner (1913–1975), let's briefly imagine Humphry
Osmond and his frequent research and writing partner John Smythies
in Zoroastrian terms. The Zoroastrian religion, one of the oldest in
history (founded c. seventh century BCE), was arguably the first to
set up a dualistic paradigm of the universe—a universe of good and
evil, light and darkness, where such diametric forces propelled all existence. Some 2,500 years after Zoroaster's death, American theologian
Reinhold Niebuhr (1892–1971) adopted this dualistic principle in his
monumental *The Children of Light and the Children of Darkness* (1944),
wherein he addressed such polarities in terms of the Second World
War. Those on the side of democracy and free thought, the children
of light, must defeat those of totalitarianism and censure, the children
of darkness.

For our purposes, if Osmond turned on Huxley, thus ushering

153

in the rediscovery—*a psychedelic Renaissance, if you will*—of an old Western paradigm regarding psychedelia,* representing the children of light, then Smythies turned on Zaehner, who sought to destroy this paradigm, representing the children of darkness.

Or rather, turned him off.

Zaehner was every bit the intellectual powerhouse as Huxley. Before reaching his twenties, he already accumulated a linguistic fluency in Greek, Latin, and Persian at Christ Church, Oxford. He later gained equal confidence in the ancient Iranian language of Pahlavi; still later, he mastered Sanskrit, Arabic, and Pali. His knowledge of primeval Persian dialects remained unmatched by his peers, earning him a reputation as the premier scholar of Zoroastrianism. These impressive languages aside, Zaehner was also the top scholar on mysticism and ancient mystical practices. His extraordinary familiarity with sacred texts from Eastern traditions had earned him the illustrious title "Spalding Professor of Eastern Religions at the University of Oxford"—the first Caucasian to have earned that title.† A deeply pious man, he enjoyed the true spoils of his academic life when he stood before admiring students, lecturing at All Souls College. The thought of taking a strange, savage drug had never occurred to Zaehner, who felt that true mystical experiences could not be self-induced through chemicals (natural or otherwise) but through rigorous contemplative practice. This proved a major setback for the Western view of the psychedelic state. Indeed, Western culture viewed each person as an individual, autonomous creature that could understand herself and her world "by the power of conscious effort and will." As one philosopher of the era observed, "A 'drugged' person is by definition dimmed in consciousness, fogged in judgment, and deprived of will."[1]

---

*Whether that goes back to the Eleusinian *kykeon* days or the Ellisian *Artificial Paradise* days.

†His immediate predecessor, Sarvepalli Radhakrishnan, went on to become the first vice president and then the second president of India (1962–1967).

~ *December 3, 1955* ~

At 11:40 a.m., under the watch of Smythies, Zaehner swallowed 0.4 grams of mescaline in his classroom at All Souls College. He had company. Besides Smythies, Mr. E. Osborn (with the Society of Psychical Research), Dr. A. Allison (of Christ Church), and Mr. Alan Tyson (a psychology major and fellow at All Souls) attended the experiment as well. Just ten minutes later, Smythies showed Zaehner a triad of Italian renaissance paintings that he would be shown again after the mescaline had taken effect.[2] Like Huxley, Zaehner proved a late bloomer when it came to the mescaline showing signs of its presence. But then—and perhaps this explains his bad experience—he also made a classic mistake. For every seasoned psychenaut knows that one must not fight the experience. Zaehner did just that. In the days leading up to December 3, he grew "increasingly uneasy." He even had three dreams about taking mescaline, one of which was more like a nightmare causing him to fear that the chemical "might be fatal, or might make [him] permanently mad." Wholly unfamiliar with this new territory, Zaehner somewhat self-sabotaged the entire experiment before it began. Even Hoch, whose tests with LSD raise a suspicious eyebrow, knew that if "[e]vasiveness, vagueness, and denial" were present in a volunteer before taking either LSD or mescaline, such feelings "were reinforced under the drug."[3] As Savage had already deduced (and as every seasoned psychenaut knows), *surrendering* to the medicine makes all the difference.

Guess what Zaehner didn't do?

"What displeased me most was 'the fact of losing control of oneself,'" he reflected. "My conscious resistance to the drug was, indeed, very strong."[4] Zaehner believed that this explained why the mescaline took so long to show any effects.

But perhaps it *really* explained his distrust of mescaline.

The paranoia soon faded until sometime later when his balls felt as if they had frozen solid, like a couple of cherries stuffed in a snowman's asshole.[5] He scrunched his legs together, as if he were about to piss snow, and thought at that moment that he just might die.

Still, notwithstanding feeling his on-again, off-again cold extremities, the effects of mescaline refused to act upon Zaehner's psyche. He suggested the team take a walk around Radcliffe Camera and enjoy a cup of coffee. When the mescaline still refused to participate in their outing, they tried walking to Tom Tower. Zaehner had hoped the mescaline would kick in by the time they got there. When he first entered Oxford at the tender age of eighteen, Tom Tower had made quite the impression upon him. He so desired to gaze upon the bell tower under mescaline (known as it was to cause abreactions—perhaps he could relive that most cherished moment in his late teens one more time).

Still nothing—no signs of any mescaline effects whatsoever.

They strolled across the boardwalk, passed Merton Chapel, and headed toward the Cathedral. By this time, Zaehner was simply giving the researchers a tour of Oxford. As they passed this and that building, he offered facts and history about the designs and architecture. His guests couldn't have been less interested. Zaehner was disappointed too. He had eagerly anticipated looking over the fine craftwork of Oxford University campus while under the influence of mescaline. But try as he might to "force" the experience, nothing much came of it.

They walked into the Cathedral. Here, slight mescaline effects finally started to emerge—it seemed to Zaehner that the historical figures depicted in the fine stained-glass pieces were trying to free themselves from the windows. And of those windows? They "seemed to expand and contract rhythmically. . . . The effect was interesting certainly, but seemed to me less beautiful than its normal state. After a short while, I found this growing and shrinking annoying."[6]

The doctors decided that it might be best to return to All Souls while Zaehner could still walk. But he was fine. In fact, his body "seemed momentarily to be leading an autonomous life." He had no difficulty walking, and led the team back to his rooms at the college.[7] Once arrived, Smythies immediately began to probe.

"I can't express myself anymore," Zaehner replied. "I'm not feeling . . . er . . . sensible at the moment."

Smythies no doubt fired off questions in Zaehner's direction, likely barraging the poor fellow with questions he couldn't begin to fathom answers to.

"Things are just *queer,*" Zaehner managed to reply.[8]

One of the Magi in the painting reached up to his head as if to take off his crown. Zaehner could feel himself cheering on the poor Magi who, due to being nothing more than a character in a painting, struggled to move at all. *Of course the Magi can't move!* Zaehner possibly thought to himself. He began to laugh uncontrollably in front of the bewildered doctors.

"What do you find so funny, Professor Zaehner?" one of them asked.

"Nothing."

This was both true and not true. It was true in the sense that Zaehner simply found *everything* funny—unlike any hilarity he had ever experienced in his life. But it was also not true because in that moment, one of the Magi was trying to bite baby Jesus's feet, and this caused more uproar in him!

"You all look so serious," he finally said once the first round of laughing subsided.

"We can't enjoy it to the same extent that you can."

"No, I suppose you can't," rejoined Zaehner wryly, which caused him to launch into a second fit of uncontrollable laughter.[9]

The doctors tried to calm him down by showing him more art and even some books. This had the opposite effect. For when they flashed Sir James Frazer's *The Golden Bough* (1890) before his eyes, Zaehner reacted like most scholars of his day toward that author and book—he ridiculed it. He held up *The Golden Bough* at a page that mentioned Diana and Virbius. "This is the silliest test I have ever had to go through. . . . Really you shouldn't be so serious. . . . It's Diana you see!" He then derided the book by reading from it: "*The Golden*

Bough . . . one of the great comic classics!" He quickly grew wary of not just Frazer's content but also his writing style: "Why doesn't he split his paragraphs? . . . They are all over the place. . . . It's all wrong. I was brought up as an undergraduate not to do such a thing. Wicked. . . . Oh, this is stupid. . . . Oh, the man's playing the fool."[10]

Mostly Zaehner disliked all the testing that occurred during his experience—a sentiment shared among many a lysergized (or in this case mescalinized) individual. It all seemed so trivial, so tragically boring. And the seriousness with which the doctors took such lackluster tasks became the cosmic joke of Zaehner's experiment with mescaline. Still, Smythies refused to give up. Perhaps he wanted to produce something in Zaehner similar to what his research and writing partner, Osmond, had awakened in Huxley. Maybe he could inspire something like *The Doors* in Zaehner.

If books and paintings did not catch Zaehner's interest, what about music? Zaehner welcomed it. The "manic" stage (as he termed it) of the experience had started to wane. A gripping piece like Berlioz's "Te Deum" might allow him to "think about religious things."[11] Alas, it had the opposite effect, slowly lulling Zaehner "back to the real world." As for the mescaline ride, Zaehner remained unimpressed. "I felt the whole experience was in a sense 'anti-religious,'" he lamented. He had transcended all right; but transcended only into a "world of farcical meaninglessness."[12]

Huxley, it turns out, had not charmed everyone.

While *The Doors* garnered impressive sales[13] and a couple of favorable reviews, one of which was drafted by Osmond himself, scores of intellectuals (unmentioned in most psychedelic history books) found Huxley's ideas, at best, laughable. One early evaluation found in *Pravda* (a Russian newspaper) reminded Huxley of George Orwell's prose, but written by "someone a good deal less clever."[14] Novelist and social commentator Thomas Mann (1875–1955) had received a copy of *The Doors* from his friend, book dealer Ida Herz (1894–1984). Herz enjoyed *The Doors* greatly and wanted to share this fantastic find with Mann. Mann returned the favor by writing Herz a letter that was not just critical of *The Doors* but scathing of its author:

> Many thanks for *The Doors of Perception,* but I cannot really share your enthusiasm for the book. It represents the last and, I am tempted to say, the rashest development of Huxley's escapism, which I never liked in him. Mysticism as a means to that end was still reasonably honorable. But it strikes me as scandalous that he has now arrived at drugs. I have a guilty conscience nowadays because I take a little seconal or phanodorm at night in order to sleep better. But to cast myself by day into a state in which everything human is indifferent to me and to succumb to wicked aesthetic egoistic pleasure would be repugnant to me. Yet this is what he recommends to everybody, because otherwise man's lot is at best idiocy, and at worst suffering. What a use of "best" and "worst"! His mystics should have taught him that "suffering is the swiftest beast that bears us to perfection," which can't be said of *doping.* And being rapt over the miracle of a chair and absorbed in all sorts of color illusions has more to do with idiocy than he thinks.[15]

Other reviewers showed little mercy, as journalist Robert Barrett's review of the book in *The Reporter* demonstrates: "Huxley's attitude in the last two decades has been to most critics an exasperating one. An intellectual of the deepest dye, he has embraced a violent anti-intellectualism."[16]

In short, many people recoiled at the fact that Huxley—the great Aldous Huxley—had taken . . . *mescaline*? Some savage synthetic sapped from the most violent of all the fruits?

Huxley had anticipated a backlash. "Some excellent persons seem to think it is a piece of propaganda for dope taking—while most seem to be quite incapable of grasping the fact that the human mind is anything more than, or different from, the every day [*sic*] self and its attached personal subconscious."[17] And there might have been some reason for critique (although disagreeable assessments much softer than Mann's would have been far classier). The problem, as some saw it, was that while Huxley did reference the "terrifying results" that can manifest with mescaline, he had not driven that point home hard enough.[18] Many readers contrasted *The Doors* with Katz's account of mescaline, which not only spoke of "terrifying hallucination[s]" but also had a three-month head start on Huxley's essay—plenty of time to circulate in the collective cultural consciousness.[19]

But of all the critics Huxley would attract with *The Doors,* none more enthusiastically panned his book than our dear friend and Zoroastrian scholar R. C. Zaehner. He dismissed Huxley's entire approach. In fact, "dismissed" might be too lenient a term here. For Zaehner absolutely loathed both *The Doors* and its animated author. So much so that Zaehner would later blame the Manson Family Murders on Huxley's reckless interpretation (as he saw it) of the mescaline experience.[20] A scholar every bit as exceptional as Huxley, he had both wrestled with the intellectual history of Eastern religious traditions (and emerged triumphantly) and had also taken mescaline himself. And Zaehner, who fit all the criteria necessary for a genuine mystical experience under mescaline, determined that Huxley's whole spiel equated to nothing more than intellectual farce. For Zaehner—skilled as he was in philosophy, religion, and the philosophy of religion—Huxley's interpretation made no sense.

And it made no sense for more than just one reason. So Zaehner marshaled several separate arguments with which to squash this pseudo-mystical pest, Huxley.

First, Zaehner noted that Huxley's adoption of the "perennial philosophy," which sought fusion with the world's mystical religious experiences, did not fully account for the many differences between said traditions. Huxley's assessment had fallen short, overlooking the mystics' "divergences not only of approach . . . but of substance; and that any arbitrary selection from their writings can demonstrate nothing except the subjective views of an individual."[21] Mysticism, so loosely defined, included every inexplicable experience from the "solipsistic Muslim" finding cosmic identity with Allah to Blake occupying a "private universe" all his own. And this didn't just cut across cultures but could be found within a specific culture as well. Consider two authors living in Western civilization at the turn of the nineteenth century as one of numerous examples. Could one really compare the self-inflicted "waking trance" of Alfred Tennyson (1809–1892), achieved through saying his name over and over silently to himself with the "trivial accidents" that sparked the experience of "boundless Being" recorded in Marcel Proust's *In Search of Lost Time*?[22]

Hardly.

The only constant between Tennyson and Proust (and countless other diverse mystic crystal revelations throughout time) was the "release from everyday, humdrum existence."[23] In other words, the differences in the great mystical writings of yore far outweighed the similarities. The "perennial philosophy" simply wasn't true with regards to the ancient mystics. And the situation seemed similar in modern days. Tennyson even took the time to clarify: "I have never had any revelations through anesthetics," a point that Zaehner enthusiastically highlighted in his own writing.[24] Although in doing so, he overlooks J. A. Symonds (1840–1893), an English poet who preferred chloroform to reach the ecstatic state. Once, while under the influence of the compound, Symonds "thought that [he] was near death; when suddenly, [his] soul became aware of God, who was manifestly dealing with [him], handling [him], so to speak, in an intense personal and present reality. . . . Is it possible that [he], in that moment, felt what some of the saints have said they always felt, the indemonstrable but irrefragable certainty of God?"[25] And anyway, could not losing oneself in a good book or surrendering one's ego to the majestic awe and natural symphony of beautiful landscapes have similar effects?

Zaehner certainly thought so.

The second problem with *The Doors* was just as intimately involved as the first. Zaehner recognized only three static kinds of mystical experience: the theistic, the monistic, and the panenhenic. Briefly, a theistic experience occurs when someone feels connected to God. Here, Zaehner reduces this category of God to one of the three classical Abrahamic religions (the Islamic Allah, the Christian God, or the Hebraic Yahweh). The panenhenic experience refers to feeling at one with nature; including feeling one's own presence as not separable from nature. The monistic experience deals with those states of awareness that transcend time, space, and self (usually induced by large group participation). To use an analogy that would irritate Zaehner: imagine you are at a rock concert and someone passes you a joint. You smoke the doob, start dancing with your new friend, and get lost in the music; soon your ego vanishes in the enormity of the crowd and the experience. *That* is a monistic mystical experience.

And of Huxley—the creases in his trousers, the breathing walls, the "Van-Goghian chair," the bejeweled bookshelves—his whole account sounded nothing like a theistic mystical experience.[26] Otherwise, his narrative would have spoken of feeling "wholly absorbed into the Deity Who is felt and experienced as . . . totally distinct and other than the objective world." Huxley never fully transcended the physical world— his idealization of mescaline closer "to that of a manic" than that of a mystic.[27]

As for the other two types of experience—the monastic and the panenhenic—Zaehner concluded that mescaline provided merely a "preternatural" experience. Sure, "preternatural" is just a five-dollar word for "bizarre"—but does a bizarre experience automatically qualify as religious or mystical? This is not that outlandish of a concern. Think about it: Is your average LSD or mescaline volunteer in the 1950s, who probably has *zero* experience with mysticism, the best person to ask about the properties of such a state? Could it not be that their ignorance of true mysticism and rapture had allowed them to fool themselves into believing that their self-induced model psychosis "through LSD and similar psychedelic drugs," which alleged to be able to produce such a deathless and timeless state, implicated true religion?[28] "Do not mistake elation for grace," Zaehner warned his readers.[29]

Perhaps.

But perhaps not. What of those genuinely theistic revelries experienced by congregants of the Native American Church? Truly, such people have deep and culturally sanctioned mystical experiences through their sacramental use of peyote, the cactus from which Western scientists synthesized mescaline. Indeed, when we consider Mooney's account of his night with the Kiowa people outlined in the first chapter of this book, Zaehner's deduction seems elementary at best, wholly ignorant at worst. Yet, he had an answer for this, too; an answer regrettably grounded in a supremacist paradigm, dismissing these early reports as "merely a vulgar error shared by many primitive communities."[30]

But perhaps Zaehner's biggest problem with *The Doors* was that the whole thing reeked of vitalism (the theory of a "vital force" that permeated all life*). Vitalism had ruled Western thought ever since ancient biologists (if one can call them that) hypothesized that inorganic matter could not rise from organic matter. Humans, indeed all living creatures, held a special place on the planet, if not the universe as a whole, for we enjoy a *spark*—a pre-human, pre-dinosaur, pre-aquatic life, pre-whatever-came-before-water *spark,* which made all life possible. Humans occupied the pinnacle of this slow, spiritually directed natural evolution. And it came with a truism: namely, non-life cannot create life.

Alas, a truism today can slowly morph into the superstition of tomorrow. And for vitalism and its supporters, that day came in 1828 when German organic chemist Friedrich Wöhler (1800–1882) created urea

---

*Also referred to as "animism."

(organic matter) by heating ammonium cyanate (inorganic salt), thus creating a natural product out of a synthetic precursor. Those who still supported the vitalist perspective quickly found themselves the target of slanders such as "quack" or "charlatan." One of those fellows who happily watched vitalism circle the drain of popular thought was Thomas Henry Huxley (1825–1895)—Aldous's grandfather—from whose thoughts Aldous represented a sharp departure. While both men could certainly crack wise over something they found silly or childish, Thomas was quite the master at sarcasm, his pugnacious rhetorical style even earning him the nickname "Darwin's Bulldog." Of vitalism, Thomas had no shortage of contemptuous analogies, famously comparing the "vital" spirit to the "aqua" spirit. In his critical essay *On the Physical Basis of Life* (1869), Thomas employed his signature snark, "We do not assume that a something called 'aquosity' entered into and took possession of the oxide of hydrogen as soon as it was formed, and then guided the aqueous particles to their places in the facets of the crystal, or amongst the leaflets of the hoar-frost."[31] Even Julian Huxley, Aldous's elder brother (and an evolutionary biologist by trade), had scoffed at vitalism, borrowing similar wit from his grandfather. Only Julian did not mockingly speak of "aquosity" but rather "force locomotion," parodying French philosopher Henri Bergson's admittedly vague concept of *élan vital* (the vital force), with his own *élan locomotif* (the locomotive force), suggesting that trains move due to an unseen energy in the universe.[32]

What a shock it must have been to Julian to discover that his younger brother—the great English gentleman and intellectual—now promoted some weird kind of proto–New Age pseudoscience! Sadly, with no vital force of which to speak, the Huxley brothers' grandfather Thomas couldn't even roll over in his grave.

We need little imagination to explain why men of science like Thomas and Julian would find Aldous's words so troubling. But what was so terrible about *The Doors* that would cause a man of faith like Zaehner to reject such a premise? Surely it was Huxley's replacement of the Christian God with an informal, vague, and (at least for Zaehner) unsatisfactory "principle of eternity."[33] Huxley had spoken of the Beatific Vision—*a strictly Christian term*. He had quoted from Meister Eckhart—*a strictly Christian mystic*. He even made the bold (and to Zaehner, rudely pretentious) claim that mescaline had allowed him to see what Adam had seen on the morning of creation. And yet not a single reference to the Christian God shone anywhere in Huxley's essay. Huxley instead spoke of the God-within, the age-old Gnostic "god" that a person finds when they turned inward in hopes of coming to know thyself. "The only kind of religion," Huxley qualified, "that is compatible with scientific thought is a religion of mystical experience—not of a Nirvana *outside* the world, but within it," he wrote.[34] This, for both Zaehner and even Carl Jung, was a cheap god. As Jung expresses, "The abstract God 'beyond all human experience leaves me cold.'"[35] With this god, there was no concern for human affairs, no ear (surrounded by a flowing, white beard) to listen to prayers, no hope of salvation through Christ.

Christ: the *only* option for those who hoped for Paradise in the hereafter. Zaehner desired such a Paradise and accepted such a gate-keeper. Perhaps images of the second century CE Valentinian Gnostic, Marcus, feeding a young woman one of his psychoactive potions crossed Zaehner's mind. Indeed, Marcus had developed an elaborate ritual for invoking Charis, the Goddess of Grace, and used psyche-magical potions to enhance the ceremony.[36]

Ah! Zaehner might have concluded. Like Marcus, *Huxley is a heretic as well*—and a vitalist heretic at that!—making the same baseless claims of salvation through chemicals as the heretics of old.

And like Irenaeus (the Church Father who condemned Marcus) before him, Zaehner (among others) felt it his responsibility to ensure that Huxley's paradigm would die with him.

◎

As the rest of this book shall demonstrate, the children of darkness failed.

13

Altar at the Center of the Universe

Psychedelics as Sacred Medicine

Isn't it possible to find some drug that will bring out this latent ability so that normal people could turn [their psychic abilities] on and off at will?

COLONEL NOLTON

KEY TO THE DOOR

~ June 17, 1954 ~

When Dr. Andrija Puharich (1918–1995) picked up the phone at the U.S. Army Chemical Center in Edgewood, Maryland, a very excited Alice Bouverie (1902–1956)* met him on the other end of the line, long distance, from New York. Bouverie's guest, paranormal investigator Harry Stone, had just started to come out of his somnambulistic state and was speaking in a pseudo-ancient Egyptian dialect. He claimed to be in contact with an ancient Egyptian priest named Ra Ho Tep. When the channeling ended, Stone looked over at Bouverie and told her "about some drug that would stimulate one's psychic faculties." Puharich found all this fascinating, of course, but had Bouverie

---

*An aristocratic medium who inherited her father's fortune after he perished on the *Titanic* in 1912. She later used her wealth to supply funds to researchers seeking grant money for paranormal experiments.

taken any notes? Such a diagnosis would be difficult without them.

"Fortunately, we took notes," Bouverie assured. "I'll send it special delivery right away."[1]

Puharich hung up the phone feeling so intrigued by the possibilities that he could barely pay attention to his patients that day. He had been interested in psychic phenomena most of his life—which was why Bouverie phoned him in the first place. His initial encounter with the phenomenal world occurred as a young boy when he took a job in Chicago delivering milk for Borden Dairy Farms. One day while on his route, an aggressive dog cornered him, its canines dripping with saliva. Instead of panicking, Puharich "sent out feelings of calmness and peace," to which the dog miraculously responded in kind. This episode instilled in him the power of psychic abilities.[2] Even after the milk boy grew into the medical doctor, Puharich's zest for the preternaturally possible never waned. Working for the Army at Edgewood Arsenal, he channeled his passion into developing a device that could intensify a sensitive's* ESP. The experiment ended in failure, so Puharich quickly sought other means of psychic amplification. *If not a device, perhaps a chemical?* "It would be nice to have a drug," Puharich confided in his friend Colonel Nolton:

> because then the research problems of parapsychology would be half solved. You see, the main problem in extrasensory-perception research is that we never know, even in a person of great talent, when this mysterious faculty will manifest itself. So we just sit around like a fisherman in a boat who puts his hand into the water every once in a while, hoping that a fish will swim into his grasp. There have been some reports of primitive peoples using such drugs extracted from plants, but I have never heard of one that worked when tested in the laboratory.[3]

---

*A "sensitive" referred to a person with paranormal abilities. The more sensitive a person, the more they could pick up the frequency of ESP, telekinesis, and such.

Bouverie was equally intrigued and wasted no time getting her report to Puharich, which arrived from New York to his home at around 9:00 p.m. that evening. Among a barrage of nonsensical utterances courtesy of Stone, Bouverie had taken the time to scrawl a crude drawing of the drug to which he referred. Stone wasn't sure of the name, but he could describe it very easily. It wasn't a drug like the kind one might find while perusing the aisles high on mescaline at the World's Biggest Drugstore, nor was it a natural plant. It was in fact, a mushroom, a large mushroom with an orange-yellow top and white flecks—the classic fairytale mushroom—the *Amanita muscaria*. Could this be the answer? Could this be the substance that would "open the doors of ESP in a big way?"[4] Puharich tested the mushroom on thirty-seven volunteers, hoping to find the thread that led a person to psychic states of awareness through a psychedelic vector.

In the autumn of 1953, Huxley continued to exhaust his numerous connections to various deep pockets hoping to secure the finances for Osmond's pending experiment (which was giving mescaline to fifty people with myriad talents). Huxley asked his friend Dr. George Maison if he would like to invest. Maison had an interest in the subject, and even had financial ties to the World's Biggest Drugstore. But he passed on investing in any psychedelic projects, for the simple fact that he couldn't think of any way to market mind-manifesting compounds to the larger public. Instead, Maison suggested that Huxley try Dr. William Malamud, who not only had an interest in psychedelics but also had an affiliation with the Ford Foundation. If this didn't work, he could always try his good friend, the medium Eileen Garrett (1893–1970), president of the Parapsychology Foundation. Garrett's foundation, while not on the same money-tier as Ford's, still had some impressive finances and could perhaps direct some Osmond's way. But the timing was off. The Parapsychology Foundation already had its assets invested in an upcoming Symposium on Philosophy and

Parapsychology, to be held in Paul-de-Vence in southeastern France that coming spring. Garrett had personally invited Huxley to speak. The foundation would cover Maria's and his travel expenses as well.[5]

Huxley would use it as an opportunity to expand on ideas outlined in *The Doors* that would explore "the fauna and flora of the deeper subconscious . . . the world from which poets and prophets have derived their descriptions of heaven and hell and other remoter areas of the Other World." He also started to merge his perennial philosophy with the psychedelic experience: "What turns up under mescaline . . . exhibits many common features, and these common features crop up in descriptions of Christian, Moslem, and Buddhist paradises and . . . in descriptions of hell."[6] Huxley brought these ideas with him to Garrett's Parapsychology Foundation's conference in Paul-de-Vence that April. He even brought his stash of mescaline for the occasion.* Huxley's speech at the conference, "A Visionary Experience," would lay the groundwork for his follow up to *The Doors,* the less praised albeit equally captivating essay *Heaven and Hell* (1956).†

Standing before his audience of eager parapsychologists, Huxley launched into his thoughts on the "dividing ocean" between two states of consciousness.[7] There existed the Old World, which encompasses our day-to-day musings, thoughts, memories, and such. And across the mental sea, just beyond the sunset, lay another world, a New World that remained impervious to colonization and conquest. We could only visit for a while—well, *some of us*. Many, Huxley maintained, would never even make the voyage. On the other paw, "naturalists of the mind," a group of which Huxley no doubt considered

---

*Which he ended up gifting to Dr. Roger Godel in Egypt after the conference. See Smith, *Letters of Aldous Huxley,* 714.

†Huxley would give this speech again at Duke University a few months after the Parapsychology Conference under the title "The Far Continents of the Mind" (Horowitz and Palmer, *Moksha,* 58). The essay would then take on another name change as he readied it for publication, "Visionary Experience and Visionary Art" (Smith, *Letters of Aldous Huxley,* 751). At some point after that, the essay gained the title it bears today, *Heaven and Hell.*

himself one of its chief navigators, sought many a visit to those far-off regions. Such sojourns required a consistent means to ferry oneself between the shores of the two Worlds. Huxley knew of two: hypnosis and psychedelics. But the latter, he assured, "carries one further into the *terra incognita.*"[8] And mind you, this terra incognita was no *terra somnia,* for people produce dreams from within themselves. The entities encountered in the New World were much like the marsupials of Australia in that they "conform to the laws of their own being, they can be classified and their strangeness possesses a certain regularity of pattern. . . . The subject does not remember or invent them; he discovers them, 'out there,' in the psychological equivalent to a hitherto unexplored geographical region." These entities were not manifestations of the Jungian collective unconscious either; they were "inhabitants of 'the Other World.'" Mescaline experiences, too, were rather predictable if the imbiber was of sound mind, body, and held a "proper degree of philosophical sophistication."[9]

And for all Huxley's talk of light, color, and "living geometrical forms," there existed an "infernal experience as well, as terrible as the other is glorious." The best way to end up in the glorious place was to, as we might say today, "trust the medicine." Foul ordeals with mescaline come "when one lacks that faith and loving confidence which alone guarantees [the] visionary experience will be blissful."[10] And then, of course, there was all the significance that mescaline gave to even the most ordinary objects—an experience that, while perhaps not religious, provided the closest kind of divine connection available to earthbound souls. Huxley held no reservations about explaining such spiritual nuances: "I am not so foolish as to equate what happens under the influence of mescaline or of any other drug . . . with the realization of the end and ultimate purpose of human life: enlightenment, the Beatific Vision. All I am suggesting is that the mescaline experience is what Catholic theologians call 'a gratuitous grace,' not necessary to salvation but potentially helpful and to be accepted thankfully."[11]

AN EXCURSION OUT OF TIME

Osmond stayed busy during this time too.

~ *December 2, 1955* ~

It started slowly.

Time and colors were rubbing against each other, causing friction like dirt and gold through a pan in a river. And before he knew it, Liberal Party Member of Parliament Christopher Mayhew (1915–1997) no longer belonged to the day everyone else was having. He could still see Osmond sitting across from him. But Osmond was part of *that* world; that world where time still exists, albeit in a vacuum. And he stood outside that vacuum. He stood outside the cameras and the lights and the microphones and the wires and all the technical accoutrements that had only a few hours ago turned his study into a sound stage. The British Broadcasting Company (BBC) had decided that filming Mayhew's journey with mescaline might prove an interesting and worthy news story. But now he stood outside of air, outside of time. What could he do? He saw all of time simultaneously and felt powerless to its whimsies. "How can I seriously claim . . . that I was aware of my eyes seeing my tea being poured out *after* I was aware of my throat swallowing it?"[12]

Time, that quirky bastard.

Now that he stood firmly outside of time, Mayhew's ego gently detached, melting away into this new land, which Osmond pulled back to our world to give a quick intelligence test.

"Will you subtract 7 from 100, and go on subtracting it until nothing is left?" he asked.

"93, 86, 79, 63 [*sic*]—whatever it is—58, 51, 44, 37, 30, 23 . . ." And then, he flew off again, deep into the Other World—but only for a moment. He was soon back in the regular world, back in the world with Osmond and BBC cameras. ". . . 34 [*sic*], 27, 20, 13, 6 . . ."

And then he was gone again.[13]

◎

With the Ford Foundation money not coming through yet, Huxley and Osmond had switched tactics. They were too excited to wait. Looking outside corporate sponsors, they hoped government officials represented another possible avenue to legitimizing psychedelics. Perhaps this would lead to attracting future benefactors. Osmond just so happened to be old friends with Mayhew, who had definitely read and enjoyed *The Doors*. In fact, it was Osmond, with whom Mayhew had been in regular correspondence, who had first mentioned how mescaline disabled the filter that protected mind from Mind at Large.[14] Even without Osmond and Huxley's influence, Mayhew had been prepping for such a mystical (as opposed to schizophrenic) interpretation of the mescaline state. He had just published his book *Men Seeking God* (1955), so felt it entirely possible "that mescaline merely enabled [him] to experience what [he] was predisposed to experience."[15]

Unfortunately, a backlash from a group of psychologists, psychiatrists, and theologians prevented the BBC footage from ever seeing the airwaves. Far from beaten, Mayhew published an account of his experience in the London *Observer*.

Therein, he pulled no punches:

Can these drugs give us fresh insight into the mysteries of human knowledge and purpose—even into the nature of Reality itself? . . . It seems as though the same detachment from the pull of our senses which characterizes religious experience can be achieved in entirely irreligious ways: mescaline, alcohol, epilepsy and hypnosis as well as by yoga, fasting, meditation, and prayer. Does this cheapen religion and invalidate the claims of the great mystics? Surely not.[16]

Things were looking up.

~ *Winter/Spring 1955* ~

Andrija Puharich busily continued his work with *Amanita muscaria* and ESP—now with LSD as a second substance for sensitives to try during his ESP experiments. He also created the Round Table Foundation in Glen Cove, Maine, courtesy of three generous grants: first from Joyce Borden Balokovic (1897–1971), heiress to Borden Dairy Farms—his former employer as a young boy! Balokovic introduced him to Bouverie. Last on board was Marcella Miller du Pont (1861–1976), who worked in chemicals and weaponry. These three women had "deep pockets and nonconformist ideas."[17] Egalitarian in nature, the new organization took its name from King Arthur's Knights of the Round Table. They invited parapsychologists like Eileen Garrett to test psychic powers on electronics devices. Could mental powers alone, say, change radio stations by tapping into unseen frequencies and moving the dial from behind the veil? Presumably (but also retrospectively) not. Another experiment was most intriguing: Tradition held that the *Amanita muscaria* did not grow in Maine. But this did not stop Round Table from trying to find it. To do so, Puharich, using a Ouija board, attempted to contact María Sabina! Timing the experiment perfectly—this was for science, after all—María Sabina ate her mushrooms at the appropriate hour* that the parapsychologists in Maine dabbled with their board. Sure enough, they contacted María Sabina and she told them where to find *Amanita muscaria* mushrooms in Maine.[18]

In any event, Puharich and the Round Table fell into Huxley's crosshairs as yet another potential donor for Osmond's research. In early March, Osmond and Bouverie received an invitation to stay with Huxley in Los Angeles to discuss such possibilities—no Round Table money exchanged. Instead, Bouverie and Puharich invited Huxley to Maine to see for himself what the foundation was up to.

---

*With help from Gordon Wasson, who acted as liaison between the two camps.

~ *August 7, 1955* ~

Huxley sat across from Stone, who tried mightily to showcase his telepathic abilities for the author, without success. Perhaps a mind as brilliant as Huxley's was too advanced to be susceptible to Stone's psychic powers? Suddenly Stone fell into a trance and, once again, channeled Ra Ho Tep. He now commanded Puharich to fetch one of his golden mushrooms. Puharich did as told, running to his lab and returning with the mushroom. Stone touched the mushroom to his tongue and then to his crown chakra in "ritualistic fashion."[19] Not long after, he regained his normal state of consciousness, though he felt somewhat tipsy. He asked Puharich if he had given him alcohol, which Puharich denied. Nonetheless, Stone began to stumble around the room like a drunk. Puharich pleaded with him to sit down, which Stone eventually did. Then Puharich convinced him to take a MAT test, which consisted of having a sensitive arrange ten picture blocks correctly with some kind of cover that stops the test-taker from seeing them. When Puharich pulled the cover away, he was astonished to see that Stone correctly paired all ten blocks. Whether Stone was failing miserably at demonstrating his telepathy to Huxley and needed an easy way out to avoid embarrassment or he legitimately fell into a trance, we don't know. But ten out of ten is pretty damn impressive either way, even though Stone hadn't even eaten the mushroom.

Unfortunately, the Round Table Foundation did not last too long after. Fighting within the group, coupled with a moratorium on all activity courtesy of "the Treasury Department for back taxes," put the foundation in "such stuff as messes are made on—and in the biggest way."[20]

But it was not just Garrett, Puharich, and Huxley who found themselves sailing into ancient fractal landscapes of "psi phenomena, visions . . . mystical experiences" and other adventures in the strange meta-reality of psychedelics.[21] By the late 1950s, they had started to influence some folks in the medical community, urging them to rethink the "model psychosis" paradigm. Osmond—who enjoyed his frequent "strays from the path of medical orthodoxy"—was changing his perspective about psychedelics in two ways.[22] First, he was falling more in line with Huxley's newfound appreciation for mescaline-induced mysticism. Second, he began exploring importing options of exotic plant specimens from Africa and South America. His goal? To try every psychedelic substance that he could get his hands on, each of which he believed "create[d] a different 'model psychosis' and open[ed] up a different area of the mind," which included "ESP possibilities."[23] His quest to import psychedelics from foreign lands had been quite successful. By 1956, he had already sampled harmala of Morocco, kavakava of the Pacific Islands, ololiuqui of Mexico, and—though not an exotic plant medicine—LSD.[24] Additionally, Huxley asked his friend Heinz Kusel, recently back in the states from Peru, if he might send some samples of ayahuasca to Osmond.[25] All of these exotic plants and cultures more deeply embedded the mystical paradigm into mid-century North American psychedelia.

Osmond also inserted himself squarely in the legal dispute between the Canadian government and the Native American Church, the latter embroiled in a fight to preserve their right to use peyote as a sacrament. The Canadian brass believed peyote a dangerous drug, not a sacred medicine.

Osmond vehemently disagreed.

~ October 6, 1956 ~

The small teepee seemed like a microcosm of the whole universe. At its center sat a decorative moon altar that held a single leaf and peyote button, the axis mundi of their celestial domain. The fire beside the altar grew larger as the participants heaped handfuls of sage and thyme into its glowing flames. The blaze caused bodies to bifurcate: faces, chests, abdomens, and legs sweltered, while backs and derrieres froze. The road man, Frank Takes Gun (1908–1988), passed sacred tobacco around, encouraging each participant to roll a cigarette. An hour later, a collection of finely ground peyote buttons wrapped in white cloths passed among the congregants. The Red Pheasant Band—the group holding the ceremony—often pulverized their peyote in a coffee grinder and folded the powder into individual cloths, as they found the bitter taste of the cactus an unnecessary exercise in religious masochism.

Once everyone had ingested, Takes Gun began to shake his rattle while "Mr. Russell" (not further named in the annals of history) reverently beat the ancient rhythms on a black iron water drum. That drum, a noble instrument—crafted with seven bulges around the side that represented the seven stars of the dippers—would surely call them home. Russell beat the skin, weaving into the teepee air the "pulsing of the galaxies."[26] Once the cactus started to take effect, Takes Gun addressed the flock:

> Dear Heavenly Father,
> We are representing our folks under this teepee.
> Dear Heavenly Father, Dear Heavenly Father,
> Bless these men that are observers here.
> Dear Heavenly Father,
> These poor people surrendered all their lands
> To the Government of Canada—their conditions
> Are pitiful.
> Dear Heavenly Father—bless my people back home.[27]

The drums and rattles sounded louder now, as they carried Takes Guns's prayers into the spirit world, the Other World. Takes Gun then exited the teepee and, using an eagle bone whistle, offered a note of salvation to the north, south, east, and west that "shrilled through aeons of space and corridors of time. It echoed to eternity."[28] Sound counted for much more than vision in these spaces—both within the ceremony and out on the plains.

The plains: so desolate, so cold, so silent. So much so that sound and music were of vital importance to the rite. You see, there was nothing much to see. The lands were barren. Therefore, *music* served as the cosmic guide to which Takes Gun ensured each prayer reach its final, heavenly destination.

But even with all this talk of Heavenly Fathers, the Red Pheasant Band also worshipped a Great Mother. And unlike the Heavenly Father, she was a physical being. A woman, who had taken the role of Mother, entered the teepee wearing a blue dress covered by a red blanket. Takes Gun welcomed her with song, which ensconced her in her role: "[S]he became superb mother earth, mother prairie, grass, cow buffalo, mare, and doe, the epitome of motherhood." It was *she* who really oversaw the entire rite. The drums, the songs, the peyote—all of it done in her honor. "She dominated the teepee," Osmond would later recall.[29]

Osmond was well aware of the challenge before him as he drove to Saskatchewan to pick up Hoffer. He had to convince a bunch of spiritual bigots of the legitimacy of the Red Pheasant Band's use of peyote to achieve "oneness with life."[30] The Minister at the House of Commons in Ottawa considered peyote a destructive force in society, akin to alcohol. Osmond found the comparison a travesty and a tragedy. So he formulated a plan. He and Hoffer, along with two reporters from Saskatoon's *Star Phoenix,* made their way to Battleford, an area just outside the Saskatchewan province. From there, they followed Red Pheasant insiders to a secret location where they would participate in an all-night peyote ceremony. They agreed that only Osmond would eat the peyote, while the others would "watch and record the ceremony." Osmond felt that if he consumed the cactus and demonstrated that it was neither a "dangerous poison" nor a "drug of addiction" (as a recent police report had stated), perhaps the government would lax its legal standing on the rites. Like ancient pagan reports of Christian sex parties,[31] the Minister at the House of Commons feared that the Native American Church's use of peyote stemmed from a desire to hold all-night orgies.[32]

Did Osmond go insane? Did he feel like he had just imbibed a lethal poison?

Hardly.

"It was a beautiful, unusual, powerful religious experience," he maintained. "I felt that every beat of the drum had a special meaning."[33]

⊚

The group setting had a noticeable effect on Osmond, as evidenced by the insights he brought into Weyburn Mental Hospital in Canada. By 1957, he was revamping the hospital *a la* Sandison at Powick Hospital in England. He started by redesigning the outfits worn by women inpatients. Or, more accurately, the women inspired his decision by consistently ripping and tearing and otherwise destroying the dull gowns they wore. Women outside the hospital wore bras; women instituted at Weyburn did not. "A woman with flabby breasts has no morale," opined Osmond, at once misogynist, albeit progressive for the late 1950s. And so he supplied all the Weyburn women with "stylish, expensive nylon gowns and brassieres."[34]

Additionally, he desegregated the ward, for Osmond harbored some misandrist ideas as well. He recalled once observing a group of male rats who grew "thin, scraggy and apathetic" when researchers removed the female rats from the pen. Moreover, when the researchers returned the female rats to the pen, the males "grew sleek, active and healthy." To Osmond, men seldom behaved differently from rats. "When there are women around," he said, "the men will shave, watch their language and mind their dress and manners."[35] Osmond wanted to turn Weyburn Mental Hospital into a "sociopetal" hospital, meaning that it would "encourage personal relationships."[36]

And so he did.

⊚

While doctors may have still spoken in psychotomimetic terms in their clinics, the mystical nature of psychedelics was slowly taking over in the public mind. Writers like Rosalind Heywood and Aldous Huxley had far deeper reach into popular culture than did medical researchers like Max Rinkel, Juliana Day, and Kiyo Morimoto. What's more, parapsychological techniques had started to infiltrate the hospital setting. One doctor at the Metropolitan State Hospital, in California, incorporated "dream analysis, spiritual readings, reincarnation discussions, a novel sort of group therapy and hypnosis."[37]

And like Osmond, even some American doctors were starting to get on board with the psychedelic state representing a positive mental experience—whatever that may entail.

It is the mid-1950s, and we are already a far cry from psychotomimeticism.

And abreaction.

And truth serums.

And wars without death.

And now it is time to take another, larger dose.

And go even deeper.

14

Scoundrels and Explorers

Eternity in an Hour

Those who advocate . . . [LSD's] use are not, in the main, after kicks, nor are they interested in antisocial activity. These advocates, who include intellectuals, professionals, and scientists, claim that the drug offers great benefits to the individual—rich inner experiences.

NEVITT SANFORD

ALL THE BEASTLY THINGS

~ *Early December 1954* ~

Two weeks after Olson had his first—and terminally last—encounter with LSD before jumping to his death in New York City, author and philosopher Gerald Heard (1889–1971) ate mescaline and raved about it with all the enthusiasm of his dear friend, Aldous Huxley. Heard took the mescaline largely for the same reason the medieval lawyer Jacopone da Todi (1230–1306) joined the Franciscan order: to achieve "a better order in all my living."[1] Heard had a "queer enigmatic way" about him.[2] He was a romantic pessimist, a hopeful doubter, an absent-minded encyclopedia—exactly what Huxley looked for in a good friend. They had much in common, including their penchant for sweeping generalizations, a trait Huxley recognized in himself and therefore knew not to totally trust. The two had worked together in

180

the past, writing on everything from metaphysics to economics and psychology, and Huxley had even written a blurb for one of Heard's books. When the situation in Europe grew too unsettling and danger-ous, Heard joined the Huxleys during the great intellectual expatria-tion of the 1930s. They made a quick visit to their friend J. B. Rhine at Duke, and after a short stay-over in Taos, New Mexico, they fin-ished their journey to Los Angeles, where Huxley would work writing for Hollywood; Heard would found Trabuco College, an institution "rooted in . . . mysticism . . . monastic inclinations . . . and [a] commit-ment to developing an elite of philosopher-kings."[3] They befriended the American astronomer Edwin Hubble and often attended university lectures "informing themselves on the latest breakthroughs in scien-tific fields."[4]

Therefore, it is not surprising that Heard (along with Russian fash-ion photographer George Hoyningen-Huene) found himself at the Huxleys' house in December of 1954. Osmond was on his way. The plan was to drive east out of Los Angeles, find a quiet spot somewhere in the desert, and take mescaline.

Huxley had a fondness for the arid air of the desert ever since 1942 when he and Maria lived in an "abandoned socialist utopia" called Llano del Rio, a small oasis in the Mojave. There, he collected his thoughts and studied the great mystic literature to pen his *Perennial Philosophy* (1945). He had remained enchanted by "this great crystal of light . . . whose height for all practical purposes is infinite."[5] Maria also had a taste for the desert. For her, the parched landscape was a place where she could have genuinely naturalistic mystical experiences—with or without any psychedelic enhancer. The Mojave was a "metaphysical reality, an unequivocal manifestation of God."[6]

Both Huxleys graciously anticipated a return to the great crystal of light.

Upon Osmond's arrival, however, he found two sick Huxleys. Aldous had recently suffered a "long siege of herpes" that eventually gave way to a bout of shingles, and Maria had taken a vitamin B complex (which neutralizes the effects of mescaline) due to having X-rays taken. She had recently been diagnosed with cancer. Instead of cancelling the engagement, Osmond gave the mescaline to Hoyningen-Huene and Heard. Of Hoyningen-Huene's experience, we cannot say much other than it was "wholly aesthetic." The rest of his experience—like so many—is lost to time. But Heard transformed from a philosopher to a medium in just a few hours. He not only heard voices, but soon they started to speak "through him from a variety of mental levels."[7] As such, he would later reflect greatly on these kinds of experiences, giving us an idea of what his visits to the Other World were like. For when he took mescaline (or, for that matter, LSD), he could hear *the pulse,* the very vibration that underlined the endless cosmos. His ego slowly dissipated into stardust until he merged with the whole of the universe. "Eternity in an hour," Heard promised of the mescaline experience.[8] He would later write that such experiences (and indeed, those of others) were "so clearly similar to the accounts given by mystics."[9]

Psychosis, aesthetic appreciation, mysticism, clairvoyance, and anything among or between: Heard and Huxley were all over such topics. They started to journey deeper—started to rediscover concepts that Huxley had wrestled with long ago: "All the beastly things from tragedy and spirituality to disgust and ennui."[10]

In the meanwhile, Osmond's plans for attracting a grant from the Ford Foundation never manifested. While he, Huxley, and now Heard saw such possible funds as nothing more than an investment in the next step in human evolution, the trustees at Ford saw a public relations nightmare waiting to happen. On this, Huxley grumbled, "whenever the Foundation gets any adverse publicity, people go to the nearest Ford dealer and tell him that henceforth they will buy Chevvies." Even Julian Huxley, who tapped Ford for far less controversial investments than his brother Aldous, received nothing from the Foundation. In light of Julian's rejection, Aldous's optimisms started to fade: "the outlook for our research in mescaline doesn't seem to be too good in this quarter," he told Osmond.[11]

So they were back to square one: many questions, lots of hope, and no money to see any of it come to fruition. Forget funds from the stuffy Ford Foundation trustees—they needed an *insider*. A wealthy benefactor who not only believed in the power of psychedelics but who would also shower their research with unlimited finances, no questions asked.

And lo! On one fine autumn day, just when all hopes of snagging an investor started to fade, Osmond received an invitation to join Alfred Matthew Hubbard (1901–1982) at the Vancouver Yacht Club for lunch. Hubbard met all the criteria Osmond and Huxley desired: he was determined, jovial, loved mescaline—*really, really loved mescaline*—and had some *very* deep pockets.

JOHNNY ACID SEED

Osmond's early work with mescaline had attracted not only Huxley to reach out to him but Hubbard as well.[12] Hubbard, affectionately known as "Al," "Cappy," or "the Good Captain" (or by any number of aliases), had a passion for psychedelics that rivaled those of Huxley and Osmond—perhaps even surpassed it. Over the course of his life, Hubbard had accumulated a fortune, and starting in the 1950s, he used his wealth to spread the gospel of LSD in a way unparalleled by anyone who had preceded him.

Ideologically situated between the CIA weapon camp (he was a retired OSS officer) and the Osmond healer camp (he later worked with alcoholics), Hubbard felt that mescaline and LSD were weapons for healing the sickness in the human soul. His unfailing Christian temperament would not permit him to quit what he considered missionary work.

Growing up impoverished in Kentucky, Hubbard learned how to make ends meet early in life. From there, it gets difficult to separate fact from fiction. For example, he claimed employment as a Prohibition agent with the U.S. Treasury Department in 1925, after which he transferred to the Bureau of Prohibition. However, a memo dated January 20, 1975, claims that both the Treasury Department and the Bureau of Prohibition have "no records concerning Matthew M. Hubbard."[13]*

The fog starts to clear around 1936 when authorities arrested him "for the crime of conspiracy to violate liquor laws" during Prohibition. An electronics expert, he had assembled the radios that rum runners used to smuggle liquor from Mexico into Los Angeles. He also claimed to drive the smuggling vehicles from time to time. He spent two years in McNeil Island Penitentiary (1936–1937). Again, his FBI file is firm: there is simply no evidence that Hubbard was ever "the subject of a criminal investigation."[14]

After his purported release from prison, he took a job in 1941 as Director of Engineering Marine Sales and Services in Vancouver, British Columbia. During this time, Hubbard's smuggling expertise once again came in handy—this time on the side of the Allied Forces just prior to America's entry into World War II. The United States was still neutral in the war at this time, although quite evidently pro-Allied, and Hubbard, now a high-level agent in the OSS, flew commercial planes and sailed ships up the United States–Canadian border where mechanics disassembled and refurbished them as military jets and naval destroyers. He then transported the individual parts to Great Britain. In 1947, Hubbard became the director of scientific research at the Vancouver-based uranium corporation, Limited.[15]

Hubbard's dealings with Great Britain did not end with the Second World War. But still unknown is how he happened upon Sandison at Powick Hospital. Given Hubbard's affiliation with the OSS, it is not improbable that he chanced upon Sandison's work via Project Paperclip or another of the agency's militarily directed intelligence gathering missions.

However, we can only speculate.

---

*Note the additional alias here.

In 1953, Hubbard swallowed his first of what would be many doses of LSD under the guidance of Sandison at Powick Hospital. Recounting that initial experience, Hubbard said LSD "was the deepest mystical thing I have ever seen. I saw myself as a tiny mite in a big swamp with a spark of intelligence. I saw my mother and father having intercourse. It was all clear."[16]

Hubbard scrambled to gain enough expertise on LSD to conduct his own sessions. In 1955, he obtained a "Doctor of Philosophy in Biocycle Dynamic Education" from Taylor University in Colorado Springs, Colorado, via correspondence courses. The courses to complete such a degree usually take two years to finish; somehow, Hubbard earned his diploma in one calendar year: December 1954 to December 1955.[17] He felt that "most people are walking in their sleep. Turn them around, start them in the opposite direction and they wouldn't know the difference."[18] His cure for human ambivalence involved a hearty dose of LSD. But without a medical degree, LSD remained out of his reach.

He sent in order forms to Sandoz for LSD before completing his "Biocycle" degree. In 1954 he encountered "no objection to . . . importing and using the drugs Mescoline [*sic*] and Lysergic acid diethylamide in the research branch of [his] laboratories." A letter dated May 31, 1955, indicated that Hubbard received "43 boxes of L.S.D." from the New Jersey branch of Sandoz Pharmaceuticals.[19]

Upon finishing his degree, Hubbard went right to work.

METANOIA

~ *January 9, 1955* ~

Almost two years after that blissful day in the Hollywood Hills with Maria, Onnie, and Osmond, Aldous ingested mescaline for the second time. Only this time around, he had company. Joining him was Heard (naturally), an unnamed person (probably Maria), and Hubbard (who supplied the mescaline). Both Huxley and Heard took 300 micrograms, while the unnamed third took 200 micrograms.* The experience still proved as remarkable as the first but in a different way. The additional bodies instigated a human connection not found in his first mescaline excursion a couple years prior. No longer was Huxley finding himself flung across the antipodes of the mind. This time the "Other World" wouldn't be found "out there," but instead layered onto this one. "[I]t was a transcendental experience within this world and with human references," Huxley said of the journey.[20]

Hubbard had formed his own research group in Vancouver that set about developing newer methods for probing the mind in a therapeutic setting using LSD. He wholly disagreed with the model psychosis theory. How else could one explain the deep insights, the galactic grooves, the cosmic unity? Hubbard's Vancouver group had started using psychedelics "as a device for raising buried guilts [sic] and traumas and permitting people to get on to better terms with themselves."[21] Mescaline, LSD— they were so much more than drugs used to mimic madness! These medicines opted to upturn old paradigms about how best to cause a person to abreact. When done with sedatives, the ego certainly loosened, but also dulled. With mescaline and LSD, awareness expanded and "the whole gamut of the psyche, up to the highest superconscious [sic] levels, is opened up."[22] Hubbard was gaining momentum in the new, burgeoning psychedelic scene. He founded the group "The Commission for the Study of Creative Imagination" and instituted a novel approach to psychedelia: re-imprinting. He believed that since a person formed their concepts about reality "based upon . . . sense experience," it surely followed that an interruption of these personal perspectives, say with something like LSD, would cause "reality ties [to be] reduced," eliminating old, harmful habits.[23] Huxley raved about Hubbard's work in Vancouver: "Delinquent boys have been totally transformed in a single sitting, and the *Metanoiai*† has

---

*As one might expect, given Hubbard's *résumé*, his dose is not recorded.
†A change in a person's perspective due to a religious conversion.

persisted. Meanwhile a considerable number of academic persons and of professional business men have all taken the stuff—and all, without exception, have declared it to be the most significant experience of their lives."[24]

And yet, neither Huxley nor Heard really cared to adopt Hubbard's approach for themselves. To be sure, they supported Hubbard's work and never spared a moment praising his abilities as a psychedelic medicine facilitator. But Heard and Huxley were more of the aloof intellectual type. They preferred to talk Tennyson, not trauma; aesthetics, not abreactions. Or maybe they would debate the underlying mystical significance of the psychedelic experience and its implications for the future of humanity. But discuss their feelings? Not even sober! How frivolous a waste of the psychedelic state!

When Hubbard would visit for a session, the two gents stealthily and successfully escaped the touchy-feely bubble that he created. Instead of participating in the group setting, they spent the night talking philosophy and mysticism between themselves, as one would expect two good, old, knowledgeable friends, who were high as a kite on mescaline, to do. "Again, neither Gerald nor I can claim to be a good experimental subject," Huxley confided to Osmond. "For we . . . seem to be too much interested in the 'obscure knowledge' of Suchness to want to be bothered with anything else."[25]

Nonetheless, Huxley remained optimistic that Hubbard would use his extensive connections to give mescaline to Nelson Rockefeller and negotiate (or con—Huxley didn't care) millions of dollars in donations to their research. There would be no trustees, board members, nor bosses. This time, the people—not corporations, nor the government, nor even the Gods—would hold the keys to eternity.

~ February 12, 1955 ~

Cancer took Maria Huxley.

She had faced her mortality bravely, even as she lost her ability to speak during those final hours. Aldous tried to ease her transition, sometimes with hypnosis, other times by sitting with Maria in silence.

When he would speak, he would remind her of the desert that she so very much loved: the sand, cacti, peyote, and coyotes that she so effortlessly transcended into naturally during their time in the Mojave. "Open the eyes of memory to the desert sky and . . . think of it as the blue light of Peace, soft and intense and yet irresistible in its tranquilizing power."[26] Sweet *Coccola*,* the skies are bluer than they have ever been, he told her. Become them. Allow yourself to merge with what you have always been—even before you were born: "a part of the divine substance, a manifestation of love, joy, and peace, a being identical with the One Reality." Step deeper into the light. "Peace now," Aldous whispered repeatedly.

> Let go, let go. Forget the body, leave it lying here; it is of no importance now. Go forward into the light. Let yourself be carried into the light. No memories, no regrets, no looking backwards, no apprehensive thoughts about your own or anyone else's future. Only the light. Only this pure being, this love, this joy. Above all this peace. Peace in the timeless moment, peace now, peace now.[27]†

Aldous hoped to offer Maria a taste of eternity in her final hour. At just about 6:00 p.m., she passed peacefully into whatever comes next. And while her son Matthew experienced great pains at his mother's passing, Aldous seemed surprisingly accepting over the loss of Maria—a

---

*Italian for "preferred one," Aldous's term of endearment for Maria.

†While it is largely believed that Aldous read portions of the *Bardo Thödol* from the *Tibetan Book of the Dead* as Maria passed on, this seems to have stemmed from a mistake originating from Jay Stevens's book, *Storming Heaven*. As the above block quote demonstrates, Aldous conjured images *reminiscent of the Bardo Thödol* (and the mysticism of Meister Eckart) but did not actually read from the book itself (the above quote is not found anywhere in the *Tibetan Book of the Dead*). So how did we come to believe otherwise? The situation was delightfully strange, as only Maria could deliver: *The Tibetan Book of the Dead* was a favorite of Maria's (recall that it was *Maria*, not Aldous, who first mentioned focusing on the "Clear Light" during the latter's first encounter with mescaline). Months after Maria passed on, she and Aldous's friend, the parapsychologist Eileen Garrett, had a dream in which Maria appeared to her. It was

point that Heard attributed to his mescaline journeys.[28] He had now seen the vastness of life, space and time, and the Clear Light, in a way that his son hadn't yet grasped. And in that way, he had reached "transcendence of the fear of death."[29]

A brief word about Maria. Not merely a secondary player during the founding of the psychedelic Renaissance, Maria contributed much to the scene—and she was the only one who did so while dying from cancer. And I cannot stress this point enough: the mystical interpretation of the psychedelic state was *her* idea, not Aldous's. She was smart, strong, a fantastic multitasker,* and an amazing cuddler. She was Aldous's eyes. His editor. His inspiration. His love. Who else would have chosen a man such as him? She ran psychedelic sessions for people with a delicate care and love unique not only in this world but in her home as well.

(*continued from page 188*) not Aldous who read the *Bardo Thödol* to Maria as she died, but rather it was Maria who recited the *Bardo Thödol* to Garrett in a dream, from beyond the grave (see Smith, *Letters of Aldous Huxley,* 746–47). Six months after Maria's passing, Aldous confided to his sister-in-law Juliette that he had spoken with Garrett about her encounter with Maria's spirit. Even here, Aldous does not claim to have read from the *Bardo Thödol,* but rather "talk[ed] to [Maria] *about it* [*italics mine*] (see Dunaway, *Aldous Huxley Recollected,* 115). Instead, he repeated a quote from Meister Eckhart: "The eye with which we see God is the same as the eye with which God sees us" (see Poller, *Aldous Huxley and Alternative Spirituality,* 84). This mistake has been repeated in Horowitz and Palmer, *Moksha,* 67; Lachman, *Turn Off Your Mind,* 96. Most recently, the claim appears in a *High Times* interview with Aldous Huxley, reprinted in 2019.

*We get a feel for how crucial Maria was to Aldous when we consider the number of friends and family members that had to replace her once she was gone. Aldous writes to Osmond: "Maria [LePut] will come [to cook] five days a week and Onnie [Wesley], the dear kind coloured woman who was with us at the time of your first visit, will come over once a week. Gerald's friend Michael will drive me wherever I want to go three afternoons a week, and one of Matthew's old schoolfellows from Dartington, a pleasant and extremely efficient young woman [Marianna Schauer], can come in the other afternoons and in the evenings, if I should need secretarial help or someone to read aloud."

After the funeral, Huxley filled his time touring, lecturing, and writing his novel, *The Genius and the Goddess* (1955), which he and his close friend Betty Wendel would also adapt for a play. And, of course, he continued his research into the deepest corners of his mind. He also grew keen on a new kind of psychedelic setting: "group mescalinization" (his term), which had a profound effect on him.[30] Recall that his second mescaline journey included other participants. On that occasion, he avoided the group facet of the setting, sneaking off with Heard to rhapsodize about any number of topics. Well, during that very journey he had visions, "luminous illustrations of the Christian saying, 'Judge not that ye be not judged.'" Buddha was also there, teaching him a most valuable lesson: the way Huxley opposed himself from the group mescalinization idea underlined every "disease of the mind."[31] Heard had changed too. True, like Huxley, he loved the deep philosophical conversations that accompanied a deep psychedelic experience. But he also came to realize what Hubbard (and indeed, many people throughout time) had known: psychedelics, particularly LSD, also offered "far reaching insights into one's own self and one's relationship[s] with others." He also stopped sneaking off with Huxley during their group sessions, later claiming, "a person intimately acquainted with LSD should be at the side of the subject as he embarks on his journey."[32]

~ *Late December 1955* ~

Courtesy of Hubbard, Huxley and Heard finally sampled LSD. Though neither gentlemen had internal visions with LSD, Heard, as per his usual psychedelic temperament, was tapping into the spirits floating around the room. Huxley's inability to reach the psychic realms led him to experiment with music, trying to use the proper sounds to fine-tune the experience.

"Bach was a revelation," he discovered through lysergized experimentation. Especially *Suite No. 2 in B-Minor,* which he urged Osmond to play for his patients undergoing psychedelic psychotherapy. "More than anything, I believe, it will serve to lead the patient's mind . . . to the central, primordial Fact . . . the memory of the understanding of which may serve as an antidote to mental sickness in the future." And perhaps one could take this use of music even a step farther? Maybe they could use the music as a guide for a spiritual experience? Huxley started to formulate ideas, visions of an elaborate ritual, wherein everyone consumed LSD. They would listen to music (preferably *Suite No. 2 in B Minor*) and let the enchanted melody guide them "to a direct, unmediated understanding of the divine nature."[33]

ONE PERSON

In 1954, Heard found himself at a library in south Palo Alto giving a speech on the remarkable nature of LSD to the Sequoia Seminar, a Bible study group headed by Stanford professor of business law Harry Rathbun and his wife Emilia, that would rechristen itself the Creative Initiative in 1962.* The Rathbuns had set up the lecture series with several big questions for each speaker to address: *Who are we? Where are we going? Are we still evolving?* And the grand inquiry: *Do we have any evidence to answer these questions?* Heard certainly had big ideas—about humanity's past, about evolution, and about psychedelia—and he felt it his duty to share them. He walked into a hexagonal room in the library, a stack of speech notes (that he never looked at once during his talk) in his hand. He then began his lecture, a finely arranged intellectual onslaught of "exquisitely composed poetic prose."[34]

One attendee listened to Heard with rapt attention. Myron Stolaroff (1920–2013) had received his degree in engineering from Stanford University and found employment as the Director of Instrumentation Marketing with the Ampex Corporation, founded in 1944 by Alexander M. Poniatoff. He had heard of this particular lecture series through his neighbor (and fellow Ampex employee) Clarence. After the

---

*In 1982 they would once again rename themselves "Beyond War." See Gelber, "Sequoia Seminar," 36.

lecture, Rathbun introduced Stolaroff to Heard, thus kicking off a life-long friendship.

The two gents hit it off so well that Heard invited Stolaroff to visit his home should he find himself in southern California. Not long after, Stolaroff flew to Los Angeles for work. Once he took care of business, he drove to Pacific Palisades to meet with Heard. He couldn't believe his ears: Heard gushed *ad nauseam* about LSD. What's more, he knew all about the great pagan mysteries of yore *and* about how different adepts used psychoactive enhancers to achieve epiphanies during the rites. There was the *Lupinus leucophyllus* that worshipers of Hecate employed to "become deprived of rational thoughts." There was also the cannabis of the Scythians; the Soma of the Vedics; the mushrooms of the Norse (by way of the Levant); and of course, the Rites of Eleusis.[35] For Heard, the "mysteries" merely represented an ancient esoteric way of saying "psychophysical therapy."[36] Modern psychedelics like LSD and mesca-line, Heard had hoped, would be the twentieth century's answer to the hopelessness felt across the world as apocalyptic weaponry churned out of arms factories from the two remaining superpowers. America needed a new myth, a new *mystery*.

For Heard, psychedelics offered the best available remedy to rein-vigorate and carry the mysteries of yore into the present day, largely for two reasons: firstly, LSD and mescaline (and mushrooms and canna-bis for that matter) "remove distractions," allowing the kind of deep inner reflection that one hundred years on a shrink's sofa couldn't provide. "The psychedelics smooth away such irrelevances and atten-tion attains to that wholeness of focus which is as flawless as that of a person under deep hypnosis," he explained. Second (now that we are all fully undistracted), our "observational construct . . . is corrected." This observational construct caused us to see the world as separable and compartmentalized. Psychedelics overturned such paradigms, leaving the lysergized or the mescalinized or the bemushroomed person to real-ize that their individual perception was "so largely influenced and dis-torted by instantaneous assumption (that is, construction-interpretation in terms of use and convenience) that it is constantly misleading the perceiver."[37]

Stolaroff was somewhat confused by all this. He had always viewed Heard as a "great natural mystic" . . . so why the need for synthetic—or even natural—enhancers?[38]

"I thought you went to all those places [in your mind] anyway," he piped up when the opportunity presented itself. "Why do you take this?"

"Oh, but it just opens the doors in so many ways to so many vast dimensions," Heard replied.[39]

As you no doubt can imagine, the rare privilege of conversing with Heard about psychedelics on a cool Southern California night in the scenic Pacific Palisades would convert anyone into a true believer. And Stolaroff was just as helpless to Heard's charm as we all would have been in that same situation. He wanted to try LSD, only he lacked a supplier. Thankfully, in a letter, Heard dropped a name—the one person he knew from up north that could certainly help the eager Stolaroff— *yep*, you guessed it . . . Al Hubbard. Coincidentally, Stolaroff's boss at Ampex, Alex Poniatoff, had just recently met with the Good Captain who couldn't stop bragging about his successes with LSD. Stolaroff fired off a letter to Hubbard and waited. Imagine his surprise when Hubbard replied by phone!

~ *February 1956* ~

Arrangements made, Hubbard traveled to Palo Alto with his "soft spoken, insightful wife," Rita, and a close family friend, Bill Galleon.[40] The trio scooped up Stolaroff at his office, and brought him back to their hotel. Hubbard gave Stolaroff a pill of Methedrine, and then a few pulls from a gas tank filled with "carbogen," a combination of 30 percent carbon dioxide and 70 percent oxygen, invented by Hungarian psychiatrist Ladislas Maduna (1896–1964), outlined in his *Carbon Dioxide Therapy* (1950). Carbogen provided Hubbard with a quick litmus test for potential LSD voyagers. First, it showed a hopeful candidate "how to let go to the experience."[41] Second, it proved a fantastic and dependable "emotional releaser." Since most people have no interplay with their subconscious mind, carbogen allowed Hubbard to gauge who was a prospective psychenaut and who was not; their reaction to the gas would let him know whether they could graduate to LSD. Stolaroff graduated immediately. For him, carbogen was a "marvelous abreactor," which released a lot of his "repressed anger."[42] And the Methedrine coupled with the carbogen afterglow was simply . . . *simply delightful.*

Stolaroff couldn't wait to try LSD, so much so that when Hubbard suggested he visit Vancouver in May for a session, the usually agreeable Stolaroff pushed for April.

~ *April 12, 1956* ~

Stolaroff laughed uproariously. "They talk about God but really know nothing of God."

Hubbard, confused, surely must have asked who Stolaroff was referring to.

"Priests," he answered, without missing a beat.[43]

Stolaroff had swallowed around 60 micrograms of LSD a few hours earlier. A close friend of Hubbard, Father J. E. Brown, had even blessed Stolaroff and promised to think of him later that afternoon when he performed Sunday Mass at the Cathedral of the Holy Rosary.

The entire experience might have been a little jarring for Stolaroff, a Jewish man, what with Hubbard flashing a picture of Jesus before his face once the LSD kicked in. Stolaroff looked in wonder as Jesus's eyes opened and shut, until his entire face morphed into a woman's face. But it didn't end there. Her face switched out for another face, and then another, until hundreds of faces, all in perfect detail, morphed one into the next. The intensity caused the LSD to turn for the worse. For several hours (each one lasting nothing short of an eternity), Stolaroff relived his birth:

> I am suddenly caught in a horribly painful stance. My head is bent over, my body is under enormous pressure, the vertebrae in my back

are crushed together as though being squeezed in a vise. The pain is unbearably excruciating. I feel I simply can't stand it. Suddenly, I am propelled forward, and I am exploded from the birth canal! . . . Next, I feel . . . an enormous burst of energy pervad[e] my body. . . . I blurt out, "They couldn't wait for me to be born!"

On Stolaroff's first LSD experience, he pierced the Great Lips. And once he had broken through, the mystical revelations began: "God is absolutely real, . . . there is only One Person, of which we are all a part."[44]

On balance, Stolaroff's experience with LSD was awful, and wonderful—and traumatizing and terrifying all at once. It had all the allure of a lucid nightmare orchestrated by Satan himself, but one that ended with a crescendo of God's grace. It was frightening, hexing, unpredictable, chaotic, unpleasant, and . . . (at least according to Stolaroff) "the greatest discovery humankind has ever made."[45]

Heard had been correct back at his home in the Pacific Palisades, Stolaroff soon realized.

LSD was the answer.

The door *and* the key.

Father Brown, who had blessed Stolaroff's maiden voyage, agreed. For Hubbard had also turned on the clergyman, who was quite taken by the psychedelic experience. In fact, Brown even sent out a mailer to his congregation titled "Introduction to LSD Experience." His words neatly lace the objectives of the scientific community with the spiritual one:

Each division of scientific knowledge has produced proof conclusive of the Supreme Being responsible for the perfection of order our scientific minds uncover. . . . We therefore approach the study of psychodelics [*sic*] and their influence in the mind of man anxious to discover whatever attributes they possess, respectfully evaluating their proper place in the Divine Economy. We humbly ask Our Heavenly Mother the Virgin Mary, help of all who call upon Her, to aid us to know and understand the true qualities of these psychedelics . . . according to God's laws to use them for the benefit of mankind here and in eternity.[46]

◎

Excited to feel the "special joy of sharing sacramental experiences with good friends," Stolaroff quickly brought his newfound Eucharist to the Sequoia Seminar group.[47] One of the first to try the Hubbard method (carbogen followed by LSD), Jeffery, was a professor of philosophy and religion at a local university who held a "deep interest in the mystical and the occult."[48] So much so that, while most in the Sequoia Seminar group approached carbogen with caution (and even anxiety sometimes), Jeffrey really enjoyed the gas. The others took fifteen inhales—twenty, tops. Jeff wouldn't stop until he drew somewhere around fifty gulps! The Sequoia Seminar crowd was quite probably the first Bible study group to turn into some kind of odd prototype for a Psychedelic Christian Church.

But there was trouble brewing. Like most robust agents of social change unused to the norms and pleasantries of polite society, Hubbard had a boisterousness about him that started to rub some of the Sequoia Seminar folks the wrong way. His big, unwavering personality upset the sensibilities of these particular Bible believers—much as he was an affirmed Catholic himself. Though some certainly warmed up to him, like Duncan Blewett (1920–2007), a portly Irish psychologist living around the Palo Alto area, who fostered such a close relationship with Hubbard that he called him "uncle Al." Blewett and Hubbard recognized each other as "scoundrels and explorers," misfits surfing the cosmos on LSD.[49] After taking LSD, Blewett had an epiphany: it should be available in every gumball machine in America! And he certainly practiced what he preached. One time he showed up to a luncheon at the Hubbard's house. Hubbard had spoken highly of Stolaroff to Blewett and to Blewett about Stolaroff. It was time they meet. Blewett arrived to the Hubbards' apartment, and as he walked up the stairs Stolaroff could see him chewing on something in his hand. Was it an apple? A plum? A pear? No—a peyote button! He entered the apartment with "a happy, fun-loving grin" on his face and offered a bite of the button to Stolaroff.[50] Is it any wonder he and Hubbard got along so well?

The Sequoia Seminar group eventually disowned Hubbard and his techniques and developed their own protocols for understanding the psychedelic state from a Christian perspective. Stolaroff left the group and continued working with Hubbard, eventually founding the International Foundation for Advanced Study (IFAS) in Menlo Park, California, in 1961. Stolaroff even left his cushy job at Ampex to work for IFAS full time. By employing a little bit of pressure, Hubbard managed to sign on Charles Savage, the ex–Operation CHATTER scientist,* as medical director. Stolaroff and Savage would go on to publish their IFAS findings, notably in an important paper "Clarifying the Confusion Regarding LSD-25." Therein, the former CHATTER scientist and the engineer sound more like Aldous Huxley and Gerald Heard than like a former CHATTER scientist and an engineer. Whereas Savage once thought in terms of pulse rates and mind weapons he now focused on the "dimensionless phenomena . . . [and] the oft reported profound philosophic and universal experiences" of the volunteers, going so far as to note the "spiritual truths" evident in some LSD sessions.[51]

SPIRITUAL DISEASE

Beginning in the late 1950s, five hospitals in the Saskatchewan District of Alberta offered a new kind of psychedelic therapy: treating alcoholism with LSD. Blewett went on to play "an active role" as an LSD facilitator at Weyburn Mental Hospital, administering LSD to countless alcoholics who couldn't tread the twelve steps. While there, in 1959

---

*Recall that Dr. Savage, despite his affiliations with the U.S. Navy, cared less about "mind control" programs and more about unlocking the secrets of LSD and mescaline for medicinal purposes.

he wrote (perhaps) the world's first medical manual for using LSD to treat alcoholism, *The Handbook for the Therapeutic Use of Lysergic Acid Diethylamide-25: Individual and Group Procedures.* Several passages in *The Handbook* even show direct influence of Huxley's psychedelic philosophies.[52] Some of the Saskatchewan brass had hypothesized that LSD might be as addicting as the Buffalo Bourbon they tried to corral. To test that possibility, Blewett (and his supervising psychiatrist) took LSD for thirty days straight. They reported no difference in their "ordinary functioning."[53]

The use of a psychedelic to treat alcoholism had its origins in the early 1900s. In the decades leading up to the synthesis of Hofmann's wonder child, anthropologists working in 1907 reported on alcoholics in the Winnebago community who had successfully given up the bottle in favor of peyote. Those who had made the transition from whiskey to dry whiskey became "successful, healthy and outstanding members" of their society. Consider the following testimonial: "Jilt [peyote] cures us of our temporal ills as well as those of a spiritual nature. It takes away the desire for strong drink[.] I myself have been cured of a loathsome disease too horrible to mention. So have hundreds of others."[54]

Modern clinical work in this area had started with Weyburn Mental Hospital psychiatrist Dr. Colin Smith, who tried to replicate the delirium tremens (DT) often felt by alcohol withdrawal, which include running a high fever, sweating profusely, nightmares, irritability, and hallucinations.* Some severe cases of DT can result in death. Smith hoped to "shock [alcoholics] into full awareness of their degradation and [generate] a desire to reform," by using LSD to simulate DT.[55] Others caught on quickly. Osmond and Hoffer both felt that alcoholics were prime candidates for LSD experimentation "because it is often easier to know whether they are improved or not."[56] Either they stopped

---

*Technically, Hubbard conceived this approach. But due to a lack of credentials, he never published any of his findings in learned journals.

drinking or they continued. And so they set out trying to find if LSD could effectively cure the "spiritual disease" of alcoholism.[57] Osmond and Hoffer gave LSD to five hundred alcoholics who had failed to sober up after receiving treatment from Alcoholics Anonymous (est. 1935) and who had had no luck with traditional psychotherapy. Thinking at the time (1954) that LSD and related compounds rested in the psychotomimetic family of chemicals, Osmond and Hoffer "conceived the idea that [LSD and mescaline] represented something very similar to delirium tremens—that a good many people who really give up alcohol do so on basis of the fact that they've had an attack of D.T.'s and been converted by them. We [thought] it might be a very good idea to give a person an 'attack' before he'd been completely destroyed."[58]

The plan backfired. Instead of experiencing DT, the patients were having "[f]avorable personality changes . . . even though this was not the purpose of the experiment."[59] Where they had tried to trigger terror, they instead triggered "illuminating" experiences.[60] Smith noted the change in alcoholics "resemble[s] the state of religious conversion." One patient sounded off about their "momentary oneness with God."[61] The alcoholics weren't "scared" straight; quite the contrary, they were actually enjoying the numinous nature of LSD. "Those who have not had the transcendental experience are not changed. They continue to drink," stated Hoffer at the Josiah Macy Jr. Conference in 1959. "The large proportion of those who had it are changed."[62] Follow-up surveys conducted after the LSD treatment revealed surprising results: "roughly half the patients either improved or stopped drinking altogether," a *Saturday Evening Post* article stated four years later. So promising was the success rate of recovering alcoholics with LSD therapy that Saskatchewan's Bureau of Alcoholism called LSD "the most helpful remedy we've known."[63]

Not bad for a chemical that supposedly makes people crazy.

15
Something Different
than Madness
Hollywood, Popular Media, and LSD

It is now generally agreed that [LSD] does
not quite mimic the naturally occurring schizophrenias.

SIDNEY COHEN

PSYCHOTOMYSTIC

~ *October 12, 1955* ~

The dose of LSD came on quickly and strongly, and Sidney Cohen (1910–1987) felt a deep, unbearable chill. So much so that he covered himself with three blankets just to warm up a little. But it wasn't the blankets that offered Cohen the most comfort and security. Nor was it the playfulness of colorful visuals, which he found uninteresting at best and disappointing at worst. It was instead the feeling of arriving "at the contemplation of eternal truth." One moment he was a doctor, interested in the physiological distortions of his body. The next moment, he was "a timeless spirit." And humorous—quipping that completing his Rorschach Test "took 200 light years, the longest on record."[1]* He didn't do much better on the Bender or Shipley-Hartford tests. He did,

---

*The editor of *The Beyond Within* notes "a light year is a measurement of distance, not of time, but this is how it was written." See Cohen, *The Beyond Within,* 108.

however, recognize the importance of setting: "I wonder whether much of the LSD experience is not dependent on the surrounding situation," he later wrote.[2]

Cohen was "a rock hard researcher who did not tolerate fools lightly."[3] Most of the time, one would find Cohen at the Veteran's Administrative Hospital in Los Angeles. Conservative in look and temperament, Cohen defaulted Delysid and mescaline strictly into the psychotomimetic category.[4] But that started to change after Cohen had read *The Doors* with great admiration for its prose, ideas, and author. Though Cohen was familiar with the psychotomimetic literature, he started to feel that LSD inspired "something different than madness," at least in the mentally stable. He had fallen in with Huxley, Heard, and Hubbard—especially Hubbard—who spoke not of model psychosis but of beatific visions. And we can see their clear influence on Cohen— it wasn't long before he too was also speaking not in clinical terms, but rather about "revelation, of great insights obtained, of feelings of profound unity and of experiences of self-transcendence."[5]

This did not mean, of course, that LSD automatically caused a mystical experience in anyone who ingested it. Take the two Zen Buddhists to whom Cohen gave LSD so as "to compare the drug state with the transcendent state achieved through meditation." Cohen had to terminate the test after the Buddhists grew too uncomfortable.[6] Another doctor at the Veteran's Administrative Hospital also tried working with LSD, giving it to one of his patients who saw no improvement in psychotherapy alone. The unnamed doctor gave a relatively low dose of 25 micrograms to the patient. "I see it all now," the patient said repeatedly once the LSD took effect. Though, every time the therapist would ask what epiphany the patient had come to, he would clam up. A few days later, he slit his wrists. He survived, but the staff kept him under careful watch. Eventually, they discharged him despite Cohen believing the unfortunate man was "essentially unimproved."[7]

Still, Cohen believed in the power of LSD and so continued to share its alchemical secrets with physicians of various sorts. One such psychologist turned on to LSD by Cohen was Dr. A. Wesley Medford. We do not have records of Medford's initial encounters with LSD, but the experiences had quite the impact on him. He soon started his own small group of LSD voyagers. And here, things got much weirder than with Huxley's group. The members of Medford's circle designed experiments to test the validity of such things as astral projection, past life regression, telepathy, and psychic powers.[8] One radiologist in Medford's circle eager to start up his own LSD therapy practice was Los Angeles–based radiologist Mortimer Hartman.

THE INFINITE MIND

"Go fuck yourself."[9] Betsy had finally said it. She was done.

Apparently so was her husband, Cary, who stormed out of bed, into the bathroom, and slammed the door. Actors Betsy Drake (1923–2015) and Cary Grant (1904–1986) had married serendipitously enough, only a year after appearing together in the romantic comedy *Every Girl Should be Married* (1948). One might expect such a quick beginning to dissolve just as quickly, but their marriage lasted thirteen years, which for Hollywood is a most impressive courtship.

But by 1957, the situation had grown unbearable. Drake had been working hard, day and night, writing her script for *Houseboat* (1958), envisioning Grant and herself as the stars. But when Grant decided that Sophia Loren (b. 1934) would instead take the female lead, Drake, as one can imagine, was crushed. She confided in her friend, the television actor Sally Brophy (1928–2007), who recommended that Drake meet a person—a specialist—that she had herself been seeing to receive help for depression. Brophy said this specialist, Mortimer Hartman, used some weird chemical to unlock the deeper recesses of her mind.

◎

We do not know how many LSD sessions Hartman ran. But it was apparently enough to whittle the therapeutic approach of LSD down to two categories (in his mind anyway). The two sides represented the classic rivalry between the Freudians and the Jungians. The Freudians abreact some early childhood memory; the Jungians transcend space and time. The Freudians largely felt that "should such a [numinous] state 'accidentally' occur," they should view it as "no such spectacular consequence," while the Jungians felt that transcendence had tremendous therapeutic value.[10] It is important to remember that, like Hubbard, Hartman was not a doctor and therefore could not get his hands on pure Sandoz LSD. He further followed Hubbard's circumvention of this problem by teaming up with a local psychiatrist named Arthur Chandler, whom he had met during his days with the Medford group. Together, they founded the Psychiatric Institute of Los Angeles, a clinic where they practiced their particular brand of "drug-facilitated psychotherapy . . . to aid repressed material to become conscious and to increase insight."[11] And they did not limit their efforts to LSD. Chandler and Hartman fully stocked the institute with Sandoz psilocybin, something called ALD-52 (another Sandoz creation), Ditran, and even ibogaine. They made sure not to intellectualize their patient's thoughts and feelings while sitting with a medicine. They drew the majority of their clientele from rich celebrities whom they charged a hundred dollars a pop for LSD psychotherapy, a move that famously earned the ire of Huxley.[12]

Like other doctors before them, Hartman and Chandler also had several of their A-list clients relive childhood memories—memories later confirmed by family members.* Fully aware that LSD (and related wonder children) "intensif[y] emotion and memory a hundred times," the shrink and the radiologist also took note of how easy it was to project the mind of the facilitator onto the mind of the lysergized during

---

*Recall from chapter 5 that "Mac," a fetishist who took LSD under the care of John Whitelaw at Powick Hospital, also experienced early childhood memories that were later confirmed by family members. So when Brophy excavated her deepest traumas, they sat silently, listening; when competitive swimmer turned actor Esther Williams (1921–2013) took LSD and started to grow a penis (in her mind anyway), Chandler and Hartman remained stoic. See Balaban and Beauchamp, "Cary in the Sky with Diamonds," 147.

these abreactions.[13] We can wonder endlessly which celebrity Chandler and Hartman had in mind—Sally Brophy? Betsy Drake?—when they spoke of one patient who "reported seeing Disney-like characters squabbling and having a fight." Like the psychiatrist Juliana Day before them, Chandler and Hartman understood that when a patient or volunteer started to wax poetic about the psychedelic experience, the proper protocol for the facilitator was to keep quiet.[14]

⊚

And so, one day after speaking with Brophy, Drake found herself in a small room at the institute, a pair of blindfolds in her hand, a hundred dollars paid. For a series of months, Drake took Delysid, covered her eyes, and went deep inside. There was so much to explore! The Other World was "like a vast ocean. You don't know where you are going to go," she exclaimed. Sometimes Hartman was attentive. Other times his hands-off approach resulted in laziness and indiscretion and he would leave Drake in the journey room while he attended other business, sometimes playing music in his absence. And for all we know, Drake preferred that scenario. Whatever happened to her during those sessions, we can only imagine. After her initial journey with LSD, one of her first orders of business was to call her mother, Ann.

"I love you," she said.

"Of course you do, darling," Ann replied sarcastically, abruptly hanging up the phone.

Still, even her inability to form a deep bond with her mother did not throw Drake off her course for self-improvement. She had seen the potential of this wondrous chemical. Even decades later, a few years before her passing, Drake still reflected fondly on her LSD sessions. "[I]t teaches you so much," she beamed to a reporter back in 2010.[15]

News of LSD's therapeutic power surged through Hollywood. American actresses like Judy Balaban (b. 1932), Polly Bergen (1930–2014), Linda Lawson (b. 1936), and Marion Marshall (1929–2018) also decided they wanted an inner tour with Hartman's strange blue pills. They had each felt the sting of what feminist scholar Betty Friedan would, in just a few years, term "the problem that has no name."[16]* This problem eventually came to be called "the feminine mystique," a draconian premise that saw women's most noble purpose as standing pregnant over a stove, waiting *oh so patiently* for her husband to get home from work. "How was your day?"—such a question was a one-way street in the 1950s. "The very condition of being a housewife can create a sense of emptiness, non-existence, nothingness in women . . . there is something about the housewife state that is dangerous," Freidan would go on to warn.[17] Upper-class white women were supposed to smile even as they slowly died inside.

As it turned out, not even Hollywood celebrities were immune.

And so one morning, as they both lie in bed, Grant asked Drake a question.

But Drake was tired of feeling dead inside, tired of smiling in front of cameras but secretly crying in front of mirrors. She was tired of the burden that had no name. No, not tired . . . *sick. So sick of it all.* With her newfound sense of liberation through LSD, instead of answering, Drake finally told Grant to go fuck himself.

Their marriage ended shortly thereafter.

Now, one might think that such an episode would have caused Grant to take a long, hard look at himself. This was not the case— although he did pay a visit to the Psychiatric Institute of Hollywood to track down Hartman.† But not to have an LSD session himself.

---

*While Friedan received some criticism for including only college-educated, "leisure-class," white women in her evaluations, that's exactly the kind of women that comprised Hollywood's elite. For criticism of this approach, see bell hooks, *Feminist Theory*, 2.
†Jay, *Mescaline,* reads "Beverly Hills psychiatrist Oscar Janiger began using Delysid . . . in which he treated Hollywood stars like Cary Grant," 206. However, all the evidence points to Grant receiving LSD from Chandler and Hartman, like the rest of the Hollywood glitterati.

Instead, Grant feared that Drake was divulging intimate details about his personal life (he had worked hard to polish his public image). Since Hartman wasn't technically an M.D., he did not have to abide by any kind of code or doctor-patient confidentiality laws. But Grant's curiosity about his former wife's gossip soon gave way to his curiosity about LSD. And so one day he decided to see what Drake had discovered.

Like many who have taken LSD, Grant felt "born again." He finally took that long, hard look at himself and "learned to accept responsibility for [his] own actions, and to blame [himself] and no one else for circumstances of [his] own creating." By the time Grant found himself talking to Joe Hyams and Lionel Crane from *Look* magazine while on set filming *Operation Petticoat* (1959), he was no longer giving his usual "amusing but scrupulously bland" interviews.[18] In fact, Grant was speaking in ways that the reporters found quite shocking. *Was this the same Cary Grant?* It didn't appear so: hence the title of the *Look* piece "The Curious Story Behind the New Cary Grant."

"I had to face things about myself which I never admitted, which I didn't know were there. Now I know that I hurt every woman I ever loved," Grant affirmed. "I was an utter fake, a self-opinionated bore, a know all who knew very little."[19]

Much to the surprise of Grant's lawyers and the suits at MGM (who all tried to stop the story from going to press), the article did not negatively affect his movie career. In fact, the public cared less about Grant taking LSD and more about their own possible LSD journeys, evidenced by the number of actors, producers, and screenwriters knocking on the doors of the Psychiatric Institute of Los Angeles.[20] Even Hyams felt the quick cultural shift, receiving over eight hundred written requests for LSD. He later confessed, "After my series came out, the phone began to ring wildly. . . . Friends wanted to know where they could get the drug. Psychiatrists called, complaining that their patients were now begging for LSD."[21]

One of those still-unknowns in Hollywood who was begging for LSD was a young actor named Jack Nicholson (b. 1937). Nicholson had "a growing collection of eclectic pals."[22] When Nicholson went looking for a doctor to facilitate a psychedelic experience, he stumbled upon either Hartman or another Los Angeles psychiatrist working with LSD at the time, Oscar Janiger* (1918–2001), though it is unclear who gave him LSD first. Maybe Nicholson was partially inspired to take LSD due to Grant's praise. But the real push came from his soon-to-be wife, Sandra Knight (b. 1940), who had already had a few LSD sessions under her belt by the early sixties and encouraged him to try it. Nicholson decided to take LSD for the same reason he first took up acting. He sought "a total abandonment, psychologically; a jumbled, speeded-up, high intensity 'emotional memory'" that would allow him to confront his own sexual problems.[23]

~ May 29, 1962 ~

Nicholson thought that LSD would be akin to smoking cannabis—something he'd done many times before. But this was no cannabis high. Nicholson "saw God," after swallowing 150 micrograms of LSD.[24] And this makes sense. His peer group at the time was using LSD as a "religious experience . . . in the sense of mind expansion and awareness," as Nicholson's friend, screenwriter, John Hackett recalls.[25] Then he felt his body dissipate as he relived his birth. Like Zaehner before him, Nicholson also felt an unnatural freeze in his genital area. Only his remedy involved something that might have made Zaehner (indeed, most men) cringe. Nicholson decided that the only way out of this testicular frost was to cut off his balls. Thankfully, he couldn't find any scissors. Instead, three weeks later, he married Knight, consummating their union righteously. Four years later, he began writing his first LSD

---

*We will meet Oscar Janiger more fully in a later chapter.

inspired movie script, appropriately titled *The Trip* (1967), starring Peter Fonda (1940–2019) as Paul Groves, and featuring supporting roles from Susan Strasberg (1938–1999) and Dennis Hopper (1936–2010). The story follows Groves, a television director, who takes LSD to deal with his cheating spouse (played by Strasberg), and gets into all sorts of mischief while under the influence. The end of *The Trip* features Groves walking onto a balcony the morning after his experience. When Glenn (played by Salli Sachse, b. 1946), asks if Paul found "what [he] was looking for? The insight?" as the sun rises, Paul replies, "Yeah, I think I . . . like I love you."

"And everybody else."

"Yeah, and everybody else."

"It's easy now, wait till tomorrow."

"Yeah, well, I'll think about that tomorrow."

At that moment, Groves's profile image freezes on screen, shatters, and the movie ends. Nicholson, Fonda, and some other cast members (who had maybe taken LSD) were infuriated. They wanted the movie to end "on the ups, not the downs."[26]

Despite the emotionally disappointing ending to the film, LSD had surely infiltrated Hollywood by the early 1960s.

But what about those earlier times—those overlooked times this book seeks to address? We tend to focus our attention on LSD success stories, those tales that epitomize the appellation *wonder child*. But there are just as many stories of no change at all, or even changes for the worse. Take, as one example, Grant's LSD therapy, which writers largely tout as a success.[27] We can sum up Grant's oft-repeated LSD conversion in three parts: first, Grant was a misogynist jerk. Second, Grant took LSD. Third, Grant was no longer a misogynist jerk. It's a great story!

But how much did Grant really change? How much had he morphed into the man he envisaged for himself? Was he really *new*? Those closest to him didn't think so. Director Stanley Donen (1924–2019), who had worked with Grant on two films by this time, *Kiss Them For Me* (1957) and *Indiscreet* (1958), recalled, "Did I notice any real changes? Not really. He was still exactly Cary Grant after LSD." Richard Brooks, whose directing debut *Crisis* (1950) starred Grant, recalls that he "did not recognize the changes [in Grant] were from taking LSD."[28]

But perhaps the best indication of how little LSD positively affected Grant comes from his fourth wife, Dyan Cannon (b. 1937, married to Grant in 1965), who testified against her soon-to-be ex-husband in divorce court three years later. Cannon charged that Grant continued taking LSD even after it became illegal. And that he was still as abusive as ever—screaming at her, hitting her, embarrassing her publicly—sometimes even while *on* LSD! Other lowlights included spanking Cannon "for reasonable and adequate causes," while laughing like a lunatic because she went to a party without his permission; trying to force-feed her LSD; and locking her in her room for wearing a skirt that Grant found too revealing. He even told Cannon's agent, Adeline Gould, "I'm going to break this girl." LSD certainly hadn't cured Grant of anything, least of all himself. In fact, Judge Wenke, who presided over Cannon's divorce from Grant, felt that far from ushering in a new Grant, LSD made him even more "irrational and hostile."[29]

As for Hartman, in August 1961, the California Board of Medicinal Examiners finally dropped the hammer on his activities, placing him under probation for ten years. The Psychiatric Institute of Los Angeles quietly closed its doors soon thereafter. But it didn't matter. He had already turned on most of Hollywood to LSD.

Popular media wasn't far behind.

◎

In 1959 Cohen, Heard, and Heard's partner and secretary, Michael Barrie, hopped aboard a flight to Phoenix, Arizona. Cohen planned to give LSD to his highest profile clients to date, Clare and Henry Luce. Both had immeasurable amounts of influence in American culture. Clare (1903–1987), the two-time congressperson and first female ambassador to Rome, was quite the political heavyweight at the time. Her play, *The Women* (1936), which featured an all-female cast, was a Broadway hit. Clare was the face of American conservatism in the 1950s, a regular feature on various late-fifties top ten "most admired women" lists;[30] Henry (1898–1967) was quite the cultural heavyweight himself, having founded *Time-Life* magazine in 1923, which by the late fifties had grown into an editorial empire.

Cohen and company couldn't have come at a worse time. The Luce's marriage was crumbling. And unlike most divorces, every sordid detail of their split graced the covers of magazines.

~ *March 11, 1959* ~

Clare's second rodeo.

She had a session with Gerald Heard in Connecticut a year prior, and so was already keen to the "burst of creative vitality" engendered by LSD.[31] So she was excited when Cohen showed up at her home in Phoenix, Arizona, with her friend Heard and a container of small, blue pills. Henry was less excited. He was too busy wondering if the American century, and indeed the entire world, would even survive. But he was also curious. Plus, LSD had the approval of Heard and Cohen, two men Henry respected. So it did not take too much nudging by Clare to persuade him to take the small, blue pills with her. He swallowed 100 micrograms of LSD and then sat at the desk in his study, lighting a cigarette with one hand as he reached for his copy of Lionel Trilling's *Matthew Arnold* (1939) with the other. Here and there, he would pick his head up from the book and discuss the finer points of Arnold and Cardinal Newman's relationship with Heard.

Clare started to feel the effects of LSD shortly after ingesting it. She grabbed a handful of flowers and, for just a moment, got lost in their geometrical perfection, their enriched color. She had to show them to Henry! She walked into his study and placed the flowers on his desk.

"Henry, can't you see how vivid the colors are on these flowers?"

"No," he replied, burying his nose back into *Matthew Arnold*.

Henry wasn't feeling anything yet; like Huxley and Zaehner before him, LSD crept up on him very slowly. At long last, nearly three hours later, he "started to see what Clare said. The aliveness . . . this perception is fantastic. Oh yes, quite wonderful. Not the visionary gleam but quite wonderful."[32] He excused himself to the yard, where an ocean appeared before him. Then, like a musical conductor, he used the melodies in his mind to draw the waves in and out of shore. He drew his friend, Father John Courtney Murray (1904–1967), over to a cactus. "Did you ever see anything more beautiful?" he asked, to which Father Murray erupted in laughter. Later that night, Henry found himself in conversation with God, who assured him that America would be just fine.[33] And while we tend to think of psychedelics as inherently "anti-conformist," Henry was on a wholly other trip. He would use his LSD insights and considerable cultural influence to become "the spokesman for the conventional values of Middle America," namely, "country, church, capitalism, and party."[34]

Clare's experience was less severe. Something about LSD always brought her back . . . back to a time when she could see the world like "a happy and gifted child."[35] She had spent the last two decades writing on religious themes, and this time around with Cohen, Henry, and Heard reminded her of an experience she had as a child, when a "religious ecstasy" overtook her as she walked along a beach.[36] Clare's aide momentarily interrupted her reflections when the phone rang. It was, of all people, Richard Nixon. She would have to phone him back later.

◎

Clare took LSD at least fourteen times after March 11. Sometimes she dropped Delysid with friends like the mosaic artist Louisa Jenkins (d. 1989). One diary entry (dated to 1961) has Clare lying around the pool at her home, dazzled by the bright, shiny colors of vibrant glass tiles provided by Jenkins. Jenkins, who first cautioned Clare about taking LSD in the first place, soon came to enjoy it as well. She would, in fact, later credit Cohen's blue pills as inspiring "my very works in the studio."

Jenkins lived with an artist community in Big Sur, California, where in between creating her beautiful mosaic pieces she studied the far-out topics of the day: Eastern religion, medieval alchemy, yoga, Jungian archetypes, and Kabbalism. She had first turned on to LSD one Sunday afternoon at Clare's house in Phoenix. Father Murray (who always seemed to be around when the LSD came out) had just finished giving a morning Mass for the household when Heard, in full mystic character, divvied up the Delysid "in a sacramental context."[37]

Other times Clare and Henry took Delysid with Father Murray, who sought to council them through their marriage. Like Hubbard's friend Reverend Brown (who blessed Stolaroff's initial LSD voyage), Father Murray also saw LSD as a sacrament—particularly a *Catholic* sacrament, which he could utilize in the fashion of Ignatius Loyola (1491–1556), who urged the faithful "to use their imaginative inner sight as a route to divine encounter."[38] It was Father Murray, in fact, who had phoned Cohen a year later, in November 1960. "LSD had seemed to improve Clare's mood in the past," he assured. Maybe Cohen wouldn't mind a return visit to Phoenix?[39] He didn't mind at all and would run several sessions for Clare. These sittings with LSD proved remarkably therapeutic for her. A smart, attractive man, Cohen soon found himself politely ignoring the advances of Mrs. Luce, who made no secret about her feelings for him. "I flirted with you, but you had not the slightest wish to flirt back," she confided to him.[40]

While biographers of Clare and Henry often skirt past the LSD issue, the truth is that both developed a strong enthusiasm for it, which was reflected in the way *Time-Life* covered LSD in the mid- to late 1950s. The first LSD article in *Time-Life* titled "Dream Stuff" had appeared in 1954 after *The Doors* hit (and quickly flew off) the shelves of bookstores. Huxley had his own thoughts about the article: "*Time* has been its usual unpleasant self—knowing, but inaccurate, Olympian but pettily malicious. And of course there is never any redress."[41]

Another article, the first published after Henry and Clare had tried LSD, titled "The Psyche in 3-D," put an additional spotlight on Grant's use and presented LSD in a very broad, but nonetheless positive light. LSD generated "vivid, colorful visions, sometimes populated by puppets or Disney characters, sometimes based on perfectly recalled childhood memories, sometimes fantasies of God and the devil."[42] The 3-D article even commended Sandoz for its "spotless" labs and "meticulous" scientists, lauding LSD as "an invaluable weapon to psychiatrists."[43] Of this article, Huxley fully approved. He also agreed with the Luces on one essential point: not everyone should have access to these small, blue pills. LSD should not be "taken like alcohol 'Just for kicks,'" the Luces affirmed.[44]

◎

~ c. July 10–13, 1972 ~

While attending the Democratic National Convention that year (held in the Miami Beach Convention Center), Clare found herself, coincidentally, on an elevator with Abbie Hoffman, cofounder of the Youth International Party (or the "Yippies"). You couldn't ask for two more polarized people: Clare, the classy conservative role model, and Abbie, the hippie-turned revolutionary. And yet, there was *one thing* that united the two.

Hoffman broke the silence: "Have you ever taken LSD?" he asked.

He meant the question as a gaff. Of course, this graceful, conservative woman had never been within one hundred miles of LSD.

But Clare was far more hip than Hoffman was aware. Her answer surely surprised him: "Oh, LSD. Why, yes, as a matter of fact, I have. But I must tell you, it was only once and quite some time ago. And it was under very controlled circumstances."

Clare wasn't truthful with Hoffman. In 1959 and the early 1960s (when the bulk of her psychedelic experiences occurred), there was nothing wrong with a conservative woman taking LSD and praising its virtues. But by 1972, promoting LSD would have been career suicide for her; indeed, at the time Clare was in the midst of planning "a whopping big party" for President Nixon, which would take place the following week. Just a year earlier, June 17, 1971, President Nixon had issued a message to Congress calling drug abuse "public enemy number one."[45]

"Did you like it?" Hoffman pressed.

"Well yes I did."

After a few more pleasantries, the two stopped on the ground floor and parted ways.

"Good-bye. It was delightful to have met you," said Clare—pleasant, classy, *elegant* as ever.

"So long. See you in Nirvana," said Hoffman as he disappeared into the hot, Florida streets.[46]

16

The Madonna and the Gingerbread Man

LSD, Psychotherapy, and Alcoholics Anonymous

Even more exciting than the therapeutic possibilities of LSD are its potentials, and those of similar drugs, for helping us to answer the many questions we have about what makes us what we are as human beings.

BETTY EISNER

CHAOS AND CONFUSION

Betty was different.

Many students no doubt walked right past the notice Sid Cohen had tacked onto one of UCLA's bulletin boards. Others perhaps scanned the post and quickly dismissed it, for it promised an "unusual" experience, but said little more.[1] It seemed scary, cryptic—not the kind of flyer that would attract the usual student that once dominated the halls of UCLA. For Cohen desired a research assistant to carry out groundbreaking experiments with this miracle drug—this *wonder child*—that both probed the deepest secrets of the mind while safely offering something different than madness. He did not even divulge the name of the unusual, experimental chemical. With too little to go on, many students glanced at the flyer and then quickly carried on with their day.

But Betty was different.

Betty Eisner (1915–2004), a thirty-five-year-old psychologist painstakingly pursuing her doctorate at the University of California Los Angeles, woke up at 4:00 a.m. every morning and devotedly carried out the tasks of motherhood and graduate studies. Perhaps this unusual drug was the same one she had read about in a recent *Look* magazine article.

"I'll bet that research is about LSD!" she exclaimed.[2]

Imagine her surprise when she found out she was correct.

Until this time, many researchers had stumbled upon Delysid "through the back door"—they harbored no particular interest in LSD but sort of just fell into it.[3] For whatever reason—perhaps she needed an escape from the exceptionally challenging juggling act of her life—Eisner found the allure of LSD irresistible. However, caught up in her own work (she hadn't yet completed her doctoral dissertation on infertility in women), she declined Cohen's offer to assist him on the project. Though, not wanting to miss the opportunity completely, she struck a deal with a colleague of hers: Lionel Fichman, or "Fish," as his friends called him, would take the position as Cohen's research assistant and Eisner, eager for the chance to explore the depths of her psyche, would volunteer as the first subject.

~ *November 10, 1955* ~

When Eisner first took LSD, the drug was still in its investigational phase. Although Huxley had already shown that psychedelics presented a deeper puzzle than a subpar term like "psychotomimetic" allowed, most doctors still handled medicines like LSD and mescaline in a reserved manner. Questionnaires superseded subjectivity. Eisner frowned on all the testing and complained that the experimental probing of her experience was "frustrating." Filling out charts and answering questions distracted her from fully engaging in the experience—a legitimate complaint we have seen before. Still, she did as expected, faithfully sketching her artistic best on the Draw-A-Person (DAP) test. The objective of the DAP is for the patient to conceptualize their Freudian ego—the rather cliché question, "Who am I?"—and draw it out. Although the test was widely known, it had a special place within the Freudian circles that believed such purging of the personality on paper exposed the inner sanctum of our deepest selves. Unsure of how to properly portray herself on paper, Betty wrestled with various alter egos ranging from Little Lord Fauntleroy to one of the Louies. Although she didn't want to admit it, she finally determined that drawing a young girl best described her inner self. The young caricature Eisner, complete with mismatched appendages (the legs were fully grown, while the face was that of a child) and a Victorian-era dress, left the real Eisner feeling embarrassed.

The other tests proved irksome as well. Struggling through the word association tests, Betty felt that each word had simply dissipated into a "great bubble of space-time," a free-floating collection of words that lacked any consistency at all.[4] Eisner simply didn't care about drawing her ID or playing with capricious words. She wanted to drift off into that "great lovely green pasture" of her mind. Yet every time she did, the doctors brought her attention back to another form or to answering another question. Disinterested in the cosmic countryside, the doctors asked Eisner to focus on the "fence" that enclosed her spacious psychic-meadow.[5] But the doctors' probing was only half the problem. Even if Eisner could have found some way to compartmentalize each word into different groups, her tongue seemed to swell up inside her mouth to the point that she felt she couldn't speak anyway. Her conscious and sub-conscious minds, once sovereign in their respective domains, now shared the same territory, leaving her to act as ambassador for each province. It was all too much. Her envoys found it impossible to keep track of all the messages going in and out of her consciousness; her "switchboard" thusly "jammed up."[6]

The best way she could describe her experience? "Chaos and confusion."[7]

If Eisner's first session was chaotic and confusing, her second (which occurred two years later* with Cohen and an unnamed friend) was harrowing. This time, she plunged into the depths of her very being. There were no dreamy green pastures there—just an apocalyptic battle waged between herself and her inner demons. As colorfully mechanized mosquitoes drilled into her skull and tried to suck out her brain, storybook characters like the gingerbread man appeared. A Madonna figure stood beside a little white church. Both the maiden and the church kept shifting from one oddity to the next. At times Eisner could only see a skeletal outline of the church, as if the walls, windows, and ceiling had disappeared completely, leaving the inside exposed. The Madonna leaning against the peculiar building morphed into a snow maiden, then an ice princess, and eventually merged with the gingerbread man. Eisner felt that she had broken through to the nucleus of all the learned behaviors she had collected throughout her life. If her first LSD experience had exposed her defenses, her second taunted them. Though Eisner also underwent a change that we have not yet seen in the annals of the wonder child fifties. LSD brought her face to face with her own deep-seated racism, allowing her to overcome it:

> I was made to feel the coldness, . . . the separateness of the myth
> that Nordic people are superior to others. I realized that this had
> been built into me from earliest childhood. I felt its austerity and its
> coldness—anyone who must be superior pays the price of snow and
> ice. And through these symbols I released the racial intolerance back
> and down to my childhood where I was brought up in the South—
> and I loosened part of my own need for feeling superior. The first
> line of defense: analysis. The second line of defense: prejudice and
> intolerance. . . . In understanding the symbols I found the Madonna
> and the gingerbread man were two halves of myself which I could

---

*Presumably at Veteran's Administrative Hospital.

not get together into a whole—they were stereotypes of my misperceptions of the masculine and feminine parts of my nature.[8]

The LSD had all but worn off and Cohen left. Not long after, Eisner's friend drove her home. But the experience had lingered longer than expected and left Eisner in a deep depression when she got home. She wanted to call Cohen but, unable to get a dial tone from her house, walked to find a payphone. She stumbled across one not too far from her home that several people were already in line to use. She forced herself to wait patiently in existential anguish until the phone became available. Thousands of years passed. Poor Betty! Every second of every minute registered in her psyche as a grueling eternity struggling uncontrollably against some hellish quantum abyss that sucked her into its nothingness. By and by the line eventually dissipated with each previous user scattering off into the air until, finally, salvation! The phone was available. Eisner reached Cohen but, much to her chagrin, he defined her experience in his usual "quiet and unspectacular terms" and acted dismissive toward her sorrowful pleas and suicide threats;[9] believing Eisner's distress to be an overstatement, he recommended she get good night's rest. *Good night's rest? How does one do that when trapped in a nightmare?!* Unable to encourage a more tender side in Cohen, she then called the friend of hers who had sat in on the session with her. The friend had just taken a sleeping pill and soon couldn't even string a coherent sentence together. It seemed that everyone Eisner cried out for trivialized the tormented thoughts going on inside her mind. Was everything that ever existed plotting against her? Eisner felt wholly alone—isolated—a tiny stitch in the fabric of the universe and decided that before the whole of the cosmos collapsed around her, she needed to find something pleasant—*anything*. Perhaps a book would ground her thoughts? Swimming through the riptides of despair she made her way back home and into her voluminous library. Immersing herself in the writings of Saint John of the Cross, Eisner later recalled that as she struggled to comprehend the passages in the tome, she "broke through to the mystical experience, which ended the depression."[10] Although she managed to hang onto Saint John and pull herself out of the dejected state during the LSD experience, Betty found that afterward she fell into the "blackest depression that anyone could dream up."[11]

One might think that such a traumatic experience would have caused Eisner to reject the psychedelic state altogether, only the opposite happened. Despite the rough edges of her first two trips, Eisner remained fascinated by LSD's potential. She spent the next year organizing a concrete routine for therapy sittings. Cohen provided many trip reports, each as captivating as the next, and Eisner worked to sift through them all. She soon developed her own unique geeky techniques.

Although common practice insisted that the doctors take LSD along with the patients during group sessions, Eisner preferred to stay lucid. She also rejected the sensory deprivation techniques used by some doctors and pioneered what she termed "eyeballing"—gazing into the eyes of her patients to conjure up sentimental emotions and access the "roots firmly meshed far below verbal levels."[12] She wanted to communicate directly with the person who existed beyond their unwanted learned behaviors and reasoned, "Words often complicate interaction rather than simplify it." And Eisner had good reason to believe this. Language can sometimes buttress more barriers than can unspoken statements. She wrote:

> It is becoming increasingly clear that a large part of the interaction between doctor and patient takes place at a non-verbal level. This is disconcerting in our highly rational, overly-intellectualized society where semantics seem to act as the cement of human relationship. However, much better results are observed to occur when the wisdom of the deep unconscious is allowed to take over—with the therapist acting more as a guide and interpreter.[13]

All those little defenses and habitual tidbits that manifested into obsessive compulsions or "quirks," mood and sexual disorders, and all-around social awkwardness, needed to be exorcised from the deep recesses of the mind of the patient who could then examine and vanquish them. Finding value in the old Ciceronian adage "The eyes are the window to the soul," Eisner would stare deeply into her patients' windows and attempt to unchain their core self.

A SINGLE OVERWHELMING EXPERIENCE

~ November 11, 1934 ~

The man sitting at the table heard enough. He had just spent the last hour or so listening to horror tales from his friend Bill Wilson (1895– 1971), who had been recovering from alcoholism until that day.

"You must be crazy!"

"I am," Wilson replied.

Wilson hadn't walked into the bar to get loaded. He simply wanted to use the telephone. The bartender, friendly albeit enabling, offered Wilson a free drink, which he accepted. After all, it was Armistice Day,* why not celebrate? What harm would one drink do? To most folks, nothing. But to Wilson all it took was one sip of the sauce to spiral south. Sure enough, that one drink turned into a month-long bender, with a brief reprise when his old friend (and drinking buddy) Edwin ("Ebby") Thatcher (1896–1966) showed up at his house in early December. Thatcher had success curbing his drinking by attending meetings hosted by the Oxford Group at the Calvary Mission. There, he had found God and lost the desire to drink.† Such notions rubbed Wilson the wrong way. "I . . . gagged badly on the notion of a Power greater than myself," Wilson later testified.[14] But Thatcher was convincing, and on December 7, Wilson made the trek to the Calvary Mission . . . hitting a number of bars along the way to socially lubricate

---

*Today called Veteran's Day.

†Sadly, his sobriety was short lived. Thatcher would battle alcoholism until the day he died. See Moore, *Alcoholics Anonymous and the Rockefeller Connection,* 71.

himself for the meeting. Once arrived at Calvary Mission, the highly inebriated Wilson found himself in something like a church. Hymns were sung, confessions made, and the priest who oversaw the meeting yapped on and on about God's forgiveness and surrender. He had been right about this place. But something remarkable also happened—not at the meeting, but rather after the meeting. On his way home, Wilson did not stop at a single bar. The next few days are fuzzy. Some reports hold Wilson drinking more than ever before, while others have him drinking just enough to stave off the DT.[15] Whatever version is true doesn't matter. What matters is that the desire to change had finally manifested in Wilson.

Exactly a month after he had fallen off the wagon, Wilson made his way to Town's Hospital . . . stopping for four beers along the way. Once admitted, he went through the "belladonna treatment" that "successfully and completely removes the poison from the system and obliterates all craving for drugs and alcohol."[16] He took pills at regular intervals, a mixture of belladonna, henbane, and prickly ash—a veritable witches' potion.* A few days into treatment, Thatcher arrived to Town's for a visit. Wilson came to the stunning realization that while he continued his downward spiral, Thatcher had started his (short-lasting) ascent. When Wilson inquired how Thatcher could stay sober, his friend responded frankly, "turn your life over to God."[17]

Perhaps he had simply "hit bottom";[18] perhaps the pills of belladonna and henbane—plants once used by ancient and medieval folks to achieve mystical visions—had awakened a spiritual center within his soul. Perhaps he took to heart the philosophies of James, whose *The Varieties of Religious Experience* he read cover to cover after Thatcher dropped off a copy at Town's Hospital. Whatever the reason, Wilson finally saw his problem. And his solution:

---

*Recall that at this time Dr. Robert House was also employing solanaceous plants to induce twilight sleep in hopes of obtaining criminal confessions.

I was at the bottom of a pit. . . . The last vestige of my proud obstinacy was crushed. All at once I found myself crying out, 'If there is a God, let Him show Himself! I am ready to do anything, anything!' Suddenly the room lit up with a great white light. I was caught up into an ecstasy which there are no words to describe. It seemed to me, in the mind's eye, that I was on a mountain and that a wind not of air but of spirit was blowing. . . . At long last, I saw, I felt, I believed. . . . Now for a time I was in another world, a new world of consciousness. All about me and through me there was a wonderful feeling of Presence and I thought to myself, 'So this is the God of the preachers!' A great peace stole over me and I thought, 'No matter how wrong things seem to be, they are still all right [*sic*]. Things are all right with God and His world.'[19]

Wilson's doctor, William Silkworth, had to assure him that he wasn't going crazy. "There has been some basic psychological or spiritual event here," the doctor said. "I've read about these things. . . . Sometimes spiritual experiences do release people from alcoholism."[20]

Sometimes spiritual experiences do release people from alcoholism. Wilson would go on to found Alcoholics Anonymous (AA) the very next year, which emphasized giving oneself over to a Higher Power— similar to the experience he had at Town's Hospital. For Wilson, the ego stood as the greatest resistance to getting sober. At the time, the greatest ego-reducer known to science was LSD.* This presented a conundrum for Wilson. As we saw in an earlier chapter, LSD was showing promising results with alcoholism at Weyburn Mental Hospital in Saskatchewan. But Wilson, and (by extension) AA, derided using chemical aids of any kind to kick the sauce—"They're even against aspirin!" Eisner joked.[21]

When Osmond and Hoffer had first brought news of LSD's success with alcoholics to Wilson's attention, he panned the idea. The formalities and privileges of his position as the head of AA came with restrictions

---

*Many would argue that, while not perfect, it still is.

and trappings—he simply *couldn't* endorse LSD (whether he wanted to or not). Though, once he stepped down as the head of AA while attending that organization's "Coming of Age" conference in St. Louis on July 3, 1955, Wilson was now free from the formalities, restrictions, and oversights that had preempted any interest in psychedelics.

Furthermore, he soon couldn't deny the research. And the statistics. And the testimonies. And the numbers, the details. Prior investigations indicated that, for many people (though, of course, not all), LSD loosened the ego instead of strengthening it. This was exactly what Wilson had been looking for, an "ego reduc[er]" that "makes the influx of God's grace possible."[22] He had earlier visited Trabuco College and met Heard and Huxley back in the winter of 1944. When *The Doors* hit bookshelves a decade later, he knew all about their interest in psychedelics, although like many, he still didn't approve (at least publicly). It wasn't until a couple years later, after he met Osmond and Hoffer, that he would change his mind.

~ *August 29, 1956* ~

Cohen, Eisner, Heard, and magazine editor Tom Powers ingested 25 micrograms of LSD, while Wilson doubled that dose. It would be his first of many, despite AA's anti-substance stance. AA was based on the theory that all alcoholics "get to a point in the program where they need a spiritual experience, but not all of them are able to have one."[23] With LSD, Wilson certainly had one. Heard faithfully jotted down notes detailing Wilson's first sitting with LSD. An hour after taking the small blue pills, Wilson felt first "a feeling of peace" that slowly gave way to pure, unbridled ecstasy. He laughed at his own pedestrian addictions, "Tobacco is not necessary to me anymore," Heard transcribes. An hour later, Wilson was asking for a cigarette. The hypocrisy didn't bother him: "people shouldn't take themselves so damn seriously," he said as he lit up the butt.[24] Wilson had visions of the world's alcoholics all coming together and helping each other. He had found "an appreciation of beauty almost destroyed by [his] years of depressions."[25]

Wilson absolutely loved his LSD experience and felt it could serve as a last effort of hope to those struggling with alcohol addiction, but could not "get the [A.A.] program."[26]* He couldn't wait to invite friends and associates to Trabuco College, where Heard sometimes held LSD sessions. To Wilson's surprise, his friends did not take to LSD as enthusiastically as did he.

While he had always believed that an afterlife awaited us after this incarnation, something about his LSD experiences proved it for him: "The public is today being led to believe that LSD is a new psychiatric toy of awful dangers. It induces schizophrenia, they say. Nothing could be further from the truth."[27] Writing to the Episcopalian priest Samuel Shoemaker, "I have come to believe proof surely exists that life goes on. . . . [T]he world badly needs this proof now."[28] LSD offered such proof. Like Father Murray, who took LSD with the Luces, and Reverend Brown, who sat with Hubbard, Wilson also gave LSD to a man of the cloth with whom he was friends, Father Ed Dowling: "The result was a most magnificent, positive spiritual experience. Father Ed declared himself utterly convinced of its validity."[29]

◎

When it came to treating alcoholics, different camps developed different approaches to achieving the numinous. We saw earlier that Osmond and Hoffer at Weyburn Mental Hospital favored the high-dose, single overwhelming experience in an attempt to generate a spiritual overhaul—the kind of experience Wilson believed acted as the key to overcoming alcohol addiction.

The high doses started with Hubbard, who, ever "Hofmann's Bulldog," had since 1953 been giving his "patients" upward of 500 micrograms of LSD, even before the doctors at Weyburn Mental Hospital were keen to this approach. Why drag out LSD psychotherapy

---

*He even used adrenochrome to successfully quell his "ex-alcoholic neurotics." See Smith, *Letters of Aldous Huxley*, 895.

for months, Hubbard wondered, when a single overwhelming experience was good enough?[30] He also appears influenced by Sandison at Powick Hospital in his attention to setting: "The appointments of the room—drapes, floor coverings and furnishings—should be tastefully combined with floral arrangements and pictures to create a harmonious atmosphere. The dominant theme of the décor should be composed of various universal symbols." If the patient showed signs of anxiety, they were not administered Thorazine (which would counteract the LSD). Instead, Hubbard gave them more LSD.[31] By the time he published his findings (coauthored by three actual doctors), Hubbard had given LSD to sixty-one alcoholics, all drawn from the Hollywood Hospital in New Westminster, British Columbia.

Successes treating alcoholism with LSD were not as high as initially hoped, and no psychedelic proved the panacea or medical magic bullet for which Hubbard had so desperately hoped. Still, some victories give us insight as to why the doctors kept pursuing this mode of addiction recovery. Take the case of a forty-four-year-old salesperson, an alcoholic for fifteen years. After 400 micrograms of LSD, he proclaimed, "This experience has given me quite an awakening and a real good look at myself. It seemed to clear a lot of garbage out of the way." Over a year later, the man was still sober. A follow-up interview revealed that he did not see LSD as a "cure all," but rather as a wake-up call to "work on oneself." LSD could only show someone the path toward healing; it was up to each person to walk it.[32] Hubbard's work with alcoholics at Hollywood Hospital kicked off a trend that would eventually reach Saskatchewan.

Other doctors like Cohen, Eisner, and Fish preferred "psycholytic"* therapy, which emphasized comparing "the functioning of an individual

---

*In other words, "loosening of the psyche," coined by Sandison at Powick Hospital, from the verb "to lyse," i.e., to "dissolve." See Abramson, *The Use of LSD in Psychotherapy and Alcoholism,* 185, 187.

under the drug and in his individual state."[33] Eisner didn't much care for the high-dose sessions she had undergone (courtesy of Hubbard) and felt that the same ends could be met without all the horrific uncertainties that might possibly befall any inexperienced LSD taker. Recovery might manifest more easily using smaller doses coupled with therapy stretched over time. The psycholytic doctors reasoned that first relaxing the psyche and then guiding the patient through the edgy corners of the mind in as comfortable a way as possible would be comparable to Hubbard's method with less possibility of an adverse reaction occurring. Eisner surely didn't want any of her patients collapsing under some mad Newtonian edict while waiting on line for a payphone. The intent was to harmonize regular therapy with the aid of small dose LSD sessions.[34] Eisner summed up psycholytic therapy thusly: "With the therapeutic study it was initially impossible to predict any given patient's experience, although with each successive session, unconscious material became increasingly manifest."[35]

They also coupled LSD with an initial dose of 50 to 100 milligrams of Ritalin or 75 to 85 milligrams of ketamine, both substances helping a person who "hit a barrier . . . blow through the barrier." Even methamphetamine, which did not have the stigma it holds today, was used (by suggestion of Hubbard). This method (an initial dose of Ritalin, ketamine, or methamphetamine followed by LSD) "enabled a person to let go as much as he or she wanted. Perhaps just a little bit at first, then a little more the next time, and finally they would allow it to happen completely." If we can believe Eisner (and there is no good reason not to), her success rates dwarfed those of Hubbard. Her patients had, in fact, achieved "resolution in all cases."[36]

Perhaps that's because Eisner was interested in slowly digging deep into the unconscious. One does not use a jackhammer in a flower bed. There wasn't just one road to the subconscious traumas of patients. Single, overwhelming experiences didn't allow time for a person to reflect, integrate, and heal as they made their way forward. Each trauma had its own unique stage of development that led back to the source—like multiple landings on a staircase leading into a secret, underground vault sitting in a dusty corner of Hell. In fact, Eisner believed that the careful observer could detect at least three distinct levels of *inferno*. The first, a "matrix consisting of the symbolic, the irrational, the primitive" served as the garden of "dreams, myths, fairy tales, and painters." These represented the Jungian archetypes. The second level represents an extension of these archetypes into the larger world. Once there, patients "work out problems in the larger framework of humanity." This represented the Freudian ego. The third landing found the patient in a space where they could deal with problems on a "cosmic level." Here, the person experiences an overwhelming sense of "order, truth, beauty, love, or any combination of these. . . . The words often used by individuals such as Is-ness,* Being, and God are much more appropriate and understandable in mystic literature than in the setting of an exploratory scientific study."[37] These represented the mystical states. Eisner's patients seem to have favored this protocol, one of them commenting on "the unrolling of the stored microfilm of her life history."[38]

Eisner also pulled from her own experience with LSD to interpret her study and refine her approach: "A state of confusion and chaos appears to be necessary for the overly intellectual, over-rationally-controlled individual" before proceeding deeply into the unconscious. Patients could easily mistake this chaos and confusion for "a state of insanity," which was the norm for researchers until they started reading *The Doors*.[39]

Despite the different trails through the wood that Hubbard and Osmond, Eisner and Cohen traversed, they all trusted that LSD would lead them to the same old, robed mystic sitting on a mountaintop. All agreed that dose, set, and setting provided the keys to success-

---

*An obvious nod to Huxley, and demonstration of his influence on the medical community.

fully unlocking the unconscious, and adopted the "special technique[s] and environment for LSD" treatment that Sandison had pioneered at Powick Hospital in England.[40] Music, once an option during some LSD voyages, now seemed a necessity to "potentiate the drug action" in all people. Moreover, all formally consented that the researchers, even if lucid during the sessions, have prior experience with psychedelics. This helped avoid "unintelligible or misinterpreted" ideas about the patients' experience.[41] They also began to map the geography of the Other World the way a cartographer charts and names newfound territories: Cosmic Limbo, the Black or Schizophrenic Belt, the Desert, and Ice Country.[42] Huxley thought of the mind as similar to "Stratified Neapolitan ice, with a peculiar flavor of consciousness at each level."[43] Therapy sessions had begun to imitate trips to a travel agent. Depending on which area of the psyche one wished to journey, Eisner, Cohen, and Fish tried to plan courses that would ensure a safe passage to their patients' chosen destination. Physical examination of the patients before administering LSD was also standard procedure. Finally, they believed that the therapy could work for anyone who recognized their own various mental problems and craved change. As Eisner liked to say, "the basic element of LSD therapy is *trust*."[44]

Hofmann came to agree with the doctors in southern California (and Hubbard). After speaking with Huxley, he described psychedelic psychotherapy as "attempts to induce a mystical-religious experience through the shock effect of LSD." Comparing his wonder child to other available chemicals, he acknowledged, "Whereas tranquilizers tend to cover up the patient's problems and conflicts, reducing their apparent gravity and importance, LSD makes them more exposed and more intensely experienced."[45]

17

An Intellectual, Fun Drug

A Strange Fraternity

LSD experiences were . . . more creative than a dream, more original than a madman.

ANONYMOUS ARTIST

PRIEST AT LARGE

Cohen did not inspire only Eisner and Fish to work with LSD. One of his former residents, Dr. Keith Ditman (1921–2001), a Jungian who did not fear the unconscious, kept regular correspondence with Huxley.[1] The two had partnered to conduct and publish two studies on LSD, one of which addressed the growing beat generation. They knew of a woman, an aspiring writer, who had taken LSD six times. And three of those occasions sound like they were facilitated by none other than Hubbard himself.

But you tell me: Cohen and Ditman write that, beyond LSD, this woman's latter three experiences also included "carbon dioxide inhalations (carbogen), methylphenidate (Ritalin), and JB-329 (Ditran), an experimental psychotomimetic drug with atropine-like effects." Who else but Hubbard would recommend such a thing (and/or had the resources) in the late 1950s? After her six sessions, the writer fell in with a group who used "marihuana, meperidine (more or less morphine), and opium" that they obtained through a Mexican source.

She claimed the substances "helped her write better." Not long after, she would leave for Mexico and join a "'beat' colony" in Guadalajara (despite having children she left in the states). As the colony in which she lived served as a trading post for illegal substances, she enjoyed a ready supply of "heroin, barbiturates, and marihuana." She eventually returned home (for the sake of her children), but couldn't decide if she wanted to "stay with them or abandon them for the amoral, irresponsible life of the 'beat' world." Cohen and Ditman felt that this aspiring beat writer's "antisocial reaction . . . may have been triggered by haphazard LSD exposure."[2]

Unlike earlier psychotomimetic researchers who only vaguely recorded the occasional ostentatious claims of some who had taken LSD, Cohen and Ditman paid special attention to it. "After the drug effects have worn off," they wrote, "the megalomaniacal belief that the individual has been chosen to convert others to the new faith has been retained." Make no mistake, they warned, "[s]mall LSD sects have been established." They even speak of one psychologist who took LSD three times. Lest I not give the account justice, I shall reproduce the write-up in full.

After his three LSD sessions:

for weeks thereafter [he] acted out grandiose plans. One was to take over Sandoz Laboratories in order to secure the world supply of the drug. He threatened his wife with a gun, then left her, wrote some songs and plays of some minor merit, and went off to live in the desert. He recovered gradually after a number of months without specific treatment.[3]

◎

When he wasn't working with Cohen, Ditman found employment at the UCLA Neuropsychiatric Institute's Alcoholism Research Clinic, and hired John Whittelsey (who also worked at the Clinic) as a statistician to gauge LSD's effects on alcoholism. Ditman's approach differed from both Hubbard and Eisner—his volunteers "received no intended psychotherapy during the LSD experience." And while some (like Hubbard, Eisner, Huxley, Zaehner, Janiger, and those at Powick Hospital) had access to music, art, "and various sensory stimuli," such practices remained uncommon in most clinical settings outside Ditman's office.[4]

The numbers don't lie. Ditman's tests included seventy-four participants; a questionnaire filled out by the volunteers revealed something rather extraordinary. Seventy-two of seventy-four felt the experience "very pleasant," and sixty-six people (or 80 percent of those tested) reported that LSD was something they "want to try again." Seven volunteers found LSD "disappointing" and only *one* labeled it "a horrible experience." However, when it came to drinking alcohol (the entire point of the study), only 36 percent of the participants reported improvement in that area. Three years later that number dropped to zero.[5] Many patients experienced a feeling not found on the questionnaires, that is, a strong sense of a "greater awareness of God or a Higher Power, or an Ultimate Reality." Ditman was familiar with spiritual writings of the time; both Raynor Johnson's *The Imprisoned Splendor* (1953) and James Leuba's *The Psychological Study of Religion* (1912) graced his bookshelf. Additionally, but in no sense inferiorly, he was also familiar with James's classic *The Varieties of Religious Experience* (1902). Unlike Zaehner, Ditman could not find much difference between religious experiences and LSD experiences. Though I suppose that would be difficult for Ditman as he listened to one of his volunteers speak of "The White Light of God," while another transformed into a "minor prophet."[6] Many of his patients saw no difference between mysticism and the LSD state either, which Ditman credited to their familiarity with *The Doors*.[7] By the end of his study, Ditman realized that those volunteers with a "religious" or "mystical orientation" found LSD "the most pleasant."[8]

One of those volunteers with a mystical orientation was a Zen philosopher named Alan Watts (1915–1973). Watts had been friends with Ditman's statistician, Whittelsey. An ordained priest since 1945, Watts always considered himself more aligned with shamanism than with priesthood (while the truth is, he was more of a bohemian philosopher than anything else). And what was a bohemian philosopher in the late 1950s like? Well, for starters, he was the kind of person who believed that if working for a boss meant high pay but even higher misery, he would rather be broke. It meant he was both a sage and a rascal; a mystic and an addict (especially to nicotine and alcohol); a holy man with an insatiable sexual appetite. He was well aware of both the public's belief in spiritual infallibility and just how fallible he was. He was the kind of person who kept in contact with people like Huxley.[9] The kind of person who harbored very liberal ideas about religion, and sought permission from his superior (in occupation, not wit or lifestyle), Bishop Wallace Edmonds Conkling (1896–1979), to act as a "priest at large" in Chicago. Bishop Conkling was to "initiate some sort of mechanism or process whereby the mystical approach to religion could become available through the Church."[10] And Watts wasn't alone. Other priests of the late fifties tried to initiate breath work as part of their Sunday Masses.

Still, Watts remained skeptical. A devotee of Zen and yoga, he, like Zaehner, didn't believe that "any mere chemical could induce a genuine mystical experience."[11] But he also loved a challenge, particularly something that might stretch the very fabric of his soul beyond the limits of space and sanity.

And so, under request from Ditman, Watts drove to the doctor's Beverly Hills office sometime in 1958 for an LSD session. Edward Halsey, who would unfortunately die in a car accident a few years later, joined him. The LSD proved "an intensely interesting aesthetic intellectual experience." However, nothing about the Other World suggested *mysticism* to Watts.[12] In fact, cannabis, which he had tried earlier, seemed a better suitor for numinous enlightenment. Like many at the time, he tape-recorded his thoughts during and after his LSD session, ending with the admission that LSD was "interesting," however, it was "hardly what [he] would call mystical."[13]

Two doctors working at the Lanley-Porter Clinic in San Francisco, Drs. Sterling Bunnell and Michael Agron, somehow caught wind of Watts's opinions and invited him to have another go at LSD. And so, one year after sitting with Ditman, Watts took LSD at the Langley-Porter Clinic. This time, he went "through states of consciousness which corresponded precisely with every description of major mystical experiences that [he] had ever read." He experimented with other substances like psilocybin and DMT, the latter of which did not tickle his fancy. He journeyed often. He journeyed deep. He came to realize that all his combined psychedelic experiences had "four dominant characteristics."[14]

He called the first characteristic *concentration in the present,* a sort of call to "be here now" before anyone was saying "be here now." This, Watts realized, was "bad for business." How can people *sell, sell, sell* if they are too busy appreciating the intricate beauty of a flower petal?

The second, he called *awareness of polarity,* an alchemical concept that referred to the way opposites create each other. For instance, there could be no me without you, no subject without object, no Heaven without Hell.

The third was the *awareness of relativity,* a nod to the fact that each of us are "a link in an infinite hierarchy of processes and beings, ranging from molecules through bacteria and insects to human beings, and, maybe, to angels and gods." Here, love and joy, revulsion and hate were constants throughout the universe. "[W]e are all in fact one being doing the same thing in as many different ways as possible. . . . As the retina enables us to see countless pulses of energy as a single light, so the mystical experience shows us innumerable individuals as a single Self."

And finally, the fourth regarded *awareness of eternal energy*. This was the "one" that people speak of when they say "we are all one." Interestingly, just as Zaehner used the Upanishads and Tennyson as examples of how mystical experiences were possible without psychedelics, Watts used them as well to demonstrate "[the] characteristics of the psychedelic experience."[15]

THE TONGUE THAT DWELLS IN THE EYES AND HEART

~ *Winter 1954* ~

Dr. Oscar and Kathleen Janiger (d. 2001) had just returned home from a trip to their summer cabin in Lake Arrowhead, a scenic backdrop about an hour and a half east of Los Angeles.

Oscar was beaming, glowing from deep inside.

At long last, he had found *it*.

Janiger had an interest in altered states of consciousness for many years. As a child he realized that while running a high fever he could "make wallpaper do all kinds of tricks." Other times, while sitting on the can, he'd "watch the tiles recompose themselves and make patterns." This led to his suspicion that there existed a part of his mind that "had certain influence over the world . . . and that, under certain conditions, it can take on novel and interesting forms."[16] In other words, *magic*. These early insights into the byways of the mind manifested an interest that led him to study both psychiatry and biology. A graduate of New York's Columbia University, he took a position at the California College of Medicine in 1949, where he taught until his death in 2001.

Back in 1954, he would stand before his classes at the University of California Irvine, lecturing on the special herbs, roots, mushrooms, and plants used for thousands of years by various peoples to induce a "strange and untoward psychic experience."[17] This inspired one of his students to bring a friend, Parry Bivens (d. 1963),* to class one day. Bivens was a doctor and professional diver who worked on the popular television series *Sea Hunt,* starring Lloyd Bridges (1913–1998), which ran from 1958 to 1961. He was also the husband of Zale Parry (b. 1933), the diving icon who gave Bridges scuba instructions so he wouldn't drown on the set of *Sea Hunt.* Zale Parry had a proclivity for exploring new turf, breaking the deep sea diving record while others "were wallowing in the shallows."[18] She also proudly graced the cover of the May 1955 issue of *Sports Illustrated*—the first woman in history to do so.† She was all too happy to cast herself into the unknown.

To return to U.C. Irvine where Bivens and Janiger first met—Bivens had mentioned that he knew how to obtain a new substance, one far more powerful than the roots and mushrooms of yesteryear. Intrigued by the possibilities, Bivens and Parry followed the Janigers to their cabin in Lake Arrowhead, where they all took LSD. Janiger's was not a "uniformly beautiful experience." Instead, he toured both Heaven and Hell. Some moments of the night were "totally and remarkably transforming." Others, not so much. One minute the experience turned "so bad" that he wanted out of the whole ordeal. Other times, the visions were "so astonishingly marvelous" that he hoped the experience would last forever.[19]

One particular sight to behold was caused not by the LSD but rather Parry's grand reentrance into the living room of the cabin once the LSD started to take effect. Or perhaps it *was* caused by the LSD? She had excused herself into one of the bedrooms for a moment, and after some time rejoined the group dressed in "a purple sweater, skin-tight vermillion pants, yellow slippers, and a long mauve scarf."[20] She proceeded to dance around the room.

Janiger was enthralled, and spent the rest of his life contemplating the enigmatic questions surrounding Hofmann's wonder child. He quickly set about looking for a research project to engage. Bivens's sup-

---

*Misnamed "Perry Bivens" in Stevens, *Storming Heaven,* 60.
†Readers of *Sports Illustrated* found Parry's cover photo so captivating that it caused that magazine to kick off its "Swimsuit Issue" series.

ply came nowhere near the amount necessary for a longitudinal study. Janiger would need a direct line to Sandoz itself, which would mean developing a research project, submitting a proposal, and hoping Sandoz accepted it. After a few days of pondering, he came up with a novel idea: why not try a purely naturalistic study? Simply give volunteers LSD and leave them alone—no testing, no pulse measuring, no prodding (albeit, "with appropriate safeguards in place").[21] He wrote to Sandoz for approval. Within weeks, he had his very own supply of Delysid.

Janiger's volunteers consisted of homemakers, clerks, assorted white- and blue-collar workers, chefs, and artists; he aimed to study the responses to psychedelics much like a field anthropologist studies subjects in a natural habitat—away from outside interference. He also encouraged his volunteers to write reports of their experiences as soon as possible, and even mailed them a questionnaire that included over fifty inquiries a month after their LSD session. His tests employed radically different methods than those of either the scientists or spies or even Hubbard, in that he avoided projecting his mind onto the mind of the volunteer altogether. And forget clinical settings. He didn't conduct his experiments in a warfare laboratory or a university hospital. The natural habitat of the modern American was a living room. Janiger would hold his LSD sessions in homes, not hospitals. He hoped more to "define the nature of the LSD experience as a special state of consciousness than [for] any specific content."[22] To achieve this goal, Janiger blocked all external stimuli from his patients by blindfolding them and drawing the shades of his office. He "did not want to program the volunteers to have any particular type of experience—not religious, spiritual, therapeutic, or creative."[23] And yet, so far as LSD and mysticism were concerned, he "found the connection to be inescapable."[24] One subject from a Janigerian trip report reads as follows: "I was raised without religion and I was not spiritual until I took LSD. I've been spiritual ever since."[25] Another claimed "the existence of some overall Creator or Order to the Universe . . . seems more possible now."[26]

Though many of his volunteers had difficulty coming to this

conclusion, reduced as they were to adjudicating "the material of consciousness which . . . cannot [be] put into words. . . . Meanwhile [they] might enchant [themselves] with the airy thought that the experience has an odd logic of its own, if [one] could but translate 'the tongue that dwells in eyes and hearts.'"[27]

But not every LSD experience led to lasting changes or mystical awakenings. Over the course of Janiger's various studies, he gave LSD to 930 people from all walks of life. Some of those volunteers were themselves physicians. Like William James before him, one physician had a taste for nitrous oxide. Only James didn't make a habit out of using nitrous oxide, which for him offered a genuine mystical experience—one to be enacted with great caution. The physician had developed an addiction to the vapor (as much as a person can be addicted to it), and saw Janiger in hopes that the 150 micrograms of Delysid he swallowed would cure his dependence. Six months later, paramedics found him dead in his home, a gasmask on his face. Others simply refused to follow Janiger's protocol. One volunteer decided that secretly eating peyote before and after an LSD session might enhance the experience. It did, but not in the way he had hoped. He fell into a "chronic LSD state for weeks," for which he was eventually hospitalized. He fully recovered six months later.[28] Still others were local artists who relished the opportunity to see how LSD might affect their painting. Janiger too, was curious. Although he refrained from publishing his poetigenic* research (he felt they teetered too close to phenomenology), his work with artists has become the definitive study on the subject in the United States.

DRY SCHIZOPHRENIA

Janiger wasn't, of course, the first psychiatrist to wonder about the relationship between psychedelics and art. Heim, the French bota-

---

*"Poetigen" means using psychedelics to inspire artistic creativity. See Hatsis, *Psychedelic Mystery Traditions*, 9.

nist who had first grown the Little Saints at his laboratory in Paris, had pondered the poetigenic question. One of the artists he gave the psilocybin to was Maitre Breitling, who had an experience fraught with "distinctly Freudian overtones." He also gave psilocybin to the graphic artist Mademoiselle Michaux. She was spellbound by the Little Saints. "I'm inspired. I've been a genius for three hours," she said of the experience. Heim didn't necessarily disagree. "We are . . . quite closer to the totemic origins of magic," he stated after seeing one of her illustrations.[29]

Max Rinkel had also wondered about odd kinds of mental phenomena beyond measuring pulse rates. In the mid-1950s, he become one of the first (and one of the few) researchers in the United States to study the effects of both LSD and mescaline on art.[30] Working with a psychiatrist at the Massachusetts General Hospital, Dr. Clemens E. Benda (1895–1975), Rinkel invited Hyman Bloom (1913–2009), an "outstanding contemporary American painter" and accomplished sitar player, to participate in artistic experiments with both mescaline and Delysid. Rinkel hoped the art would reveal "a progressive, almost schizophrenic deterioration."[31]

Like all other volunteers, Bloom took his Delysid in water at 8:00 a.m. As he drifted deeper into the experience and continued to draw, he mumbled words like "etheric colors" and "luminosity itself." By 10:00 a.m., Bloom was fully lysergized, writing the words "Hindu religion" on the corner of one of his drawings of monsters and kitty-cat creatures, and now feeling "divisions of space and sensations of excitement and rapture." He was lighter than air—high. Looking at Rinkel he admitted, "I could go off in complete fantasy."[32]

Simply float away . . .

Instead, Bloom remarked on the experience that may have surprised the Boston Psychopathic team: "I always connected insanity with a feeling of misery, but this is not a feeling of insanity. It is just a feeling of, well, being in another world, a sleepier world, sleepy in the sense of being absolutely removed."[33]

Still, Bloom was remarkably judicious in keeping with the integrity of the experiments—regularly asking Rinkel for the time to mark changes in his mood, body, and consciousness. His pictures show an interesting volley between meticulous detail and incomprehensible doodles. These artistic fluctuations, psychologist Eliot Rodnick (1911–1999) deemed at the Second Conference on Neuropharmacology in 1955, were "not unlike the type of behavior one frequently sees in the psychological testing of schizophrenic patients. One of the most revealing aspects of schizophrenic behavior is variation from a rather high level of quality to a poor level of quality. When such inconsistent and extreme variation occurs, it is frequently apt to be indicative of the schizophrenic type of response."[34]

Rinkel couldn't agree more. His tests with Bloom served for him as nothing more than a way to determine what *kind* of "psychotic" LSD generated in an artistic person. Over in Italy, researchers Tonini and Montanari had experimented with LSD on artistic expression back in 1955. They too felt that drawings and paintings made after taking LSD "reflected psychopathological manifestations markedly similar to those observed in schizophrenia."[35]

But by the late 1950s, when Janiger began his longitudinal study on creativity, Rinkel's model psychosis interpretation of both LSD and the art produced under its influence was fading, and would soon be lost to historical memory.

A Rinkel in time.

Dry schizophrenia. That's what Janiger called the artistic mind.[36]

In the 1950s, the going consensus among doctors was that mental instability and art went hand-in-hand. In fact, one doctor even lamented the "culturally noxious assumption . . . that one must be sick to be creative."[37] Janiger had once read that Lucia Joyce, daughter of author James Joyce, suffered from schizophrenia. Desperate, Joyce (despite his distrust of psychiatrists) took her to see the great

Carl Jung. During the visit, James confided in Jung that he believed Lucia harbored a *far more impressive* creative mind than did he.

"That may be true," Jung replied. "But the two of you are like deep sea divers. You go into the ocean, a rich, interesting, dramatic setting, with your baskets, and you fill them up with improbable creatures of the deep. The only difference between the two of you is that you can come up to the surface, and she can't." *Dry schizophrenia*—the "difference between being able to swim in the ocean or being [c]aught by the waves and dashed to pieces."[38]

◎

It all unfolded rather coincidentally.

One of Janiger's volunteers just so happened to be an artist. During one LSD session, the artist noticed a Hopi doll sitting on Janiger's bookshelf and lit up, quickly asking Janiger for a pencil and sketchpad.[39] As the artist carefully drew out the doll, Janiger started to formulate ideas for a new investigation, which would differ from Rinkel's in at least two ways. First, Janiger would dedicate an entire study to the creative and artistic potentials of LSD; Rinkel only gave LSD to Bloom. Secondly, Janiger asked that the artist paint before, during, and *after* the LSD session to see if there were any noticeable changes in style, whereas Rinkel wanted to see how well an artist manipulated a paintbrush while on LSD. If Rinkel wanted to see how LSD affected the *artist,* then Janiger wanted to see how LSD affected the *art.* One of Janiger's volunteers felt that an LSD experience was comparable to "a four-year course in art school."[40]

A THOUSAND DREAMS INTO ONE

One of the artists who painted Janiger's kachina doll while under the spell of Delysid was Gil Henderson. Henderson had been a member of a deep-rooted artistic community in Los Angeles that gathered every now and then at the Instant Theater. The theater was drenched with surrealistic performances and improvisations—a vanguard of the avant-garde in Los Angeles. Actors would pull double-duty, one moment reciting a soliloquy on stage and then rushing to the sound booth to enhance the lighting effects, and then back on stage again to finish the lines. And they all shared a single, worn copy of *The Doors*. The poet Michael McClure (1932–2020) remembers the reason his bohemian clique gravitated toward that famous essay, "For alchemical, hermetic, understanding of ourselves or of the universe." Multimedia artist and jazz enthusiast Robert Alexander (1923–1987), founder of *Press Baza* (an artists' zine), sums up the fervor that spread through the Los Angeles art scene in the mid-1950s: "If you were any kind of artist, you would wonder if maybe this chemical would give you space in your own body that would give you room to work, because you know you're locked in there and can't get out."[41]

One member of this artistic enclave was the noted novelist Anaïs Nin (1903–1977). Like the others at Instant Theater, Nin had her chance to sit with the copy of *The Doors*. Unlike the others, she found herself none-too-impressed with it. She was far more interested in Henderson's two sessions with the kachina doll. "The difference between [Henderson's sketches] was astonishing," she recalled. "The first version was rigid and photographic. The second, impressionistic and emotional."[42] How desperately she wanted to see if LSD might influence her writing similarly! And she knew Huxley personally. But Huxley blew her off, ignoring her repeated requests to try LSD.[43]*

Coincidentally, Janiger had already been looking for an author with whom to give Delysid, a message that Henderson relayed to Nin, who jumped at the chance. Henderson even signed on to act as her "sober pilot" through the byways of the experience.[44]

---

*Nin was not the only artist with whom Huxley refused to share the psychedelic experience. He also disregarded the repeated requests from novelist and playwright Christopher Isherwood (1904–1986) to try mescaline. See Dunaway, *Aldous Huxley Recollected,* 96.

~ *Autumn 1955* ~

Janiger held a number of blue pills—maybe five, maybe eight, Nin couldn't remember—in one hand and a glass of water in the other. She washed the pills down and waited. Now, for some (like Huxley and Zaehner) the chemical rather took its time showing its effects. Not with Nin, who within twenty minutes noted how the fibers in the rug had begun to flow like wheat stalks in a cool, late summer breeze. Corners and the sharp ends of tables began to soften until they liquefied. Doorknobs "melted and undulated like living serpents."[45] The experience intensified quickly. The "current of vibrations" became too great—pulling her in two directions: one of mind, where she experienced the condensation of "a thousand dreams into one"; the other, her body, which seemed completely out of sync with the increased rhythm of outer space. The filters that protect us all from Mind at Large exist for a reason. Throw open the valves too quickly and the "metaphysical energies" can overwhelm a person.[46]

Nin felt an intense cold. She needed air. Warm air. Fresh air. *Less intense air.* She walked down a long hallway, where Henderson opened a door that led to a bountiful garden in Janiger's backyard. As it turned out, the air outside proved just as intense. "Trees, clouds, lawns, heaved and undulated too, the clouds flying at tremendous speed." What's more, the golden sheen of the autumn-dipped SoCal sun put a blinding yellow veneer over the world. But that radiance . . . that radiance was the very glow that turned the *world* into the *Other World*. There was power here. There was magic here. *If she could just get her body in flow with the air, she could dance with it.* This alone proved a revelation. She relaxed. Focused. She honed the energy of the space—all the artists who had taken LSD there, including her good friend Henderson—and used it to project intricate "Persian designs, flowers, mandalas, patterns in perfect symmetry" on the door. She couldn't believe her eyes! She held up her hand to draw a line into her fractal designs and watched as a stripe of orange emitted from her fingertips like a magic wand.[47] What's more— the fractals created music as they formed, and Nin was the conductor.

She had found the connection. Her intensity finally matching that of the air, that of the Other World.

> My body was both swimming and flying. I felt gay and at ease and playful. There was perfect connection between my body and everything that was happening. My senses were multiplied as if I had a hundred eyes, a hundred ears, a hundred fingertips. The murals which appeared were perfect, they were Oriental, fragile, and complete. . . . I felt myself becoming a full percussion orchestra. . . . I could see a new world with my middle eye, a world I had missed before. I caught images behind images, the walls behind the sky, the sky behind the infinite. . . . I looked at a slender line curving over into space which disappeared into infinity. I saw a million zeros on this line, curving, shrinking in the distance.

She could only laugh and tell Janiger, "Without being a mathematician I understood the infinite."[48]

Janiger was aloof and unresponsive for some reason. Perhaps he had heard this kind of talk before and considered it frivolous? Or maybe that was just Nin's perception of him from a million light-years away? Who knows. Whatever the cause, Janiger's dismissive temperament sent poor Nin floating through space, with only the rotations of cold and lifeless planets as company. The loneliness was crushing, so she called out to Henderson from the outer regions of the Milky Way: "Are you sure that I will find my way back?"

"Of course, I found my way back. I am here."[49]

But in that moment, Nin wasn't so sure. The air had intensified past her body's capabilities again. And this time, it overwhelmed her. She fell short of breath and Henderson immediately called Janiger, who suggested Nin lie down on the couch. She lit a cigarette and once again that familiar blazing gold veneer had taken over the room. Only this time, the gold started to overtake her too! All those trials—the coldness, feeling discarded in space, feeling small in size *a la* Alice in

Wonderland—had caused her to transmute. *Solve et coagula*—separate and join together. "[M]y body was becoming GOLD, liquid gold, scintillating, warm gold. I was gold. It was the most pleasurable sensation I had ever known, like an orgasm. It was the secret of life, the alchemist's secret of life."[50]

Nin wasn't the only one to feel this way. Something new, something inspired, something magical, something exciting was happening in Los Angeles—something that no one could quite explain.

Yet everyone wanted to take part.

FAR-THINKING VISIONARIES

Back at Janiger's pad, a third, *underground study* started to form. This analysis represented something less scientific and more . . . *well* . . . he had begun to create a sort of secret society based around taking LSD. *Secret*—because none of this activity had been approved by Sandoz. *Society*—well, let's take a look.

During the mid-1950s, Hubbard was seeking an accredited doctor to help him administer LSD. Janiger admired his enthusiasm. Together, the shrink and the Good Captain held regular LSD sessions at Janiger's home in Los Angeles for several years. Janiger wanted to take LSD with the "intelligent, progressive, and far thinking visionaries" of the day.[51] Hubbard had just spent the last few years forming LSD cells up and down the West Coast. The number of people that he gave some form of a psychedelic (LSD, carbogen, mescaline, or otherwise) remains unknown. Acting as a guide, Hubbard joined Janiger's therapeutic sessions and held people's hands as they walked through the farthest reaches of their psyches. He never charged for his services and spent hundreds of dollars traveling all over America, Canada, and parts of Europe on, as he puts it, "a mission."[52] And this passion project evolved into nothing short of a new kind of psychedelia with a "specifically Catholic frame of reference."[53]

At least, that's how Huxley saw it. But Hubbard's plan was more nuanced. His idea of a deity seemed to straddle the line between Zaehner's Christian God and Huxley's Gnostic God:

Hubbard stated:

> I am perfectly aware that most of our people with their little personal God do now know my God of the Galaxies, and there is such a vast chasm between their God and my God that in most cases it would be impossible to bridge. The small group of mystics in our church who know what I am talking about and within whose authority I operate, are not very many compared with the five hundred million members.[54]

From Paul the Apostle to Marcion to Martin Luther, Hubbard stood in a long line of revisionists working diligently to create a new version of the faith. In all likelihood, Hubbard might be the name redacted from a letter Huxley wrote to Osmond in January 1958. Huxley speaks of someone he knew who wanted to use LSD "as an instrument for validating Catholic doctrines" and set up a form of "anti-alcoholism project . . . under Roman Catholic auspices."[55] Whether Huxley referred to the Good Captain or not, Hubbard was the interstellar adhesive that united various dimensions: Janiger and Nin, Huxley and Heard, Cohen and Eisner, Ditman and Watts, Osmond and Hoffer, and even actors like the so-called "King of Hollywood," Clark Gable.[56]

This network of colleagues and friends comprised the first large group to enjoy LSD as a social medicine.[57] They would assemble at Janiger's or Huxley's house and wait for Hubbard to show up with his psychedelic doctor's kit.[58] After he arrived, the guests would eat LSD or mescaline or whatever odd chemical stew Hubbard had mixed and attempt to find the "'essential' or 'active' ingredients of the mystical experience," as Watts remembered.[59] Ditman remarked of those days, "LSD became for us an intellectual fun drug."[60]

Janiger had no delusions about his gatherings of far-thinking visionaries. He was rather candid about the main objective he had for these soirées: to reproduce "the ritual created by the Greeks at Eleusis."[61] This was the next level in group mescalinization, and every one of them, like the initiates at Eleusis, wanted a share in the secret.

Janiger reflects:

> In those days, when you made contact, it was like two people look at each other from across the room, and with a sort of nod of the head that acknowledged that "you too." It was so different then, you know, like "Welcome brother, you have now entered the Mysteries." That was your ticket to admission. Nothing else. That knowing look, and from then on you were part of a sort of strange fraternity. We saw ourselves as members of a consciousness clan that goes back through history to Eleusis and the Sufis and the Vedic Hindus.[62]

Janiger remained wary of the psychotomimetic model. He believed that researchers should "look beyond psychosis. For . . . the drug experience [has] its own unique rewards."[63] His Eleusinian gatherings in some ways prefigured the "acid parties" of the 1960s (Janiger's on a much smaller scale, and with a sense of responsible use of psychedelics). And yet, he wrote in 1959 (somewhat humorously to our contemporary sensibilities), that due to the "intense and unpredictable nature [of LSD], it is not likely to be sought after as a divertissement."[64]

Several years before the Haight-Ashbury scene in San Francisco became the top stop for all things psychedelia, an artist-philosopher enclave of mind-expanding futurists was forming a community in Los Angeles. But to some, like Cohen, LSD had already become too recreational. At some point, *he did not know when exactly,* everything had gotten a lot less scientific and a lot more syrupy. His jaw dropped when he read an article that briefly mentioned the "LSD 25 social parties" of his colleagues.[65]* He stopped showing up to the LSD gatherings. Eisner had

---

*Theirs was not the only group to explore these mystical states of awareness outside a clinical setting. None other than ex-CHATTER operative Savage made note of "Some religious groups [that] have developed around the LSD experience." See Savage, "Uses and Abuses of LSD in Psychotherapy," 466.

already disassociated from the clique. She never found much use for the group sessions (or soirées, depending on who you asked) anyway.[66]

Nonetheless, those in the circles of Janiger, Huxley, and Hubbard made their way across the United States, Canada, and Europe promoting the new psychedelia. Giving a lecture on psychedelics *here,* taking psychedelics with so-and-so *there,* the group was awash with various offers to come to various places and speak about various far-out topics. At one point, Heard made his way to Harvard and delivered a speech on ideas that would comprise a small section of his forthcoming book, *The Five Ages of Man* (1963). That is, the role of psychedelics in ancient pagan mystery rites. He ended his speech with a somber prediction to his audience, "This is the future of the human race."[67]

It all seemed so promising by the late 1950s. Osmond was recording impressive success rates treating alcoholics; Eisner was taking psychedelic psychotherapy into newer, more focused and compassionate places; Huxley and Heard continued testing the next frontiers of human evolution; artists were finding new ways of self-expression; and movie stars raved about the healing effects of LSD.

And then suddenly . . . suddenly it was all gone.

What happened?

18
The Fall
The Tragedy of Timothy Leary

It certainly would be a huge misfortune if [LSD] ever got loose in the general public without a careful preparation as to what the drug is and what the meaning of its effects may be.

BILL WILSON

We're going to have to write a Bible about this.

TIMOTHY LEARY

AN EDUCATED SAVAGE

Cuernavaca, Mexico, had come a long way since its days as a haven of "soothsayers, wise men, and magicians."[1] About an hour drive south of Mexico City, the small city now served as a sanctuary for "sophisticated Aztecs, corrupt politicians, and wandering scholars."[2] To those vacationers visiting for the summer, the days were serene but predictable: "Crystal clear summer days, swimming trunks around the pool before breakfast, cold grapefruit, hot discussions. . . . The sudden cooling splash of evening rain. . . . Margaritas. Candlelight dinners."[3] It was here where Timothy Leary (1920–1996) had spent his previous four summers. Earlier that spring, he had taken a psychology lectureship at Harvard University, impressing the department chairperson, David McClelland (1917–1998), with both his book *The Interpersonal Diagnosis of Personality* (1957) and his experiment to test the validity of psychotherapy at Kaiser Hospital, which he ran with friend and colleague Frank Barron (1922–2002).

About Kaiser: In 1955 Leary and Barron had received a generous grant from the Kaiser Foundation to investigate the interpersonal core of personality. They assembled a group of patients who were receiving psychotherapy and compared their progress with a group of patients who had been put on a waiting list and anticipated similar treatment in the future. Kaiser yielded disappointing, if not downright shocking, results. After nine months, Leary and Barron found that both groups "showed similar ratios of improvement: a third had gotten better, a third had gotten worse, and a third had stayed about the same . . . [confirming] that what passed for therapy was merely a collection of techniques and tricks that worked sometimes, but failed just as often."[4] The Kaiser experiment validated Leary and Barron's theory: that below the awareness of everyday living, the unconscious mind was still an ineffable area of uncharted personality. Somehow, the two psychologists desperately wanted to find a way through the veil of waking consciousness.

The villa Leary had rented in Cuernavaca provided the ideal setting for either lounging around or exploring one's mind. A "rambling white stucco house with scarlet trim" in the design of Spanish-Muslim architecture sat adjacent to the Acapulco golf course. The perfect hideaway for an "educated savage."[5] And he had plenty of company as he drank local beers and lounged around all day. Nurse Ruth Dettering and her husband, psychologist Richard Dettering, lived at the villa with Leary. Ralph Metzner (1936–2019, who would play a key role in Leary's public life) and Barron were expected to arrive to the villa in a few days. David McClelland lived only ten miles away in Tepoztlan and would make frequent visits to the villa. Finally, there was anthropologist Gerhart Braun who came with both an expertise in Nahuatl (the preconquest language of the Aztecs) and his girlfriend Joan, along with her witty, poet friend Betty.[6]

Braun's visits courted the most excitement. He had been lecturing on *teonanácatl,* or "God's flesh," the sacred mushrooms of the Aztecs at the University of Mexico. He told of the visions, the prophecies, the healing, and the ceremonies that accompanied mushroom use. He spoke of how humans had "lost" the thread of sacred mushrooms in Mexico, the result of such strict Catholic repression that modern scholars had denied such fungi had ever existed at all.

At Leary's urging,[7] Braun, Leary, and Bruce Conner (a logician friend of Braun) hopped into Braun's car and drove to the marketplace in the village of San Pedro. Going from shop to shop, Braun and Leary inquired where they might procure teonanácatl. One merchant told them to wait at his shop for Señora Juana, who he expected within the hour. Not long after, an elderly, hunched-over woman— *Señora Juana!*—walked right past them. Braun caught up to her and asked about the mushrooms. Cuernavaca sits at the foot of three volcano summits: the Popo, Ixtacihuatl, and Toluca. Señora Juana would have to climb the sides of the volcanoes—she pointed up at them for emphasis—*that's where the mushrooms grow.*

Braun returned to the others, a fulfilling smile on his lips. "Okay. It's all set. She'll get the mushrooms next Wednesday and I'll meet her in the marketplace next Thursday."

As instructed, Braun returned to the bustling San Pedro market the following week. Señora Juana returned as well, this time with a satchel of mushrooms in her hand.

"And you are sure these are safe to eat?"[8]

Juana said nothing. Instead, she opened the bag and threw two mushrooms down her throat. Convinced of their harmless constitution, Braun took the bag from Juana, and thanked her for her troubles. He hurried home, washed the remaining bits of dirt off the mushrooms, and stored the bag of divinity in his refrigerator.

~ *August 9, 1960* ~

A beautiful Mexican sun shone brightly overhead that Saturday morning. Eight people had assembled at Leary's villa to try the mushrooms, save two who abstained: Ruth, who was pregnant (incidentally, Leary was happy to have a sober nurse on-hand for the experiment), and "Whiskers," a college dropout suffering from anxiety, whom Braun "appointed scientist" to take copious notes of the day's unfolding.[9] The others—Leary, Joan (Braun's girlfriend), Joan's daughter Mandy, Betty, and Richard Dettering—gathered around the patio table as Braun separated the female mushrooms from the male mushrooms. He then instructed them on dosage, "six females and six males," further commenting that the males were innocuous, serving only a symbolic ceremonial role.[10] With that, Braun picked up a mushroom and ate it. Then he ate another.

Then Joan ate, then Mandy, then Richard. Next was Leary's turn. He picked up a mushroom, the damp smell of which reminded him of a "New England basement."[11] He ate it, but followed up with a swig of Carta Blanca to ease the shock of the taste. Once everyone had partaken, the group nervously waited.

They were not disappointed . . .

With the end of summer, Leary returned to Harvard full of ideas, eager to start some kind of research project with mushrooms. He wanted to use psychedelics in a new kind of psychotherapy called "existential transaction," largely based on a book he was writing of the same name. In short, "existential" referred to studying events as they unfolded without placing any prior judgment on the situation or tainting the natural flow of things with preconceived notions about what *ought to be*. "Transactional" meant regarding the research direction as a social mesh—"the psychologist doesn't stand outside the event but recognizes his part in it, and works collaboratively with the subject toward mutually selected goals."[12] Now couple this approach with psychedelic mushrooms. It may seem radical today, but in 1960 it was the next, logical evolution in psychedelic psychotherapy. Leary had no interest in giving a patient some kind of natural or synthetic agent, sitting back, and observing only their external reactions. Like Hubbard before him, Leary wanted to take the dive with the patient "to study any and all aspects of psychology, aesthetics, philosophy, religion, life."[13] But Leary had other ideas, too. One of which sounded like a reverse form of Rinkel's "negative logic" theory. To refresh, Rinkel wanted to know how to counteract LSD's effects on the brain so he could chart a similar course for schizophrenics. Leary wanted to uncover "new circuits of the brain . . . by drugs, [so] one could learn how to re-activate the experience without drugs."[14]

His first day back on campus that September, Leary ran into a graduate student, George Litwin. The previous spring semester, Litwin had told Leary about his own experiments with mescaline. Back then, Leary had met Litwin's prospects with censure. This time, Leary was pulling Litwin into his office and chewing his ear off about his Mexican mushroom adventures. Litwin signed on as Leary's first volunteer and provided him with copies of *The Doors* and *Heaven and Hell*. The next question was *where to get the mushrooms*? Leary tried a few leads. The Public Health Service in Washington had recently synthesized psilocybin. He fired off a letter to them. *No response.* Maybe Braun could find Señora Juana who could procure a sizable amount of the fungi and send it to Leary? *No response.* Or maybe doctors at the University of Mexico, who had just cultivated the mushrooms, might be interested in sharing? *Sigh . . . no response.* Thankfully, due to Litwin's prior interest with mescaline, he was also hip to the fact that the New Jersey branch of Sandoz Pharmaceuticals had recently restocked their supplies of psilocybin, the active ingredient in the mushroom. Leary pulled out some Harvard letterhead and sent his request to Sandoz.

Response!

A few days before Thanksgiving 1960, a small brown box appeared on Leary's doorstep. Nestled inside the box lay several brown bottles marked "PS 39," each containing little pink pellets and a pamphlet specifying that they were "not to be sold" and should be used for "research investigation" only.[15] And of course, like the instructions that came with Delysid, those who planned to give the psilocybin to volunteers should first test it on themselves.

Leary didn't like cocktail parties—the pretense, the conformity, the elitism, the forced laughter. He didn't like the high-brow ass-kissing: *How interesting! You don't say? Fascinating! Tell me more.* But he was certainly happy that he attended one that October. Amid the usual boring cocktail party chitchat, one of Leary's colleagues mentioned that Huxley had recently accepted a visiting lectureship at Massachusetts Institute of Technology (MIT). The coincidence was not lost on Leary. He had just finished reading Huxley's essays on psychedelics (courtesy of Litwin) and couldn't wait to start a professional relationship. Since the two gents would practically be neighbors, Leary wrote Huxley a long letter explaining his research interests. A couple of days later, Huxley phoned him directly. A lunch date was set.

Leary picked up Huxley from the MIT apartments, which overlook the Charles River, and the two arrived just before noon at the Harvard Faculty Club, where, in an auspicious prophecy, they both ordered a bowl of the soup of the day—mushroom soup! In between talks of global revolution and mental autonomy, one question kept coming up: How should the Harvard team introduce these medicines to the larger society? Huxley had a solution: "Why don't I come over to your place tonight? We'll take the drug and ask our expanded brains that question."[16]

In anticipation of Huxley's arrival that evening, Leary built a large fire to stave off the bitter Massachusetts winter. Huxley plopped a stack of books on Leary's coffee table and sat before the inviting flames.

Once the fire roared, Leary broke out his record collection—everything from Bach and Mozart to African drums and Indian chants to Ravi Shankar. Leary had one thing on his mind: the *plan*. He once again asked Huxley the same question he had asked only hours earlier at the Harvard Faculty Club. *How do we turn on the masses?*

As Shankar's sweet sitar guided Huxley back to reality, he busily reached for insights the way one tries to recall the last memories of a dream. He channeled the echoes of the alchemists, the magicians, the village wise-women: "In the past this powerful knowledge has been guarded in privacy, passed on in the subdued, metaphorical obscurantism of scholars, mystics, and artists." Leary claims to have rejected this idea. "But society needs this information," he protested.

"These are evolutionary matters," Huxley replied. "They cannot be rushed. Work privately. Initiate artists, writers, poets, jazz musicians, elegant courtesans, painters, rich bohemians. And they'll initiate the intelligent rich. That's how everything of culture and beauty and philosophic freedom has been passed on."[17]

~ *January 1961* ~

By this time, Leary had given psilocybin to fifteen volunteers, the beginning of what he called the Harvard Psilocybin Project. Besides Huxley and a handful of colleagues, Leary's first subjects were comprised mostly of graduate students. With each passing day, the trickle of students turned into floods of curious people seeking enlightenment from Leary's magic bullets. One of those curious folks was Allen Ginsberg (1926–1997), who arrived at Leary's house sometime just before 1960 turned into 1961. During the session, Ginsberg and his lover, Peter Orlovsky (1933–2010), stripped naked and danced around Leary's house proclaiming themselves messiahs. The murmurs on campus indicated that the mushroom session had been some kind of bohemian orgy. This was not the kind of publicity Harvard wanted, and although they did not abort the Psilocybin Project altogether, they did seize all of Leary's PS 39 supplies.

Other researchers might have taken pause, reflected, and reevaluated their strategy. But Leary loved the attention. For him, the incident meant discarding established psychedelic practices worked out by a series of trials and errors over the previous wonder child decade. He threw out the playbook: "No selecting subjects. No testing them before or after. No explaining the mushroom effect in terms of my favorite variables or your favorite variables . . . I'd like everyone who takes the mushrooms to write down afterwards what he saw and felt and envisioned and how the whole scene affected his life."[18] Yet Leary didn't even abide by the irresponsible rules he created. For example, let's momentarily put aside that not selecting or testing subjects before a psychedelic experience is wholly reckless; notwithstanding, Ralph Metzner, who had signed on to the Harvard Psilocybin Project early on, noticed that while Leary made it "preferred policy to not stress the role of guide," he acted very differently during session. In fact, "Tim generally set the tone of the experience," he recalled.[19] As for not "explaining the mushroom effect in terms of my favorite variables," Leary arranged the décor of his office in a way that he hoped would prompt a certain *hip* experience. Hindu art graced the walls; jazz played on the stereo. And then he would brief each volunteer with his interpretation of what the psychedelic state was all about. Even Hubbard, whose cavalier approach to LSD irked some of the other experimenters, still believed in holding a carbogen session to test candidacy for LSD. Whether LSD, mescaline, or PS 39, these chemicals were not run-of-the-mill analgesics or relaxants, and users needed to treat them with utmost respect and responsibility.

Leary didn't even pretend to respect them. In one such case, Metzner reflected on a harsh trip he had during one of his first psilocybin sessions with Leary. As reality collapsed all around him, Metzner lost control and had a "deep psychotic experience." The rest of the group gave no care; they administered no sedatives. Metzner recalls, "Tim and the others simply laid me out on a bed and hoped for the best."[20] Metzner was interrupting the party; he had to go. Leary carefully omits any sour reactions from the discussion in *High Priest,* asserting of the same session the bogus claim that "there were no discordant notes, no anxiety, depression, or friction."[21] Or consider the testimony of another woman (unnamed in the source) involved in the Harvard Psilocybin Project. Not much is known about her. Leary never mentions her. Her account would have gone altogether untold had not *The Saturday Evening Post* interviewed her in 1963: "I cannot convey the horror of it except through analogy. . . . Imagine you were forced to look on helplessly while monsters hacked your children to bits. Intensify that emotion a thousandfold [*sic*] and you'll have some inkling of my ordeal."[22] We can never know how many people experienced various kinds of negative reactions under Leary's supervision simply because he never reported them. His exclusion of both Metzner's and the anonymous woman's bad reactions to psilocybin leaves one wondering how many more were omitted. Just about everyone—Hubbard, Cohen, Eisner, Ditman, Harman, and Stolaroff—disagreed with Leary's approach.[23]* At best it was wholly unscientific. At worst, it was dangerous. He would run two major psilocybin studies while at Harvard. The setting for each experiment couldn't be more dissimilar: Concord Prison and Marsh Chapel.

In the former experiment, which commenced in March 1961, Leary wanted to try to lower the recidivism rate.† The recidivism rate at Concord Prison stagnated at 70 percent—the majority of parolees returned. Like most people, Leary reasoned, criminals acted as they did due to social games caused by Pavlovian reflexes to negative societal stimuli that had been imprinted in their psyches. He aimed to prove that psilocybin wiped away the ego and produced a state of detachment from learned behavior roles. The prisoners, along with Leary and

---

*While Leary doesn't mention Huxley, I suspect the great novelist and philosopher disagreed with Leary's methods as well, considering he "often expressed caution against dramatizing or glamorizing psychedelic drugs in the mass media" (see Horowitz and Palmer, *Moksha*, 185). At the same time, we must also recognize that Huxley often found the "'scientific' approach" limiting and frustrating, even complaining to Leary that such "Pavlovian" methods were the protocols of "idiots" (Horowitz and Palmer, *Moksha*, 186).
†The recidivism rate calculates how likely it is that a person will return to prison after release.

his crew, could then re-imprint new, socially acceptable, behaviors. In Leary's accounts—most notably his autobiographies *High Priest* (1968) and *Flashbacks* (1983)—the Concord Experiment proved successful. However, a follow-up study conducted by MAPS* founder Rick Doblin has shown that Leary falsified the data.[24]

However, with the "Good Friday Experiment" that took place at Marsh Chapel in 1962, Leary scored a victory. Originally, the study was the idea of Walter Pahnke (1931–1971) who wanted to see if he could induce a purely religious experience in a purely religious setting for purely religious graduate students—twenty from Harvard's divinity school. However, the study had been terminated when Dr. Dana Farnsworth (1905–1986), director of the Harvard Medical Service, decided that Leary was too irresponsible to work with psilocybin after the Ginsberg incident. Leary decided to violate university protocol and push through with the experiment anyway. And so on April 20, 1962—Good Friday—a group consisting of twenty divinity students along with Chairperson of M.I.T's philosophy department, Huston Smith (1919–2016), Professor Emeritus in the psychology department at Andover-Newton Seminary, Walter Clark (1902–1994), and Leary assembled in the basement of Marsh Chapel, where Howard Thurman's (1899–1981) Good Friday sermon pumped through a set of speakers.

The study was double-blind, meaning neither the researchers nor the volunteers knew who received the PS 39 and who received a placebo (nicotinic acid, which causes mild, somatic effects). Though, within an hour, such measures proved fruitless and it became obvious who took the psilocybin and who took the nicotinic acid. While one student, Randall Laarko, had an adverse reaction and ran out of the chapel (and had to be injected with Thorazine), the rest of the experimental group seems to have experienced a positive encounter with PS 39.[25] But Leary's decision to move forward with the experiment—successful as is was—after Farnsworth had put the kibosh on it only added weight to his

---

*Multidisciplinary Association of Psychedelic Studies.

being fired from the university (along with Metzner and Alpert)* in the spring of 1963.

Leary's departure from Harvard merely kicked off a spiral that dragged him, and the academic pursuit of psychedelia, into disrepute.

THE PUPPET SHOW OF REALITY

~ *Winter 1961 or Spring 1962*† ~

Leary ingests LSD for the first time.

In those days, Leary thought LSD had a "dubious reputation." He felt the same way about cannabis. Nonetheless, when the "divine rascal" Michael Hollingshead (b. 1931) showed up at his door with a mayonnaise jar filled with LSD, plans quickly changed. Rather fatefully, Leary took a hefty spoonful from the jar. He could see the past and future, "tumbling and spinning, down soft fibrous avenues of light that were emitted from some central point."[26]

It all became clear. Life was all a game. Writing books. Marriage. Children. Harvard. Society. The Kaiser experiment had taught him so. But the lesson hadn't stuck until he ate a spoonful of LSD from that divine rascal's mayonnaise jar. Now, Leary saw the pawns, the queens, the kings, and the chessboard itself. He had always felt that society was a lie of some sort. A "cosmic costume," if you will. There was *something* lurking beneath the veneer—call it rebelliousness, call it intuition, call it whatever you want. Designations for this sentiment aside, Leary just never imagined that he was every bit a part of it. And now he saw the cold, hard truth: he epitomized the whole game. He too wore a costume. He was another marionette who couldn't see his strings, dancing to the "puppet show of reality."[27]

---

*Metzner was let go for giving psilocybin to a student off-campus; Alpert was canned for giving psilocybin to an undergraduate student (they were only allowed to give PS 39 to graduate students).

†Leary gives two different times for his first LSD experience. In *High Priest* the voyage took place in December 1961 (244–46) and in *Flashbacks* it happened in spring 1962 (116).

Here's how it all unfolded: at some point along that initial LSD journey he thought of Susan (1947–1990), his daughter, and ran upstairs to her bedroom to check on her. He walked into her room and felt a "shock of terror." There she sat; there he stood: daughter and father. "A shallow superficial stereotyped meaningless exchange of Hi, Dad, Hi Sue, How are you Dad? How's school? What do you want for Christmas? Have you done your homework? The plastic doll father and the plastic doll daughter both mounted on little wheels, rolling past each other, around and around, on fixed tracks."[28]

While Leary's earlier experiments with psilocybin had "opened up sensory awareness, pushed consciousness out to the membranes," LSD was a different beast. It flipped Leary's "consciousness into a dance of energy, where nothing existed except whirring vibrations and each illusory form was simply a different frequency."[29] But what about the rest of the Harvard Psilocybin Project team? Those closest to him—Barron, Metzner, Richard Alpert (1931–2019)*—grew "a bit scared" by Leary's reaction to LSD. Alpert worried about the "blank look of someone who is seeing too much" now cast in Leary's eyes.[30]

LSD does not always dissolve the ego. In Leary's case, LSD inflated his ego straight into the upper stratospheres. He was, in fact, a psychopath, remembers Charles Slack, a drinking buddy of Leary's.[31] For he now felt himself chosen to lead all of humankind to cellular salvation. The avenue to such salvation was the International Foundation for Internal Freedom (IFIF), a nonhierarchical† organization of psychologists, mystics, drug enthusiasts, and various other scientists in the vein of Stolaroff and Hubbard's International Foundation for Advanced Study. Its *raison d'être:* "IFIF would be a cluster of autonomous cells,

---

*Like Metzner, Alpert would play a major role in promoting Leary's work. Later in life, he would change his name to Ram Dass.

†Leary wasted no time inaugurating himself as the president of the nonhierarchal organization.

each built around the nucleus of an IFIF-trained guide. These cells, as they grew, would divide, forming other cells, until the world was speckled with mini-Islands."[32]

These "mini-Islands" of Leary's derived directly from the recently published Huxley novel *Island* (1962), the last work of his successful career. The novel tells of a group of people, the Palanese, who ingested a sacred medicine, *moksha,* for "enlightening and liberating grace."[33]* However, it remained up to them to "cooperate with the grace and take those opportunities" that they had seen while on moksha.[34] IFIF needed a home base, away from the disbelievers, away from the stale academic model of psychedelia. Leary decided on Mexico. After all, this is where his long strange trip had begun.

Zihuatanejo, Mexico, seemed the ideal location. Described in IFIF literature as "unspoiled by commercial civilization . . . the inhabitants are friendly, honest and happy . . . life is open, and is close to the sea, palms, and sun." It was here that the Hotel Catalina, a forty-room motel, was transformed into "Freedom House," a research center that would astutely probe the mystery of the psychedelic state—the Other World.[35] The doors to Freedom House swung open for one month to anyone who could pay the $200 fee. While in Zihuatanejo, Leary toyed with the idea of clinically deconstructing the *Tibetan Book of the Dead* into a manual for guiding people through the visions of the psychedelic experience. At least that's what Leary hoped it to be—a guidebook that would allow inexperienced people to aid the lysergized during their journeys. He remembers the time as a positive triumph that had "given us a glimpse of utopia."[36] Metzner remembered the time as a vacillating energy cycle. Some days were indeed enjoyable—taking psilocybin, body surfing, playing baseball, beach bonfires complete with booze, guitars, and flutes—but on other days "the tension lay in the air like dynamite with a crackling fuse."[37] At one point a man named Foster tried to burn down Freedom House. Leary, of course, never mentions the semi-daily tensions or the

---

Moksha is a Sanskrit word that means "liberation."

arson attempt in any of the several books he wrote about himself. He also doesn't mention how Freedom Center came to an end. Two *federales,* one of whom sampled LSD at Freedom House, infiltrated the quasi-utopia posing as reporters for a local Mexican newspaper. Within days after the "reporters" departed Freedom House, Leary received word that the group was being deported for operating a business on a tourist visa. On June 18, Freedom Center closed and IFIF relocated in Dominica. After a brief meeting with the governor they were expelled from there too.

Undeterred, IFIF found a home on Antigua, an island in the Caribbean. During an experiment, one IFIF-er had a psychotic reaction to the LSD and ran away. He had apparently felt that a "sacrifice was needed to free IFIF from its bad luck," and chose himself as the *sacraficee.*[38] Alpert found him several days later in a mental asylum deep in the Antiguan jungle. The incident reached the colonial governor of Antigua and IFIF was deported.

In less than three months, IFIF had been kicked out of Harvard and three countries. Leary saw the incidents as further proof of religious persecution. Returning to America, he announced to a crowd of doctors gathered for the American Psychologists Association in Philadelphia that they were "witnessing a good, old fashioned, traditional religious controversy."[39]

Fellow IFIF-ers weren't so encouraged by these words, but rather by William "Billie" Hitchcock, the vice president of Lehman Brothers, a global financial services company. Billie had sampled LSD and wondered if the secrets of the Other World could teach him how to make more money.[40] Leary and the group were invited to reestablish their home base in Dutchess County in upstate New York. Leary's acceptance of Billie's offer further demonstrated his hypocrisy. After all, he first chose Zihuatanejo due to its detachment from commercial enterprise, and now here he was accepting an estate from the vice president of one of the largest commercial firms in America, and in fact, the world (at the time). Leary even admitted "a weekend in Millbrook was the chic thing for the hip young rich of New York."[41]

THE SELF-FULFILLING PROPHET SEES

Millbrook, the name of the four-thousand-acre estate, was home to Leary's last attempt to prove to the world that he was not a quack. He saw the promise of Millbrook as a "stable, mentally enriching environment detached from the stresses of the modern industrial state," . . . all on the penny of the modern industrial state![42] The property consisted of a sixty-room mansion (called the "Big House"), horse stables, forests, tennis courts, polo fields, a small private lake, a gatehouse, and a fountain. A royal bounty of LSD, marijuana, hashish, speed, cocaine, DMT, opium, heroin, and just about every other ecstasy under the psychedelic sun could be found at the estate.

Where the Harvard Psilocybin Project had tried to cure society's ills—like criminal rehabilitation and a crisis of spirituality*—the Millbrook experiments made a mockery of the study of psychedelia. For example, one test involved tripping for days on end to see what would happen.

Nothing happened.

Leary often likened Millbrook to a cosmic marketplace, where hundreds of inner-galaxy voyagers could reconvene and fuel up. He also claimed his paradise was the epicenter of a new-age social movement. In reality, Millbrook was not a utopian cosmic weigh station, but rather a massive dump. Garbage littered the hallways. The residents fed cats, dogs, goats, and other animals the same substances they imbibed, inhaled, and injected, leading to the poor beasts defecating on the floors. Journalist Marya Mannes reported: "The rooms [were] dirty, the sinks piled with dishes, floors spattered with mud, and closets crammed with junk."[43] A three-year-old was once seen chugging a beer while his mother looked on approvingly.[44] The driveway had been reduced to rubble on account of "that legendary trip when

---

*The cover story for the April 8, 1966, issue of *Time* magazine would ask the question, "Is God Dead?"

Timothy and Co. had decided to get rid of all the pavement in the world."[45]

Most people who visited the manor didn't care for Leary's rhetoric and were merely freeloading junkies of varying degrees who decided that Millbrook was the perfect place to hide from the world. In and out these people came. Some stayed two days; some stayed two months, made a scene, and then vanished. Hollingshead made it a point to dose everyone who visited Millbrook with LSD, a dangerous and heinous practice.

Leary simply could not see (or refused to see) the disgrace that his "studies" had become. And neither could two members from the Food and Drug Administration (FDA), "a medico and an enforcement type," that visited the ongoing party at Millbrook.[46] After informing Leary that the U.S. government was already working to make LSD illegal so that they could pounce on him, Leary reportedly replied, "The government should license, supervise, and educate people to use drugs effectively."[47] But using these medicines with even the slightest amount of respect had eluded the researchers at Millbrook.

When asked to testify in the hearings before the Special Subcommittee of the Committee on the Judiciary United States Senate on LSD and Marijuana Use on College Campuses in 1966, Leary told Teddy Kennedy (1932–2009), who oversaw the hearing, that regarding LSD, "special types of legislation are needed . . . legislation which would license responsible adults to use these drugs for serious purposes."[48] But this was hardly what was happening at Millbrook.

The whole thing was a complete farce.

No pioneer of LSD research advocated such carelessness with the human psyche; some vocalized their disapproval. Janiger explained how he felt about Leary's haphazard LSD-taking and dispensing: "The whole goddamn climate changed. Suddenly you were conspirators out to destroy people. I felt like Galileo. I closed my practice and went to Europe. I felt violated. . . . If you want to know, it was Leary and the others who were ruining what we had worked so hard to build."[49] Betty

Eisner echoed similar remarks: "I think Tim Leary was mainly responsible for things going wrong."[50]*

They were not alone.

The media also began to turn against Leary. Where only a few years
ago the newspapers and magazines held a relatively neutral stance on
Leary's shenanigans (and psychedelics in general), by 1966 LSD scare-
stories became common.[51] One of the media denouncers of Leary was
Henry Luce, who, as we saw, once held a favorable view of LSD. But an
article in the March 1966 issue of *Life* shows his change of mind: "A
person . . . can become permanently deranged through a single terrifying LSD experience . . . it brings about the worst in some people."[52]

Leary needed a break from it all. In late December 1965, he
embarked on a road trip with his new girlfriend Rosemary Woodruff
(1935–2002) and children Susan and Jack (b. 1949). The four hopped
into Leary's station wagon and headed for Mexico. The New York
publishing house New American Library had offered Leary a $10,000
advance for an autobiography; Mexico would provide the perfect environment for him to put pen to paper. After a few days of driving, they
arrived in the border town of Laredo, Texas, where immigration agents
found a small cannabis seed on the floor of their station wagon. This
invited a search of the vehicle. U.S. agent Helen Loftis searched Susan
and found a tiny amount of cannabis buds in a small, silver box hidden between her legs. Leary took responsibility for the cannabis. All
were arrested for violating the Marihuana Tax Act of 1937.[53] Eventually
released, they drove back to Dutchess County, tails between their legs.

While Leary tried to remain optimistic, many at Millbrook
couldn't help but notice that his confidence sounded "more and more
hollow."[54] The party would last all but a month more. Sheriff Lawrence
M. Quinlan had heard enough complaints from the other residents of
Dutchess County and raided the Big House, arresting everyone too

---

*To Leary's credit, he did eventually apologize for his thoughtless actions (at least he did
to Eisner). See Eisner, "The Birth and Death of Psychedelic Therapy," 93.

inebriated to run away. Accompanying him was G. Gordon Liddy (1930–2021), who was running for district attorney in Dutchess County and would later play a lead role in Richard Nixon's Watergate Scandal. Quinlan informed *Newsweek* that the raid commenced after he and his men saw "a great many people dancing wildly around a bonfire . . . that's not normal."[55] Clearly more of an excuse for an arrest than an actual reason for one, but it didn't matter to the people of Dutchess County who pressured the Poughkeepsie Police Department to remove Leary from their neighborhood. In an odd twist of fate, the arrest did not stick on a technicality; no one at Millbrook had been read their Miranda Rights, the case of which was still being debated at the time of the bust. When Miranda was finally written into law on June 13 of that year, all the charges were dropped. Not that it mattered, as Leary still faced a thirty-year sentence and a thirty-thousand dollar fine (the highest in drug history at the time) for his arrest at Laredo.

~ July 15, 1965 ~

The Drug Abuse Control Amendments were signed into law. The amendments concerned and expanded upon the FDA's Food, Drug, and Cosmetics Act of 1938, the very law that first oversaw the manufacture and distribution of Delysid nearly two decades earlier. The original act only mentioned five commodities: food, drugs, medical devices, tobacco products, and cosmetics. In 1951, the law was amended to include "a written prescription of a practitioner licensed to administer such drug,"[56] which is where LSD came into the picture—two years *after* Hyde took the first hundred micrograms of LSD on U.S. soil. However, by 1965, section 201 of the Food, Drug, and Cosmetic Act was once again amended, now including "any drug which contains any quantity of a substance which . . . has been found to have . . . a potential for abuse because of its . . . hallucinogenic effect."[57] But the first laws to mention LSD by name were drafted by governors Grant Sawyer (1918–1996) of Nevada and Edmund Brown (1905–1996) of California, who both officially outlawed the "manufacture, sale, and possession of LSD" in 1966. Leary responded by urging Sawyer and Brown to try LSD.[58] The governors ignored Leary's good advice. LSD was now defined as a "Schedule 1 Drug," under the hasty, definitive, and absolutely brainless assumption that it had "no currently acceptable medical use and a high potential for abuse."[59]

All the pioneering triumphs of the wonder child decade vanished. Leary was out of defenses. He continued to lecture despite the mounting criticism that followed him everywhere he went. The academic world had dismissed him and the psychedelic veterans had shunned him. Then, in 1970, Superior Court Judge Byron McMillan (1928–2016) slammed the gavel down on Leary, calling the disgraced psychologist an "insidious menace," and sentencing him to ten years in prison.[60] Judge McMillan intended this stretch to run consecutively with his earlier ten-year sentence for the Laredo bust.

Leary's journey rather reminds one of the words of the late missiologist of the Dutch Reformed Church, Hendrik Kraemer (1888–1965), who warned:

> The mystic who triumphantly realizes his essential oneness with God, or the World-Order, or the Divine, knowing himself in serene equanimity the supreme master of the universe and of his own destiny . . . nonetheless, in the light of Biblical revelation, commits in this sublime way the root-sin of mankind—"to be like God." In other words, *he repeats the fall.*[61]

The psychedelic Renaissance was over.

For the while . . .

19

A Far-Gone Conclusion

Resurrecting the Renaissance

Ralph Metzner and Ram Dass's enjoyable work *Birth of a Psychedelic Culture* (2010) dates the founding years of psychedelia (as many do) to the 1960s. I was not immune to the allure of the 1960s either; when I first began my studies in psychedelic history some twenty years ago I too operated under that premise. So far as I knew, LSD just *appeared* sometime before the Summer of Love, caused the boomer generation to flip out, and was all but tarnished by the disco age. But as I hope this book has demonstrated, the 1960s decade seems to have represented not the childhood days of psychedelia, but rather its tumultuous teenage years, so to speak. No one referred to LSD as a "problem child" during the 1950s.

The *true* origins of psychedelic culture as we understand it in the twenty-first century began in the early to mid-1950s, around the time Juliana Day was paying attention to the proper setting of each room during LSD sessions and Roland Sandison was dedicating a whole wing of Powick Hospital to LSD therapy; when Maria Huxley was advising her husband to focus on the Clear Light of the Tibetans and the Wassons were finally sitting in a traditional mushroom rite with a legit curandera. When ideas like "set," "setting," "integration," "psychedelic therapy," and "psychedelic mysticism" swirled within intellectual and artistic circles creating a fantastic and unprecedented cross-pollination among chemists and poets, psychiatrists and philosophers, parapsychologists and reverends, spies and screenwriters. Psychedelia was born and evolved slowly and amorphously among thousands of tiny interactions, changes in attitudes, definitions, and philosophical epiphanies—the building blocks of culture.

◎

Of course, the 1950s decade also had its dark side.

The attempt by the CIA's MKUltra program to weaponize medicines like LSD and psilocybin should rightfully be dismissed as unconscionable. The lives destroyed or otherwise irreparably damaged by surreptitious dosing and maniacal—dare I say *evil*—subterfuge courtesy of George Hunter White and others during the early 1950s was certainly more appalling than any careless use of LSD by college students during the latter half of the 1960s. And Isbell's drug bartering system at the Lexington narco, which he subsequently both lied about on medical documents and omitted from later personal testimony, was highly unethical—to say nothing of the blatant immorality of it all.

But we also should not paint every CIA scientist or doctor under the agency's payroll with a broad brush—or even with the same brush. While White's safehouses in Manhattan and San Francisco, Isbell's secret drug-bartering program at Lexington, Hoch's medical murder of tennis player Harold Blauer,* and Gottlieb's cover-up of Frank Olson's death leave a sour flavor in the mouth of anyone with good taste, there were, of course, counterweights to their malicious handlings of LSD. Recall that Charles Savage, one of the earliest medical doctors tapped by the Navy to carry out MKUltra-like experiments, was more interested in uncovering the true healing power of LSD and mescaline. He even later worked with compassionate researchers like Myron Stolaroff, addressing the spiritual side of the psychedelic experience and its role in curing social ills like alcoholism, instead of any "mind

---

*Hoch, you will recall, didn't know whether he injected tennis pro Harold Blauer with mescaline or "dog piss."

control" initiative. Moreover, at least one CIA agent (but perhaps at least a few more) had an experience with LSD analogous to Huxley's first encounter with mescaline. Whereas Huxley found "Eternity in a flower, Infinity in four chair legs and the Absolute in the folds of a pair of trousers,"[1] this particular CIA agent spoke of "seeing all the colors of the rainbow growing out of the cracks in the sidewalk . . . the cracks became natural stress lines that measured the vibrations of the universe." The agent did not experience a model psychosis, nor did he feel he would make a superb assassin after taking LSD. He told his colleagues as the chemical's effects began to wane that he "didn't want to leave it." He felt he "would be going back to a place where [he] wouldn't be able to hold onto this kind of beauty."[2] Another operative remarked something that would have caused the McCarthyists to soil their britches: "I found it awfully hard when stoned to maintain the notion: I am a U.S. citizen—my country right or wrong. . . . You tend to have these good higher feelings."[3] And then there were those statements made by some patients under the observation of a CIA-contracted psychiatrist, Gerald Klee (1927–2013). One had an out-of-body experience ("I feel like I'm a bystander watching myself"), while another remarked how she felt "blended with the universe."[4]

None of this held any interest to American intelligence.

Try as they might, government employees could not find a tactical program with which to fit LSD. The CIA, U.S. Army, and U.S. Navy failed to turn Hofmann's wonder child into a war child. But the truth is that the majority of academics tapped by the CIA had nothing to do with such violations (the obvious bad actors notwithstanding). Most were merely happy to accept large checks for engaging in work that had already interested them prior to any government involvement. For example, it is highly doubtful that even someone as unethical as Harris Isbell knew anything about White's safehouses. The majority of the "academic espionage" camp was simply fascinated by LSD and graciously accepted money from CIA fronts, some knowingly and some unknowingly. Thankfully, this kind of immoral misuse of both synthetic and natural medicine has not survived in the present day—at least, that's the official story.

◎

What did survive in our own day were the two other paradigms of the phantastic fifties: the use of LSD as a therapeutic medicine and its role as a sacrament. Today we are seeing our all-knowledgeable, always compassionate and moral government finally begin to recognize the healing benefits of these medicines. In 2018, nine U.S. cities entered Phase 3 testing for MDMA-assisted therapy. Just days before I wrote these words, Cambridge, Massachusetts, decriminalized "all Entheogenic Plants [sic] and plant-based compounds."[5]* In November 2020, my home city of Portland, Oregon, became the first municipality to legalize psilocybin for therapeutic use. Even without this step in legalization, many people are discovering the healing benefits of microdosing to deal with depression, trauma, and anxiety. The medical model is on a revival—an upswing even.

As to the second surviving paradigm from the phantastic fifties— the sacramental use of these plants, fungi, and synthetics—I don't actually care what any human law says about it. No one should. We have a *natural right* to utilize them in spiritual practice; case closed. This, of course, is not meant to endorse the irresponsible employ of these medicines. It means that we learned a lot about using psychedelics responsibly during the phantastic fifties and it would be unwise to ignore such lessons. Those of sound mind and body, who follow at least the basic format of dose, set, and setting, have little to fear even when and if the ride gets bumpy.

Maria Huxley's suggestion that her husband Aldous focus on the Clear Light outlined in the *Tibetan Book of the Dead* initiated an old (but forgotten) paradigm in our culture, a way to dance in the mystic space. Afterword, when Huxley wrote *The Doors,* he was reintroducing

---

*Eight to one in favor. This ratio is important.

that forgotten paradigm into the twentieth century. He further strengthened this connection in a *Saturday Evening Post* article from 1958, reminding us that in "many societies at many levels of civilization attempts have been made to infuse drug intoxication with God intoxication."[6] Moreover, Hubbard was around to offer these mystic states to Bible-believing Christians. Whether a person preferred the liberal spiritualities of Huxley or the more conservative Christian beliefs of Hubbard, both served to reinforce the mystical paradigm in the United States and Western Europe. Additionally, the curandera María Sabina's ceremonial use of her Little Saints also influenced and reinforced this paradigm once Valentina Wasson's *This Week* magazine article "The Sacred Mushroom" and her husband Gordon's *Life* article "Seeking the Magic Mushroom" both hit the newsstands in March and May of 1957.

We can today say with confidence that Zaehner was wrong. If it was our ignorance of mystical experiences that led us to fooling ourselves that LSD could mimic such states (as Zaehner argued), then how does he explain the deep plant and fungi traditions that dot the globe throughout time? His view that only "primitive" people found use for these otherworldly states as prompted by plant medicines (and therefore did not invite genuine mysticism) strikes this author as deeply ignorant at best and racially supremacist at worst.

There are, of course, those sides of the 1950s that strike our modern sensibilities as outdated relics of bygone years. For example, Sandison, Martin, and the larger medical culture of the 1950s saw homosexuality and sexual deviances as mental disorders rather than as natural expressions of healthy adults. Obviously, this paradigm does not fly today (with good reason), but we must also consider the times—*society* as a whole had embraced these notions, and for some, LSD therapy was their last resort for living a happy life. And while it can be disconcerting to read about closeted homosexuals who were "cured" of their "disorder" via LSD we can at least hope that such psychedelic therapies helped them deal with the oppressive, heteronormative societal structures of their day. And please consider that all those doctors—

Sandison, Whitelaw, Martin, countless unnamed nurses and other hospital staffers—believed they were doing the right thing. They treated the issues not with shame and guilt (as more Abrahamic "conversion" therapies might utilize) but rather with deep compassion and tolerance for their non-heteronormative patients. And from what we can tell from the literature, at least some of those patients appreciated that.

Along that nuanced gray-scale of LSD investigation during the phantastic fifties, I hesitate to out-rightly dismiss the tests that sought to find the hidden powers of the mind. Experiments with psychedelics to find the source of ESP and other supernormal activity conducted by Heywood, Garrett, Puharich, Huxley, and others may seem preposterous to us now, but even our government took such matters seriously at that point in time.[7] Removing my historians' hat for a moment and speaking from a personal perspective, I have had enough interesting experiences with these medicines to know (well, "know" in a *soft* way) that the human mind is far more powerful and capable than we can currently measure on a chart or a graph. So while I don't agree that Puharich's medium friend Harry Stone was indeed channeling the Egyptian priest Ra Ho Tep, I am all in favor of us weirdoes using LSD or mushrooms to swim in the sacred. When we consider all the ideas that were once scoffed at by the smartest people on the planet (i.e., we live in a heliocentric universe; only birds can fly; X-rays are impossible; and invisible electronic signals cannot be transmitted through the air) we should take pause. The history of science is the history of uncovering prejudiced fallacies among humans about the nature of reality. So who knows what doors in the mind LSD might unlock in the future? Consider how psychiatrists once argued that lysergized people *couldn't* be abreacting experiences from their infancy (as the cerebral cortex hadn't developed enough yet) only to have their volunteers' stories corroborated by other family members. Does this mean that telekinesis is real and that celebrity "psychics" like James van Praagh and Theresa Caputo are not parasitic grief-mongers? Of course not. It is merely my suggestion to keep an open mind about the powers we have available to us when we connect to the Infinite through psychedelic medicines. Christopher Bache's *LSD and the Mind of the Universe* (2019) is hopefully just the first of many future accounts that will address and explore our true common ancestor—the Cosmos itself.

Such principles, however, can sometimes be taken to the extreme, as the tragedy of Timothy Leary indicates. He wasn't a hero. He was a hypocrite who preached "ego loss" from the media pulpit while using LSD to inflate his own ego in private; who "rejected" academia all while including his Ph.D. credentials on the covers of his many books about himself; who promoted safety protocols in public as he turned Millbrook into a hazardous dump; whose ideas of "free love" included unabashed misogyny and infidelity; whose cure for a broken society was to ignore it by "turning on, tuning in, and dropping out." He tapped the Weather Underground to help spring him from prison only to testify against that organization in exchange for a reduced sentence when he was later apprehended. And his ignoble use of LSD sent all research and legitimate inquiry back to the dark ages.

Not a hero, my friends.

Mind you, this is certainly not meant to suggest that the psychedelic sixties did not give rise to meaningful advances in art, music, and spiritual philosophies. Who would want to live in a world without peace, love, and music? And I totally reject Allan Bloom's acerbic summation that "Enlightenment in America came close to breathing its last [breath] during the sixties."[8] My critiques of the kind of lazy, escapist hedonism that Leary promoted aside, I happen to find the aesthetic of the 1960s powerfully moving. Such ideas like "drop acid, not bombs" and Flower Power will forever hold special places in my heart. And I certainly respect and champion the antiauthoritarianism, Civil Rights, anti-war, free speech movements of that decade. But if a lesson can be learned from the problem child years of LSD, I feel it is this: using these medicines to "drop out" of society (as Leary recommended) is a waste of good medicine. Instead, the establishment, or the system, or the matrix (or whatever you want to call it) must be permeated by compassionate, insightful, clever people who will gut it, sage it, and reinvent it from within the bowels. Feel-good *kumbaya* colonics won't work.

⊚

While we consider that, let's leave both the psychedelic sixties and the phantastic fifties for a moment and focus our attention on today's cultural climate: decriminalization of psilocybin in Denver, Colorado, Oakland and Santa Cruz, California, and Somerville and Cambridge, Massachusetts (with dozens of other cities working toward similar goals). Most impressively, Oregon just decriminalized all substances in the entire state—go us! All this is to say nothing of the recent semi-paroling of that beautiful, medicinal, philosophical, and magical plant, cannabis, after spending a century as the target of numerous nonsensical and vicious misinformation campaigns resulting in the immoral and callous incarceration of the innocent. Or simply consider the recent boom in microdosing. We are truly resurrecting the psychedelic Renaissance! As we watch the oppressive structures of the last fifty years—which sought to infringe our natural right to cognitive and spiritual liberty—crumble all around us, the nuances between the psychedelic sixties and the phantastic fifties will prove evermore paramount. If these medicines are to reenter Western society safely and with a keen eye toward harm-reduction and self-improvement, we must look to the groundbreaking medical work of those like Day, Sandison, Osmond, and Eisner (among others) and the spiritual philosophies rendered by Maria Huxley and Heard, while simultaneously reevaluating our romance of LSD's teen-age years—the problem child years (even though there are some artistic aspects of that time worth cherishing and preserving). Which brings me to my theme—a theme I have been thinking about for twenty years. A theme that is evident throughout the phantastic fifties.

So allow me to unpack it here, before I forget again.

"Psychedelia" (for lack of a better term) seems to pop up here and there in different times and places with no set rules or boundaries. The only confines seem to be those of the cultures that discover psychedelics and the way people within those cultures interpret the experiences. As I have tried to show in all my published works in this area, the "psychedelic" experience changes depending on the time, the culture, and the needs of the person using these substances.

So for example, to the people living in the ancient city of Dendera (Upper Egypt), the experience meant drinking a special beer mixed with mandrake* in honor of Hathor, who had come to earth to butcher the whole of humanity. She finally stopped her slaughter after drinking a mandrake-laced beer, which mellowed her harsh. In antiquity, on her feast day every year, the people of Dendera drank the same mandrake drink to celebrate her change of heart. That's the experience they needed at the time.

And for those early modern people living in the cities, towns, and backwoods of Western Europe, Solanaceae plants provided an escape from the oppressive realities of life. In that somniferous space they could achieve some kind of spiritual satisfaction by walking in the trail of a fertility goddess.[9] When we consider the Church's attempted eradication of those female-centric beliefs that survived the fall of Rome, access to the goddess through somnitheogenic† plants provided a path to Her. That's the experience those people needed at the time.

When James Mooney participated in a Kiowa peyote ceremony, he did so to form a conscious link between that people (and, by extension, other First Nations peoples of this continent) and those of European descent. The Temperance Movement was clearly making life miserable for everyone in those days and Mooney wanted to show that peyotism had nothing to do with the problems associated with opium or alcohol. That was what was needed at the time.

---

*Mandrake, a highly psychoactive plant, is a member of the Solanaceae family, a sibling of other powerful plant medicines like deadly nightshade, henbane, and datura, and cousin of the more common tobacco, tomato, and eggplant.
†I.e., to "generate divinity in dreams."

For more modern practitioners like María Sabina, mushrooms provided a way to access medical information and magical cures that were otherwise cut off from people living in remote parts of the world. To a materialist mindset, such things seem ridiculous. However, María Sabina's success rate is not to be scoffed at. Her clients certainly believed in her abilities. And so did she. For in the highland of Huautla de Jiménez—far removed from scientific reductionism—her relationship with the Principal Ones, accessed via the Little Saints, was what the people needed at the time.

Leary's fall, as outlined in this book, is not my attempt to place all the blame squarely on him. But he definitely played a role in bringing about the demise of LSD, illustrating a *small* fraction of how things can go wrong quickly if we do not respect the power of these medicines. However, of the three models envisioned for Hofmann's wonder child by various experimenters during the 1950s (as a weapon, as a therapeutic medicine, or as a sacrament), only the latter two survive to the present day. Perhaps this is no coincidence. The modern world, for all its luxuries and comforts that I personally enjoy and wouldn't want to live without, comes with a price.

Well, two prices: a price of the *mind;* a price of the *soul.* At least in my life, medicines like mushrooms and ayahuasca have reimbursed some of that cost. They have kept me sane when the world around me has gone crazy, and they have reinvigorated my connection with the dance of existence. And I'm not alone in feeling that way.

As we attempt to resurrect the psychedelic Renaissance, let's remember that we don't have to hearken back to the tumultuous problem child years of psychedelia that occurred during the 1960s for answers—back when Leary falsely claimed that LSD was a magic bullet for self-improvement. *No preparation, no integration, little respect—a simple "trip" to cure what ails ya.* Let's instead look back to more reasonable and responsible medical and spiritual models that shone a brighter light on the true wonder of medicines like LSD. In those days, preparation, respect, set, setting, and integration ruled the day—even if such principles were violated by bad actors.

So let's pick up the story at this, our turn—our moment in history. Let's not "turn on, tune in, and drop out," but instead "turn on, tune in, and *help* out"—with a focus on healing and a deeper connection to our place in this mad infinity that is the perpetual cycle of life. Let's grant that these medicines can both enlighten a prepared mind and destroy an ill-equipped one. Let's admit that the outcome of a successful psychedelic experience isn't predicated on the substances—like LSD, cannabis, mushrooms, or otherwise (as the psychedelic sixties would have us believe)—but has far more to do with the value given to them (as the phantastic fifties compel us to consider). And let's not forget that the real labor comes *after* the experience has ended. Natural and synthetic medicines are not magic bullets, despite Leary's insistence to the contrary. They can only connect you with the deeper mysteries of All That Is. It's up to you to integrate those lessons upon your return.

Above all, let's remember that most awesome lesson from the phantastic fifties. Namely, that people choose to engage with psychedelics for either therapeutic or spiritual practices for one reason . . .

They work.

Notes

BEFORE I FORGET . . . AGAIN

1. Strassman, *DMT: The Spirit Molecule,* 28.

1. PHARMACIES OF FAIRYLAND: VICTORIAN PSYCHEDELIA

1. Mitchell, "Remarks on the Effects of Anhelonium Lewinii (the Mescal Button)," 1626.
2. Tainter and Marcelli, "The Rise of Synthetic Drugs in the American Pharmaceutical Industry," 392.
3. Quoted in Otis, *Membranes,* 43.
4. Mitchell, *Characteristics,* 13.
5. Davenport-Hines, *The Pursuit of Oblivion,* 120.
6. Von Bibra, *Plant Intoxicants,* 96.
7. Courtwright, *Dark Paradise,* 63.
8. De Quincey, *Confessions of an English Opium Eater,* 70–71.
9. De Quincey, *Confessions of an English Opium Eater,* 88.
10. Palmer and Horowitz, *Sisters of the Extreme,* 29.
11. Palmer and Horowitz, *Sisters of the Extreme,* 27.
12. Quoted in Davenport-Hines, *The Pursuit of Oblivion,* 102–3.
13. Perrine, "Visions of the Night," 30.
14. Quoted in Mitchell, "Remarks on the Effects of Anhelonium Lewinii (the Mescal Button)," 1628.
15. Quoted in Perrine, "Visions of the Night," 35.
16. *The American Encyclopaedic Dictionary: Volume 4* (Chicago: W. B. Conkey and Company, 1896) s.v. "whiskey root," 4502; for the use of "white mule," see Perrine, "Visions of the Night," 18–19.
17. Prentiss and Morgan, "Therapeutic Uses of Mescal Buttons (*Anhalonium lewinii*)."
18. Quoted in Perrine, "Visions of the Night," 16.

19. Quoted in Perrine, "Visions of the Night," 16.

20. Perrine, "Visions of the Night," 17.

21. Lewin, *Phantastica*.

22. Perrine, "Visions of the Night," 22.

23. Mooney, "The Mescal Plant and Ceremony," 9.

24. Quoted in Mooney, "The Mescal Plant and Ceremony," 9.

25. Mooney, "The Mescal Plant and Ceremony," 8.

26. Mooney, "The Mescal Plant and Ceremony," 10.

27. Mooney, "The Mescal Plant and Ceremony," 11.

28. Quoted in Perrine, "Visions of the Night," 21.

29. James, ed., *The Letters of William James Vol. I*, 296.

30. James, *The Varieties of Religious Experience*, 319.

31. Quoted in Perrine, "Visions of the Night," 35.

32. James, *The Varieties of Religious Experience*, 320.

33. James, *The Varieties of Religious Experience*, 321.

34. James, *The Letters of William James Vol. II*, 37.

35. Quoted in Croce, "Physiology as the Antechamber," 309.

36. James, *The Varieties of Religious Experience*, 326–27.

37. James, "Subjective Effects of Nitrous Oxide," 359.

38. Croce, "Physiology as the Antechamber," 303.

39. Croce, "Physiology as the Antechamber," 308.

40. Quoted in James, *The Varieties of Religious Experience*, 328.

41. Ellis, *The Art of Life*, 95.

42. Ellis, "Mescaline," 537.

43. Jay, *Emperors of Dreams*, 97.

44. Partridge, *High Culture*, 91.

45. Jay, *Emperors of Dreams*, 98.

46. Partridge, *High Culture*, 92.

47. Partridge, *High Culture*, 93.

2. MOTHER'S GRAIN:
A BRIEF HISTORY OF THE ERGOT FUNGUS

1. Quoted in Lapinskas, "A Brief History of Ergotism," 203.

2. Quoted in Stone and Darlington, *Pills, Potions, and Poisons*, 109.

3. For a list of the years ergot epidemics were reported in Europe, see Packer, "Jewish Mystical Movements and the European Ergot Epidemics."

4. Quoted in Kavaler, *Mushrooms, Mold, and Miracles*, 150.

5. Schiff, "Ergot and Its Alkaloids," 1.

6. Hatsis, *The Witches' Ointment*, 110.

7. Wasson, *The Road to Eleusis,* 36.

8. Quoted in Ginzburg, *Ecstasies,* 304.

9. Quoted in Alm, "The Witch Trials of Finnmark, Northern Norway, During the 17th Century," 409.

10. Kilbourne Matossian, *Poisons of the Past,* 77.

11. Kilbourne Matossian, *Poisons of the Past,* 74.

12. Packer, "Jewish Mystical Movement and the European Ergot Epidemics," 227–39.

13. Packer, "Jewish Mystical Movement and the European Ergot Epidemics."

14. Hatsis, *Psychedelic Mystery Traditions,* 50 *ff.*

15. Quoted in Starkey, *The Devil in Massachusetts,* 56.

16. Quoted in Starkey, *The Devil in Massachusetts,* 56.

17. Caporael, "Ergotism," 23.

18. Quoted in Kilbourne Matossian, *Poisons of the Past,* 115–16. Printed as originally published.

19. Lawson, *A Brief and True Narrative of Some Remarkable Passages Relating to Sundry Persons Afflicted by Witchcraft, in Salem Village: Which Happened from the Nineteenth of March, to the Fifth of April, 1692.* Accessed via archive.org.

20. Starkey, *The Devil in Massachusetts,* 42.

21. Starkey, *The Devil in Massachusetts,* 46.

22. Hofmann, *LSD: My Problem Child,* 39–40.

23. Logan, *Air,* 61.

24. Quoted in Goodwin, "Drug Took Stevenson Face to Face with Hyde."

25. "Cinema: The New Pictures," *Time Magazine.*

3. A PECULIAR PRESENTIMENT: BIRTH OF THE WONDER CHILD

1. Hofmann, "LSD: Completely Personal," 49.

2. Hofmann, "LSD: Completely Personal," 36.

3. Hofmann, *LSD and the Divine Scientist,* 17.

4. Stoll, "The Impact of Studies of Natural Products on Chemical Industry," 357.

5. Hofmann, "LSD: Completely Personal," 1–2.

6. Hofmann, "Stan Grof Interviews Dr. Albert Hofmann," 3.

7. Hofmann, *LSD: My Problem Child,* 47.

8. Hofmann, "Stan Grof Interviews Dr. Albert Hofmann," 3.

9. Hofmann, *LSD: My Problem Child,* 47.

10. High Times, "Interview with Albert Hofmann."

11. Hofmann, *LSD: My Problem Child*, 48.

12. Hofmann, "Stan Grof Interviews Dr. Albert Hofmann," 24.

13. Hofmann, *LSD: My Problem Child*, 49.

14. Hofmann, "Stan Grof Interviews Dr. Albert Hofmann," 24.

15. Hofmann, *LSD: My Problem Child*, 49.

16. Hofmann, "Stan Grof Interviews Dr. Albert Hofmann" 25.

17. High Times, "Interview with Albert Hofmann."

18. Quoted in Hofmann, "How LSD Originated," 60.

19. Quoted in Shroder, *Acid Test*, 10.

20. Quoted in Shroder, *Acid Test*, 20.

21. Geronimus et al. "Effects of LSD-25," 39.

22. Stevens, *Storming Heaven*, 11.

23. Sandison, *A Century of Psychiatry*, 35.

24. W. Stoll, "Ein neues in sehr kleinen Mengen wirksames Phantastikum," ". . . therapeutischen Effekt vermuten konnte."

25. Condrau, "Klinische Erfahrungen an Geisteskranken mit Lyserg-saure-diathylamid," 1.

26. Condrau, "Klinische Erfahrungen an Geisteskranken mit Lyserg-saure-diathylamid," 2.

27. Condrau, "Klinische Erfahrungen an Geisteskranken mit Lyserg-saure-diathylamid," 2.

28. "Medicine: Happiness Pills" (July 28, 1947). See also Stevens, *Storming Heaven*, 11.

29. High Times, "Interview with Albert Hofmann"; Shroder, *Acid Test*, 11.

30. Quoted in Davenport-Hines, *The Pursuit of Oblivion*, 299.

31. Horowitz and Palmer, *Moksha*, 146–47.

32. Quoted in Sandison, *A Century of Psychiatry*, 35.

33. From the pamphlet Sandoz Pharmaceuticals sent to researchers along with the LSD, reprinted in Hofmann, *LSD: My Problem Child*, 73.

34. Ott, *The Age of Entheogens and the Devil's Dictionary*, 82.

4. DELYSID:
SEEKING A MODEL PSYCHOSIS

1. Stevens, *Storming Heaven*, 14.

2. Stevens, *Storming Heaven*, 16–18.

3. Lightner, *Bilirubin*, 113.

4. Rinkel, "Experimentally Induced Psychosis in Man," 235. See also Hofmann, *LSD: My Problem Child*, 73.

5. Rinkel, "Experimentally Induced Psychosis in Man," 236.

6. Rinkel, "Discussion at Annual Meeting of the American Psychiatric Association in Detroit, May 1st, 1950," 42.

7. Rinkel, "Experimentally Induced Psychosis in Man," 235.

8. Marks, *The Search for the Manchurian Candidate,* 57.

9. Rinkel, "Experimentally Induced Psychosis in Man," 235.

10. Rinkel, "Experimentally Induced Psychosis in Man," 235.

11. Rinkel, "Experimentally Induced Psychosis in Man," 236.

12. Rinkel et al., "Experimental Schizophrenic-Like Symptoms," 574.

13. Rinkel, Hyde, and Solomon, "Experimental Psychiatry III," 264.

14. Graham and Khalidi, "The Actions of d-Lysergic Acid Diethylamide (L.S.D. 25) Part II," 44.

15. Huxley, *The Doors of Perception,* 20.

16. Henderson, "Salvage," A4047.

17. Henderson, "Salvage," A4045.

18. Henderson, "Salvage," A4045.

19. Proceedings of the American Psychiatric Association, "The 106th Annual Meeting, Detroit," 283.

20. Rinkel, "Discussion at Annual Meeting of the American Psychiatric Association in Detroit, May 1st, 1950," 42.

21. Rinkel, "Discussion at Annual Meeting of the American Psychiatric Association in Detroit, May 1st, 1950," 42.

22. Rinkel, "Discussion at Annual Meeting of the American Psychiatric Association in Detroit, May 1st, 1950," 42.

23. Rinkel et al., "Experimental Schizophrenic-Like Symptoms," 575.

24. Rinkel, "Experimentally Induced Psychosis in Man," 237.

25. Busch and Johnson, "LSD as an Aid in Psychotherapy," 241.

26. Busch and Johnson, "LSD as an Aid in Psychotherapy," 241.

27. Busch and Johnson, "LSD as an Aid in Psychotherapy," 243.

28. Busch and Johnson, "LSD as an Aid in Psychotherapy," 243.

29. Busch and Johnson, "LSD as an Aid in Psychotherapy," 243.

30. Quoted in Katz, "Dr. Osmond's New Deal for the Insane," 10.

31. Osmond, "On Being Mad," 22.

32. Osmond, "Research on Schizophrenia," 202.

33. Quoted in Katz, "Dr. Osmond's New Deal for the Insane," 10.

34. Katz, "Dr. Osmond's New Deal for the Insane," 10.

35. Osmond, "Research on Schizophrenia," 203.

36. Rinkel, Hyde, and Solomon, "Experimental Psychiatry III," 263.

37. Rinkel, Hyde, and Solomon, "Experimental Psychiatry III," 264.

38. Hoffer, "Nicotinic Acid Modified Lysergic Acid Diethylamide Psychosis," 9.

39. Hoffer, "Studies with Niacin and LSD," 45.

40. Hyde, Von Mering, and Morimoto, "Hostility in the Lysergic Psychosis," 266.

41. Rinkel, "Experimentally Induced Psychosis in Man," 237–38.

42. Rinkel, "Experimentally Induced Psychosis in Man," 241–42.

43. Cholden, Kurland, and Savage, "Clinical Reactions and Tolerance to LSD in Chronic Schizophrenia," 219.

44. Quoted in Cholden, Kurland, and Savage, "Clinical Reactions and Tolerance to LSD in Chronic Schizophrenia," 217.

45. Day, "The Role and Reaction of the Psychiatrist in LSD Therapy," 437.

46. Day, "The Role and Reactions of the Psychiatrist in LSD Therapy," 437.

47. Forrer and Goldner, "Experimental Physiological Studies with Lysergic Acid Diethylamide (LSD-25)," 588.

48. Forrer and Goldner, "Experimental Physiological Studies with Lysergic Acid Diethylamide (LSD-25)," 584–86.

5. THE GREAT LIPS:
AN INTENTIONAL APPROACH TO SET AND SETTING

1. Sandison, "The Clinical Uses of Lysergic Acid Diethylamide," 27.

2. Sandison, *A Century of Psychiatry*, 36-7.

3. Caldwell, *LSD Psychotherapy*, 92.

4. Sandison, *A Century of Psychiatry*, 30.

5. Sandison, *A Century of Psychiatry*, 31.

6. Sandison, Spencer, and Whitelaw, "The Therapeutic Value of Lysergic Acid Diethylamide in Mental Illness," 504.

7. Quoted in Sandison, "Psychological Aspects of the LSD Treatment of the Neuroses," 512.

8. Sandison, "The Clinical Uses of Lysergic Acid Diethylamide," 28.

9. Sandison, "The Clinical Uses of Lysergic Acid Diethylamide," 28.

10. Sandison, "Psychological Aspects of the LSD Treatment of the Neuroses," 508.

11. Sandison, "The Clinical Uses of Lysergic Acid Diethylamide," 31–32.

12. Martin, "L.S.D. Treatment of Chronic Psychoneurotic Patients Under Day-Hospital Conditions," 194.

13. Ball, "The Nursing and Care of Mentally-Ill Patients Under d-Lysergic Acid Diethylamide," 1532.

14. Ball, "The Nursing and Care of Mentally-Ill Patients Under d-Lysergic Acid Diethylamide," 1532.

15. Sandison, "The Clinical Uses of Lysergic Acid Diethylamide," 32.

16. Sandison, *A Century of Psychiatry*, 49.

17. Cutner, "Analytic Work with LSD 25," 715.

18. Quoted in Sandison, *A Century of Psychiatry,* 40.

19. Melechi, "Drugs of Liberation: From Psychiatry to Psychedelia," 38–39.

20. Cohen, "Lysergic Acid Diethylamide: Side Effects and Complications," 33.

21. Whitelaw, "A Case of Fetishism Treated with Lysergic Acid Diethylamide," 575.

22. Whitelaw, "A Case of Fetishism Treated with Lysergic Acid Diethylamide," 573.

23. Whitelaw, "A Case of Fetishism Treated with Lysergic Acid Diethylamide," 574.

24. Whitelaw, "A Case of Fetishism Treated with Lysergic Acid Diethylamide," 574.

25. Whitelaw, "A Case of Fetishism Treated with Lysergic Acid Diethylamide," 574.

26. Whitelaw, "A Case of Fetishism Treated with Lysergic Acid Diethylamide," 575.

27. Whitelaw, "A Case of Fetishism Treated with Lysergic Acid Diethylamide," 575.

28. Martin, "The Treatment of Twelve Male Homosexuals with 'L.S.D.,'" 400.

29. Martin, "A Case of Psychopathic Personality with Homosexuality Treated by LSD," 113.

30. Martin, "The Treatment of Twelve Male Homosexuals with 'L.S.D.,'" 400.

31. Martin, "A Case of Psychopathic Personality with Homosexuality Treated by LSD," 112.

32. Martin, "A Case of Psychopathic Personality with Homosexuality Treated by LSD," 112.

33. Martin, "The Treatment of Twelve Male Homosexuals with 'L.S.D.,'" 398.

34. Martin, "A Case of Psychopathic Personality with Homosexuality Treated by LSD," 113.

35. Martin, "A Case of Psychopathic Personality with Homosexuality Treated by LSD," 113.

36. Martin, "A Case of Psychopathic Personality with Homosexuality Treated by LSD," 114.

37. Martin, "A Case of Psychopathic Personality with Homosexuality Treated by LSD," 114.

38. Martin, "A Case of Psychopathic Personality with Homosexuality Treated by LSD," 114.

39. Martin, "The Treatment of Twelve Male Homosexuals with 'L.S.D.,'" 399.

40. Martin "A Case of Psychopathic Personality with Homosexuality Treated by LSD," 114.

41. Martin, "The Treatment of Twelve Male Homosexuals with 'L.S.D.,'" 399.

42. Martin, "L.S.D. Treatment of Chronic Psychoneurotic Patients Under Day-Hospital Conditions," 193.

43. Martin, "L.S.D. Treatment of Chronic Psychoneurotic Patients Under Day-Hospital Conditions," 191.

44. Martin, "Schizophreniform Reactions Under Day Hospital L.S.D. Therapy," 320.

45. Sandison, "The Clinical Uses of Lysergic Acid Diethylamide," 29.

46. Sandison, *A Century of Psychiatry*, 51.

6. MIND FIELDS:
WEAPONIZING LSD

1. Marks, *The Search for the Manchurian Candidate*, 15.

2. Novak, "LSD before Leary," 90, note 9.

3. *Hearings before the Subcommittee on Health and Scientific Research of the Committee on Human Resources United States Senate* (statement of Sidney Gottlieb), 207.

4. Marks, *The Search for the Manchurian Candidate*, 23.

5. Geis, "In Scopolamine Veritas," 353.

6. Geis, "In Scopolamine Veritas," 350.

7. Geis, "In Scopolamine Veritas," 350.

8. Hatsis, *The Witches' Ointment*, 139–44.

9. Muehlberger, "Interrogation Under Drug Influence," 513.

10. Quoted in Geis, "In Scopolamine Veritas," 348.

11. Muehlberger, "Interrogation Under Drug Influence," 514.

12. Muehlberger, "Interrogation Under Drug Influence," 513.

13. Quoted in Geis, "In Scopolamine Veritas," 354.

14. Muehlberger, "Criminal Confessions Under Narcosis," 449.

15. Muehlberger, "Interrogation Under Drug Influence," 524.

16. Lee and Shlain, *Acid Dreams*, 6.

17. Quoted in "Recruitment of Germans: Project Paperclip," 1.

18. Quoted in "Recruitment of Germans: Project Paperclip," 6.

19. "Recruitment of Germans: Project Paperclip," 6.

20. *Foreign and Military Intelligence: Book 1, Final Report of the Select Committee to Study Governmental Operation with Respect to Intelligence Activities* (Church Committee Drug Testing Report), 399.

21. Quoted in Marks, *The Search for the Manchurian Candidate*, 38.

22. *Hearings Before the Subcommittee on Health and Scientific Research of the Committee on Human Resources United States Senate,* "Statement of Dr. Sidney Gottlieb," 170.

23. *Hearings Before the Subcommittee on Health and Scientific Research of the Committee on Human Resources United States Senate,* "Statement of Dr. Sidney Gottlieb," 167.

24. Marks, *The Search for the Manchurian Candidate,* 70.

25. Quoted in Lee and Shlain, *Acid Dreams,* 27.

26. Marks, *The Search for the Manchurian Candidate,* 71.

7. ACADEMIC ESPIONAGE:
LUCY IN DISGUISE WITH DOCTORS

1. Kinzer, *Poisoner in Chief,* 58.

2. *Hearings Before the Subcommittee on Health and Scientific Research of the Committee on Human Resources, United States Senate,* "Statement of Sidney Gottlieb," 185.

3. Marks, *The Search for the Manchurian Candidate,* 76.

4. Savage, "The Resolution and Subsequent Remobilization of Resistance by LSD in Psychotherapy," 434–35.

5. Savage, "Lysergic Acid Diethylamide (LSD-25)," 896.

6. Savage, "Lysergic Acid Diethylamide (LSD-25)," 897.

7. Cholden, Kurland, and Savage, "Clinical Reactions and Tolerance to LSD in Chronic Schizophrenia," 217.

8. Quoted in Cholden, Kurland, and Savage, "Clinical Reactions and Tolerance to LSD in Chronic Schizophrenia," 217.

9. Cholden, Kurland, and Savage, "Clinical Reactions and Tolerance to LSD in Chronic Schizophrenia," 217.

10. Quoted in Lee and Shlain, *Acid Dreams,* 27.

11. Savage, "Variations in Ego Feeling Induced by d-Lysergic Acid Diethylamide (LSD-25)," 11.

12. Savage, "Variations in Ego Feeling Induced by d-Lysergic Acid Diethylamide (LSD-25)," 1.

13. Savage, "Lysergic Acid Diethylamide (LSD-25)," 898.

14. Roberts, "Reservoir Drugs," 16.

15. Quoted in Roberts, "Reservoir Drugs," 17.

16. Marks, *The Search for the Manchurian Candidate,* 234.

17. Quoted in Marks, *The Search for the Manchurian Candidate,* 64–65.

18. Quoted in Marks, *The Search for the Manchurian Candidate,* 66.

19. Marks, *The Search for the Manchurian Candidate,* 129.

20. Abramson, ed., "Introductory Remarks," 475.

21. Abramson, "Lysergic acid diethylamide (LSD-25)."

22. Novak, "LSD before Leary," 91, note 12.

23. Lee and Shlain, *Acid Dreams,* 20.

24. Hoch, "Experimental Psychiatry," 788.

25. Hoch, Cattell, and Pennes, "Effects of Mescaline and Lysergic Acid (d-LSD-25)," 580.

26. Hoch, "The Production and Alleviation of Mental Abnormalities by Drugs," 430.

27. McGlothlin, "Social and Para-Medical Aspects of Hallucinogenic Drugs," 42.

28. Lubasch, "$700,000 Is Made in '53 Secret Test Death."

29. Quoted in United Press International, "$702, 044 Awarded in Drug-Research Death."

30. Quoted in Marks, *The Search for the Manchurian Candidate,* 72.

31. Lubasch, "$700,000 Is Made in '53 Secret Test Death."

32. "Living History Project: William J. C. McCurdy."

33. *Hearings Before the Subcommittee on Health and Scientific Research of the Committee on Human Resources, United States Senate,* "Human Drug Testing by the CIA," 172.

34. Collins, *Sleep Room,* 58.

35. Quoted in Marks, *The Search for the Manchurian Candidate,* 64

36. *Hearings Before the Subcommittee on Health and Scientific Research of the Committee on Human Resources, United States Senate,* "Human Drug Testing by the CIA," 171–72.

37. Wall, *From Healing to Hell,* 186–87.

38. *Foreign and Military Intelligence: Book 1, Final Report of the Select Subcommittee to Study Governmental Operation with Respect to Intelligence Activities* (Church Committee Drug Testing Report), 391.

39. Wall, *From Healing to Hell,* 187.

40. Kosten and Gorelick, "The Lexington Narcotic Farm," 22.

41. Isbell et al., "Studies in Lysergic Acid Diethylamide (LSD-25)," 469.

42. Ketchum, *Chemical Warfare,* 123.

43. Marks, *The Search for the Manchurian Candidate,* 68.

44. Quoted in Marks, *The Search for the Manchurian Candidate,* 68.

45. Isbell et al., "Studies in Lysergic Acid Diethylamide (LSD-25)," 469.

46. *Report on Alcohol, Drug Abuse, and Mental Health Administration Involvement in LSD Research, Kennedy Subcommittee Hearings,* 993.

47. American Medical Association, Judicial Council, "Supplementary Report of the Judicial Council."

48. Atomic Energy Commission for Biology and Medicine, transcripts of meeting, 10 November 1950. See chapter 1 note 57.

8. ENLIGHTENED OPERATIVES:
THE BLOOD OF PATRIOTS

1. *Hearings Before the Subcommittee on Health and Scientific Research of the Committee on Human Resources, United States Senate,* "Human Drug Testing by the CIA," 187.
2. Stratton, "Altered States of America," *Spin Magazine.*
3. Information on George White comes from letters, diaries, and interviews released by his wife after his death in 1973 to Foothills Junior College, Los Altos, California (now at Stanford University) and/or from what Ike Feldman disclosed in his 1994 interview with Richard Stratton. Sidney Gottlieb also discussed White's operating role in the safehouses during his testimony at the 1977 Subcommittee hearing.
4. Quoted in Lee and Shlain, *Acid Dreams,* 73.
5. "Deep Creek Memo."
6. Quoted in Lee and Shlain, *Acid Dreams,* 31.
7. Scott, "Family Blames CIA for Father's Death," A1.
8. Marks, *The Search for the Manchurian Candidate,* 85.
9. Starr and Ramsland, *A Voice for the Dead,* 107.
10. Colby, *Honorable Men,* 425.
11. Marks, *The Search for the Manchurian Candidate,* 88.
12. Edwards, "The Sphinx and the Spy."
13. *Foreign and Military Intelligence: Book 1, Final Report of the Select Subcommittee to Study Governmental Operation with Respect to Intelligence Activities* (Church Committee Drug Testing Report), 401.
14. Quoted in Stratton, "Altered States of America."
15. *Hearings Before the Subcommittee on Health and Scientific Research of the Committee on Human Resources, United States Senate,* "Human Drug Testing by the CIA," 100.
16. Ketchum, *Chemical Warfare,* 223–24. Additional information on Wayne Ritchie can be found in his legal complaint, accessible at law.justia.com.
17. Ritchie v. Ira Feldman.
18. See Wayne Ritchie's complaint on law.justia.com.
19. *Joint Hearing before the Select Committee on Intelligence and the Subcommittee on Health and Scientific Research of the Committee on Human Resources* ("Truth Drugs in Interrogation, Project MKULTRA, The CIA's Program of Research in Behavior Modification"), 32.

20. Lee and Shlain, *Acid Dreams,* 14.
21. *Testimony before the Presidential Advisory Committee on Human Radiation Experiments* (statement of Christine deNicola).
22. *Testimony before the Presidential Advisory Committee on Human Radiation Experiments* (statement of Claudia Mullen).
23. Ketchum, *Chemical Warfare,* 3.
24. Lee and Shlain, *Acid Dreams,* 36.
25. Quoted in Kobler, "The Dangerous Magic of LSD," 36.
26. Lee and Shlain, *Acid Dreams,* 37.
27. Cohen, *The Beyond Within,* 233.
28. Ketchum, *Chemical Warfare,* 44.
29. Quoted in Lee and Shlain, *Acid Dreams,* 41.
30. United States Congress House Committee on Foreign Affairs, *Chemical-Biological Warfare: US Policies and International Effects,* 60.
31. Furst, *Hallucinogens and Culture,* 60.
32. Quoted in Lee and Shlain, *Acid Dreams,* 39.
33. Lee and Shlain, *Acid Dreams,* 39–40.
34. Quoted in Marks, *The Search for the Manchurian Candidate,* 75.

9. THE WORLD WHERE EVERYTHING IS KNOWN: MARÍA SABINA'S GIFT

1. Estrada, *María Sabina,* 48.
2. Halifax, *Shamanic Voices,* 133.
3. Quoted in Estrada, *María Sabina,* 38.
4. Estrada, *María Sabina,* 39.
5. Estrada, *María Sabina,* 39.
6. Halifax, *Shamanic Voices,* 132.
7. Halifax, *Shamanic Voices,* 131.
8. Quoted in Halifax, *Shamanic Voices,* 131.
9. Estrada, *María Sabina,* 40.
10. Wasson and Wasson, *Mushrooms, Russia, and History, Vol II,* 289.
11. Quoted in Halifax, *Shamanic Voices,* 133.
12. Halifax, *Shamanic Voices,* 133.
13. Estrada, *María Sabina,* 47.
14. Quoted in Halifax, *Shamanic Voices,* 134.
15. Estrada, *María Sabina,* 48.
16. Estrada, *María Sabina,* 71.
17. Wasson, "Seeking the Magic Mushroom."
18. Wasson, "Seeking the Magic Mushroom."

19. Wasson, "Seeking the Magic Mushroom."

20. Estrada, *María Sabina*, 72.

21. Wasson, "The Sacred Mushroom," 10.

22. Letcher, *Shroom*, 193.

23. Quoted in Marks, *The Search for the Manchurian Candidate*, 117.

24. Quoted in Marks, *The Search for the Manchurian Candidate*, 118.

25. Wasson and Wasson, *Mushrooms, Russia, and History, Vol II*, 269.

26. Quoted in Marks, *The Search for the Manchurian Candidate*, 123.

27. Estrada, *María Sabina*, 73.

28. Quoted in Letcher, *Shroom*, 193.

29. Hofmann, *LSD: My Problem Child*, 126.

30. Isbell, "Comparison of the Reactions induced by Psilocybin and LSD-25 in Man," 7–8.

31. Isbell, "Comparison of the Reactions induced by Psilocybin and LSD-25 in Man," 9.

32. Estrada, *María Sabina*, 91.

33. Quoted in Letcher, *Shroom*, 98.

10. VOICES FROM BEHIND THE VEIL: ESP AND LSD

1. Hays, *The Selected Writings of Maurice O'Connor Drury*, 31.

2. Heywood, *ESP*, 63.

3. Heywood, *ESP*, 65.

4. Heywood, *ESP*, 65.

5. For "Voices from behind the Veil," see Heywood, *ESP*, 97; for "Orders," see, Heywood, *ESP*, 119 *ff*.

6. Heywood, *ESP*, 112.

7. Quoted in Heywood, *ESP*, 101.

8. Dilley, *Philosophical Interactions with Parapsychology*, xii.

9. Quoted in Huxley, *The Doors of Perception*, 22–23.

10. Quoted in Heywood, *ESP*, 125.

11. Heywood, *ESP*, 125.

12. Heywood, *ESP*, 113.

13. Heywood, *ESP*, 113–14.

14. Quoted in Heywood, *ESP*, 30.

15. Quoted in Heywood, *ESP*, 31.

16. Heywood, "Some Recent Mescaline Experiments," in Zaehner, *Mysticism*, 208.

17. Heywood, *ESP*, 203.

18. Heywood, "Some Recent Mescaline Experiments," in Zaehner, *Mysticism*, 209.

19. Heywood, "Some Recent Mescaline Experiments," in Zaehner, *Mysticism*, 209.

20. Heywood, *ESP,* 208.

21. Heywood, "Some Recent Mescaline Experiments," in Zaehner, *Mysticism,* 210.

22. Heywood, *ESP,* 209.

23. Heywood, *ESP,* 210.

24. Heywood, *ESP,* 210.

25. Heywood, *ESP,* 211.

26. Heywood, *ESP,* 211.

27. Heywood, "Some Recent Mescaline Experiments," in Zaehner, *Mysticism,* 209.

11. TO SOAR ANGELIC: BIRTH OF THE PSYCHEDELIC RENAISSANCE

1. Horowitz and Palmer, *Moksha,* 9.

2. Horowitz and Palmer, *Moksha,* 3.

3. Lewin, *Phantastica,* 112.

4. Huxley, *The Doors of Perception,* 72.

5. Smith, *Letters of Aldous Huxley,* 389.

6. Quoted in Horowitz and Palmer, *Moksha,* 33.

7. Horowitz and Palmer, *Moksha,* 34.

8. Quoted in Horowitz and Palmer, *Moksha,* 32–33.

9. Horowitz and Palmer, *Moksha,* 31.

10. Stevens, *Storming Heaven,* 44.

11. Quoted in Berg and Freeman, *Conversations with Christopher Isherwood,* 95.

12. Horowitz and Palmer, *Moksha,* 36.

13. Huxley, *The Doors of Perception,* 15.

14. Huxley, *The Doors of Perception,* 18.

15. Huxley, *The Doors of Perception,* 30.

16. Huxley, *The Doors of Perception,* 19, 21.

17. Huxley, *The Doors of Perception,* 17.

18. Huxley, *The Doors of Perception,* 57.

19. Quoted in Huxley, *The Doors of Perception,* 57.

20. Huxley, *The Doors of Perception,* 60.

21. Dunaway, *Aldous Huxley Recollected: An Oral History,* 97.

22. Smith, *Letters of Aldous Huxley,* 676–77.

23. Bedford, *Aldous Huxley: A Biography,* 529–30.

24. Quoted in Horowitz and Palmer, *Moksha,* 42.

25. Quoted in Katz, "Dr. Osmond's New Deal for the Insane," 11.

26. Katz, "My Twelve Hours as a Madman," 69.

27. Katz, "My Twelve Hours as a Madman," 70.
28. Smith, *Letters of Aldous Huxley,* 679.
29. Smith, *Letters of Aldous Huxley,* 679.
30. Smith, *Letters of Aldous Huxley,* 681.
31. Huxley, *The Devils of Loudun,* 322.
32. Huxley, *The Devils of Loudun,* 326.
33. Huxley, *The Devils of Loudun,* 324.
34. Horowitz and Palmer, *Moksha,* 22.
35. Huxley, "Mescaline and the 'Other World,'" 46–47.
36. Becker, "Psychopathologie der Lysergsäurediathylamidwirkung," 1.
37. Quoted in Rinkel, "Experimentally Induced Psychosis in Man," 240.
38. Smith, *Letters of Aldous Huxley,* 729.
39. Osmond, "A Review of the Clinical Effects of Psychotomimetic Agents," 429.
40. Horowitz and Palmer, *Moksha,* 107.
41. Callahan, *A Love Supreme,* 18.
42. Horowitz and Palmer, *Moksha,* 107.
43. Horowitz and Palmer, *Moksha,* 107.

12. THE VITALIST HERETIC: CRITICS OF CHEMICAL MYSTICISM

1. Watts, "Psychedelics and Religious Experience," *California Law Review,* 74.
2. Zaehner, "The Author's Experience with Mescaline," in *Mysticism,* 212.
3. Hoch, Cattell, and Pennes, "Effects of Mescaline and Lysergic Acid (d-LSD-25)," 580.
4. Zaehner, *Mysticism,* 213.
5. Zaehner, *Mysticism,* 213.
6. Zaehner, *Mysticism,* 214–15.
7. Zaehner, *Mysticism,* 216.
8. Zaehner, *Mysticism,* 216-17.
9. Zaehner, *Mysticism,* 218.
10. Zaehner, *Mysticism,* 219.
11. Zaehner, *Mysticism,* 225.
12. Zaehner, *Mysticism,* 226.
13. Horowitz and Palmer, *Moksha,* 55.
14. Smith, *Letters of Aldous Huxley,* 715.
15. Mann, *Letters of Thomas Mann 1889–1955,* 463–64.
16. Quoted in Watt, *Aldous Huxley,* 28.
17. Smith, *Letters of Aldous Huxley,* 703.

18. Horowitz and Palmer, *Moksha,* 55.

19. Katz, "My Twelve Hours as a Madman," 69.

20. Zaehner, *Our Savage God.*

21. Zaehner, *Mysticism,* 15.

22. Zaehner, *Zen, Drugs, and Mysticism,* 46–47.

23. Zaehner, *Mysticism,* 15.

24. Quoted in Zaehner, *Zen, Drugs, and Mysticism,* 42.

25. Quoted in James, *The Varieties of Religious Experience,* 329.

26. Huxley, *The Doors of Perception,* 34.

27. Zaehner, *Mysticism,* 22.

28. Zaehner, *Zen, Drugs, and Mysticism,* 44.

29. Zaehner, *Mysticism,* 26.

30. Zaehner, *Mysticism,* 24.

31. T. Huxley, *On the Physical Basis of Life,* 16.

32. Shermer, *The Believing Brain,* 112.

33. Zaehner, *Zen, Drugs, and Mysticism,* 43.

34. Sexton, *Selected Letters of Aldous Huxley,* 477.

35. Quoted in Ulanov, "Jung and Prayer," 91.

36. Bennett, *Liber 420,* 49–52.

13. ALTAR AT THE CENTER OF THE UNIVERSE: PSYCHEDELICS AS SACRED MEDICINE

1. Quoted in Puharich, *The Sacred Mushroom,* 9–10.

2. Jacobson, *Phenomena,* 23.

3. Puharich, *The Sacred Mushroom,* 14–15.

4. Smith, *Letters of Aldous Huxley,* 738.

5. Bedford, *Aldous Huxley,* 548.

6. Smith, *Letters of Aldous Huxley,* 693.

7. Horowitz and Palmer, *Moksha,* 58.

8. Horowitz and Palmer, *Moksha,* 59.

9. Huxley, "Mescaline and the 'Other World,'" 47–49.

10. Horowitz and Palmer, *Moksha,* 60.

11. Huxley, *The Doors of Perception,* 73.

12. Quoted in Ebin, *The Drug Experience,* 297.

13. Ebin, *The Drug Experience,* 296–97.

14. Ebin, *The Drug Experience,* 294.

15. Ebin, *The Drug Experience,* 299.

16. Quoted in Ebin, *The Drug Experience,* 300.

17. Jacobson, *Phenomena,* 30.

18. Smith, *Letters of Aldous Huxley,* 761.

19. Puharich, *The Sacred Mushroom,* 118.

20. Smith, *Letters of Aldous Huxley,* 810.

21. Huxley, *The Doors of Perception,* 154.

22. Katz, "Dr. Osmond's New Deal for the Insane," 10.

23. Smith, *Letters of Aldous Huxley,* 718.

24. Osmond, "Peyote Night," 70.

25. Smith, *Letters of Aldous Huxley,* 806.

26. Aaronson and Osmond, *Psychedelics,* 78.

27. Quoted in Aaronson and Osmond, *Psychedelics,* 72–73.

28. Aaronson and Osmond, *Psychedelics,* 75.

29. Aaronson and Osmond, *Psychedelics,* 80-81.

30. Aaronson and Osmond, *Psychedelics,* 82.

31. See Cohn, *Europe's Inner Demons.*

32. Aaronson and Osmond, *Psychedelics,* 68.

33. Katz, "Dr. Osmond's New Deal for the Insane," 11.

34. Katz, "Dr. Osmond's New Deal for the Insane," 11.

35. Katz, "Dr. Osmond's New Deal for the Insane," 11.

36. Katz, "Dr. Osmond's New Deal for the Insane," 41.

37. Cohen, "Lysergic Acid Diethylamide: Side Effects and Complications," 35.

14. SCOUNDRELS AND EXPLORERS: ETERNITY IN AN HOUR

1. Heard, "Can This Drug Enlarge Man's Mind?" 3.

2. Smith, *Letters of Aldous Huxley,* 347.

3. Toy, "The Conservative Connection," 67.

4. Higham, "Isherwood on Hollywood," 47.

5. Reid, "The Possessed," 209–10.

6. Smith, *Letters of Aldous Huxley,* 735.

7. Smith, *Letters of Aldous Huxley,* 717.

8. Quoted from the short film, William Whitley et al., "Focus on Sanity" (Los Angeles, Calif., 1957).

9. Quoted in Novak, "LSD before Leary," 93.

10. Smith, *Letters of Aldous Huxley,* 322.

11. Smith, *Letters of Aldous Huxley,* 684.

12. Eisner, *Remembrances of LSD Therapy Past,* 9.

13. Federal Bureau of Investigation/Privacy Acts Release, "Subject: 'Michael' M. Hubbard."

14. Federal Bureau of Investigation/Privacy Acts Release, "Subject: 'Michael' M. Hubbard," 6.

15. Lee and Shlain, *Acid Dreams*, 44–45.

16. Quoted in Lee and Shlain, *Acid Dreams*, 45.

17. Federal Bureau of Investigation/Privacy Acts Release, "Subject: 'Michael' M. Hubbard," 12.

18. Quoted in Adams, "Psychosis," 83.

19. Herb Museum, "History of Sandoz Pharmaceuticals."

20. Horowitz and Palmer, *Moksha*, 69.

21. Horowitz and Palmer, *Moksha*, 69.

22. Smith, *Letters of Aldous Huxley*, 720.

23. MacLean et al., "The Use of LSD-25 in the Treatment of Alcoholism and Other Psychiatric Problems," 42.

24. Smith, *Letters of Aldous Huxley*, 720.

25. Smith, *Letters of Aldous Huxley*, 799.

26. Smith, *Letters of Aldous Huxley*, 735.

27. Smith, *Letters of Aldous Huxley*, 737.

28. Stevens, *Storming Heaven*, 51.

29. Smith, *Letters of Aldous Huxley*, 863.

30. Horowitz and Palmer, *Moksha*, 69.

31. Horowitz and Palmer, *Moksha*, 68.

32. Heard, "Can This Drug Enlarge Man's Mind?" 3–4.

33. Horowitz and Palmer, *Moksha*, 86–87.

34. Stolaroff, *Thanatos to Eros*, 21.

35. Heard, *The Five Ages of Man*, 236. For Hecate-worshipers use of *leucophyllus*, compare with Plutarch's *Moralia*, 483.

36. Heard, *The Five Ages of Man*, 244.

37. Heard, *The Five Ages of Man*, 238-39.

38. Stolaroff, "How Much Can People Change," 55.

39. Quoted in Stevens, *Storming Heaven*, 70.

40. Eisner, *Remembrances of LSD Therapy Past*, 10.

41. Stolaroff, "How Much Can People Change," 58.

42. Stolaroff, *Thanatos to Eros*, 122.

43. Stolaroff, *Thanatos to Eros*, 23.

44. Stolaroff, *Thanatos to Eros*, 24.

45. Stolaroff, "How Much Can People Change," 58.

46. Quoted in Stevens, *Storming Heaven*, 71.

47. Stolaroff, *Thanatos to Eros*, 141.

48. Stolaroff, *Thanatos to Eros*, 122.

49. Stolaroff, *Thanatos to Eros,* 119.

50. Stolaroff, *Thanatos to Eros,* 121.

51. Savage and Stolaroff, "Clarifying the Confusion Regarding LSD-25," 218, 220.

52. Blewett and Chwelos, *The Handbook for the Therapeutic Use of Lysergic Acid Diethylamide-25,* 8, 21, 37.

53. Stolaroff, *Thanatos to Eros,* 121.

54. Quoted in Savage, "LSD, Alcoholism, and Transcendence."

55. Kobler, "The Dangerous Magic of LSD," 39.

56. Littlefield, *Hofmann's Potion* (documentary).

57. Kurtz, *Not-God,* 136.

58. Quoted in *Pass It On,* 369.

59. Chwelos et al., "Use of d-Lysergic Acid Diethylamide in the Treatment of Alcoholism," 577.

60. *Pass It On,* 369.

61. Quoted in Dyck, "Flashback," 385.

62. Quoted in Stevens, *Storming Heaven,* 86.

63. Quoted in Kobler, "The Dangerous Magic of LSD," 39.

15. SOMETHING DIFFERENT THAN MADNESS: HOLLYWOOD, POPULAR MEDIA, AND LSD

1. Cohen, *The Beyond Within,* 107–8.

2. Cohen, *The Beyond Within,* 110.

3. Eisner, *Remembrances of LSD Therapy Past,* 13.

4. Novak, "LSD before Leary," 89.

5. Cohen, *The Beyond Within,* 84.

6. Cohen, "Lysergic Acid Diethylamide," 32.

7. Cohen, "Lysergic Acid Diethylamide," 33.

8. Stevens, *Storming Heaven,* 64.

9. Quoted in "Betsy Drake Was an Actress, LSD Advocate, Shipwreck Survivor, Novelist and Cary Grant's Third Wife," *National Post.*

10. Unger, "Mescaline, LSD, Psilocybin, and Personality Change."

11. Chandler and Hartman, "Lysergic Acid Diethylamide (LSD-25) as a Facilitating Agent in Psychotherapy," 286.

12. Smith, *Letters of Aldous Huxley,* 881.

13. Balaban and Beauchamp, "Cary in the Sky with Diamonds," 173.

14. Chandler and Hartman, "Lysergic Acid Diethylamide (LSD-25) as a Facilitating Agent in Psychotherapy," 293.

15. Quoted in Balaban and Beauchamp, "Cary in the Sky with Diamonds," 174.

16. Freidan, *The Feminine Mystique*, 57 *ff.*
17. Friedan, *The Feminine Mystique*, 422.
18. McCann, *Cary Grant*, 174.
19. Quoted in McCann, *Cary Grant*, 174–75.
20. Stevens, *Storming Heaven*, 65.
21. Quoted in Novak, "LSD before Leary," 103.
22. MacDougal, *Five Easy Decades*, 44.
23. McGilligan, *Jack's Life*, 142.
24. MacDougal, *Five Easy Decades*, 45.
25. Quoted in McGilligan, *Jack's Life*, 141.
26. McGilligan, *Jack's Life*, 143.
27. For the latest perpetuator of the "LSD changed Cary Grant" myth, see Pollan, *How to Change Your Mind*, 157.
28. Quoted in McCann, *Cary Grant*, 176.
29. Quoted in Eliot, *Cary Grant*, 357–58.
30. Siff, "Glory Visions," 147.
31. Quoted in Brinkley, *The Publisher*, 433.
32. Quoted in Brinkley, *The Publisher*, 434.
33. Quoted in Herzstein, *Henry R. Luce, Time, and the American Crusade in Asia*, 240. See also Lee and Shlain, *Acid Dreams*, 71; Stevens, *Storming Heaven*, 72.
34. Herzstein, *Henry R. Luce, Time, and the American Crusade in Asia*, 240.
35. Quoted in Siff, "Glory Visions," 147.
36. Morris, *Rage for Fame*, 79–80.
37. Osborne, *American Catholics and the Church of Tomorrow*, 140.
38. Osborne, *American Catholics and the Church of Tomorrow*, 138.
39. Morris, *Price of Fame*, 517.
40. Quoted in Brinkley, *The Publisher*, 433.
41. Smith, *Letters of Aldous Huxley*, 889.
42. Siff, "Glory Visions," 155.
43. Quoted in Balaban and Beauchamp, "Cary in the Sky with Diamonds," 173.
44. Quoted in Siff, "Glory Visions," 149.
45. Barber, "Public Enemy Number One."
46. Quoted in Morris, *Price of Fame*, 571.

16. THE MADONNA AND THE GINGERBREAD MAN: LSD, PSYCHOTHERAPY, AND ALCOHOLICS ANONYMOUS

1. Eisner, "The Birth and Death of Psychedelic Therapy," 91.
2. Eisner, *Remembrances of LSD Therapy Past,* 5.
3. Abramson, "Introductory Remarks," 11.
4. Eisner, *Remembrances of LSD Therapy Past,* 7.
5. Eisner, "The Birth and Death of Psychedelic Therapy," 92.
6. Eisner, *Remembrances of LSD Therapy Past,* 4.
7. Eisner, *Remembrances of LSD Therapy Past,* 15.
8. Eisner, *Remembrances of LSD Therapy Past,* 17–18.
9. Caldwell, *LSD Psychotherapy,* 116.
10. Eisner, "The Birth and Death of Psychedelic Therapy," 92.
11. Eisner, *Remembrances of LSD Therapy Past,* 15.
12. Caldwell, *LSD Psychotherapy,* 76.
13. Eisner, "The Influence of LSD on Unconscious Activity," 143.
14. Quoted in Pittman, *The Roots of Alcoholics Anonymous,* 153.
15. Moore, *Alcoholics Anonymous and the Rockefeller Connection,* 72.
16. Markel, "An Alcoholic's Savior."
17. Quoted in Moore, *Alcoholics Anonymous and the Rockefeller Connection,* 73.
18. Moore, *Alcoholics Anonymous and the Rockefeller Connection,* 72.
19. Quoted in Pittman, *The Roots of Alcoholics Anonymous,* 153.
20. Quoted in Pittman, *The Roots of Alcoholics Anonymous,* 153.
21. Eisner, "The Birth and Death of Psychedelic Therapy," 94.
22. Quoted in *Pass It On,* 370.
23. Eisner, "The Birth and Death of Psychedelic Therapy," 94.
24. Quoted in Cheever, *My Name Is Bill,* 241.
25. Quoted in Hill, "LSD Could Help Alcoholics Stop Drinking, AA Founder Believed."
26. Quoted in Kurtz, *Not-God,* 137.
27. Quoted in *Pass It On,* 375.
28. Quoted in *Pass It On,* 372.
29. *Pass It On,* 371.
30. MacLean et al., "The Use of LSD-25 in the Treatment of Alcoholism and Other Psychiatric Problems," 35.
31. MacLean et al., "The Use of LSD-25 in the Treatment of Alcoholism and Other Psychiatric Problems," 36.
32. MacLean et al., "The Use of LSD-25 in the Treatment of Alcoholism and Other Psychiatric Problems," 42.

33. Eisner, *Remembrances of LSD Therapy Past,* 4.
34. Eisner and Cohen, "Psychotherapy with Lysergic Acid Diethylamide," 529.
35. Eisner, "Observations on Possible Order within the Unconscious," 439.
36. Eisner, "The Birth and Death of Psychedelic Therapy," 95–96.
37. Eisner, "Observations on Possible Order within the Unconscious," 440.
38. Eisner, "Observations on Possible Order within the Unconscious," 439.
39. Eisner, "Observations on Possible Order within the Unconscious," 441.
40. Eisner and Cohen, "Psychotherapy with Lysergic Acid Diethylamide," 529.
41. Eisner and Cohen, "Psychotherapy with Lysergic Acid Diethylamide," 531.
42. Eisner, *Remembrances of LSD Therapy Past,* 116.
43. Smith, *Letters of Aldous Huxley,* 714.
44. Eisner, "The Birth and Death of Psychedelic Therapy," 93.
45. Hofmann, *LSD: My Problem Child,* 75.

17. AN INTELLECTUAL, FUN DRUG: A STRANGE FRATERNITY

1. Watts, *In My Own Way,* 323.
2. Cohen and Ditman, "Prolonged Adverse Reactions to Lysergic Acid Diethylamide," 478.
3. Cohen and Ditman, "Prolonged Adverse Reactions to Lysergic Acid Diethylamide," 479.
4. Ditman, Hayman, and Whittlesey, "Nature and Frequency of Claims Following LSD," 346.
5. Ditman, Hayman, and Whittlesey, "Nature and Frequency of Claims Following LSD," 352.
6. Ditman, Hayman, and Whittlesey, "Nature and Frequency of Claims Following LSD," 349–50.
7. Ditman, Hayman, and Whittlesey, "Nature and Frequency of Claims Following LSD," 351.
8. Ditman, Hayman, and Whittlesey, "Nature and Frequency of Claims Following LSD," 347–48.
9. Smith, *Letters of Aldous Huxley,* 481.
10. Watts, *In My Own Way,* 174–75.
11. Watts, "Psychedelics and Religious Experience," 75.
12. Watts, *In My Own Way,* 324.
13. Watts, *In My Own Way,* 324.
14. Watts, "Psychedelics and Religious Experience," 76.
15. Watts, "Psychedelics and Religious Experience," 76 *ff.*
16. Quoted in Janiger, "Psychiatric Alchemy."

17. Dobkin de Rios and Janiger, *LSD,* 15.

18. Gilliam, "Zale Parry: First Lady of Diving."

19. Quoted in Leary, *Flashbacks,* 132.

20. Stevens, *Storming Heaven,* 60.

21. Dobkin de Rios and Janiger, *LSD,* 16.

22. Janiger, "Personal Statement by Oscar Janiger," 5.

23. Dobkin de Rios and Janiger, *LSD,* 16.

24. Dobkin de Rios and Janiger, *LSD,* 2.

25. Quoted in Dobkin de Rios and Janiger, *LSD,* 70.

26. Quoted in Dobkin de Rios and Janiger, *LSD,* 56.

27. Janiger, "The Use of Hallucinogenic Agents in Psychiatry," 253.

28. Cohen, "Lysergic Acid Diethylamide: Side Effects and Complications," 34.

29. Quoted in Letcher, *Shroom,* 190–91.

30. Letcher, *Shroom,* 187.

31. Rinkel, "Experimentally Induced Psychosis in Man," 255.

32. Rinkel, "Experimentally Induced Psychosis in Man," 244.

33. Rinkel, "Experimentally Induced Psychosis in Man," 252–53.

34. Quoted in Rinkel, "Experimentally Induced Psychosis in Man," 256–57.

35. Tonini and Montanari, "Effects of Experimentally Induced Psychosis on Artistic Expression," 225–39.

36. Janiger, "Psychiatric Alchemy."

37. Quoted in Novak, "LSD before Leary," 98–99.

38. Janiger, "Psychiatric Alchemy."

39. Dobkin de Rios and Janiger, *LSD,* 22.

40. Quoted in Dobkin de Rios and Janiger, *LSD,* 22.

41. Quoted in Hackman, *The Los Angeles Art Scene of the Sixties,* 34.

42. Nin, *The Diary of Anaïs Nin, Vol. 5,* 255.

43. Hackman, *The Los Angeles Art Scene of the Sixties,* 34.

44. Nin, *The Diary of Anaïs Nin, Vol. 5,* 255.

45. Nin, *The Diary of Anaïs Nin, Vol. 5,* 256.

46. Nin, *The Diary of Anaïs Nin, Vol. 6,* 3.

47. Nin, *The Diary of Anaïs Nin, Vol. 5,* 256.

48. Nin, *The Diary of Anaïs Nin, Vol. 5,* 257.

49. Quoted in Nin, *The Diary of Anaïs Nin, Vol. 5,* 257.

50. Nin, *The Diary of Anaïs Nin, Vol. 5,* 258.

51. Dobkin de Rios and Janiger, *LSD,* 16.

52. Quoted in Lee and Shlain, *Acid Dreams,* 50.

53. Smith, *Letters of Aldous Huxley,* 862.

54. Quoted in Eisner, *Remembrances of LSD Therapy Past,* 11.

55. Smith, *Letters of Aldous Huxley*, 843.

56. Dobkin de Rios and Janiger, *LSD*, 24.

57. Dobkin de Rios and Janiger, *LSD*, 16.

58. Lee and Shlain, *Acid Dreams*, 51.

59. Watts, "Psychedelics and Religious Experience," 75.

60. Quoted in Novak, "LSD before Leary," 99.

61. Janiger, "Personal Statement by Oscar Janiger." 6.

62. Quoted in Leary, *Flashbacks*, 132.

63. Janiger, "The Use of Hallucinogenic Agents in Psychiatry," 258.

64. Janiger, "The Use of Hallucinogenic Agents in Psychiatry," 256.

65. Quoted in Novak, "LSD before Leary," 99.

66. Eisner, "The Birth and Death of Psychedelic Therapy," 93.

67. Quoted in Stevens, *Storming Heaven*, 143.

18. THE FALL:
THE TRAGEDY OF TIMOTHY LEARY

1. Leary, *High Priest*, 12.

2. Leary, *Flashbacks*, 29.

3. Leary, *Flashbacks*, 30.

4. Stevens, *Storming Heaven*, 20.

5. Leary, *High Priest*, 62.

6. Leary, *High Priest*, 15.

7. Leary, *Flashbacks*, 30.

8. Quoted in Leary, *High Priest*, 16.

9. Leary, *High Priest*, 19.

10. Leary, *High Priest*, 17–18.

11. Leary, *High Priest*, 18.

12. Leary, *High Priest*, 13.

13. Leary, *Flashbacks*, 37.

14. Leary, *Flashbacks*, 38.

15. Leary, *High Priest*, 68.

16. Quoted in Leary, *Flashbacks*, 43.

17. Leary, *Flashbacks*, 44.

18. Leary, *High Priest*, 63–4.

19. Metzner, "Initial Experiences from the Harvard Psilocybin Project," 179.

20. Metzner, "Initial Experiences from the Harvard Psilocybin Project,"186.

21. Leary, *High Priest*, 182.

22. Quoted in Kobler, "The Dangerous Magic of LSD," 34.

23. Leary, *High Priest,* 11–12.
24. Doblin, "Dr. Leary's Concord Prison Experiment."; Doblin, "Pahnke's 'Good Friday Experiment.'"
25. Doblin, "Pahnke's 'Good Friday Experiment," 12.
26. Leary, *Flashbacks,* 117.
27. Leary, *Flashbacks,* 117.
28. Leary, *Flashbacks,* 118.
29. Leary, *Flashbacks,* 118.
30. Leary, *Flashbacks,* 120.
31. Stevens, *Storming Heaven,* 132–33.
32. Stevens, *Storming Heaven,* 189.
33. Huxley, *Island,* 173.
34. Huxley, *Island,* 173.
35. Stevens, *Storming Heaven,* 192.
36. Leary, *Flashbacks,* 143.
37. Quoted in Stevens, *Storming Heaven,* 194.
38. Stevens, *Storming Heaven,* 201.
39. Timothy Leary, *The Politics of Ecstasy,* 55.
40. Stevens, *Storming Heaven,* 214.
41. Leary, *Flashbacks,* 190.
42. Stevens, *Storming Heaven,* 261.
43. Mannes, "The Raid on Castalia."
44. Di Prima, "The Holidays at Millbrook—1966," 345.
45. Di Prima, "The Holidays at Millbrook—1966," 344.
46. Leary, *Flashbacks,* 197.
47. Leary, *Flashbacks,* 198.
48. Leary, *The Politics of Psychopharmacology,* 37–38.
49. Quoted in Stevens, *Storming Heaven,* 171.
50. Eisner, "The Birth and Death of Psychedelic Therapy," 97.
51. Stevens, *Storming Heaven,* 274.
52. Luce, "LSD."
53. Lerner, "Leary Gets 30 Years," in *The Harvard Crimson.*
54. Quoted in Stevens, *Storming Heaven,* 269.
55. "On and Off," *Newsweek.*
56. FDA Food, Drug, and Cosmetic Act of 1938, Pub. L. 215, 649.
57. FDA Food, Drug, and Cosmetic Act of 1938, Pub. L. 89–74, 227.
58. "Control Law Set on LSD," *Desert Sun,* May 31, 1966, 1.
59. U.S. Department of Justice, "Drug Scheduling."

60. Roberts, "Leary Goes to Prison on Coast to Start Term of 1 to 10 Years," *New York Times,* March 20, 1977, 27.

61. Quoted in Zaehner, *Zen, Drugs, and Mysticism,* 85.

19. A FAR-GONE CONCLUSION:
RESURRECTING THE RENAISSANCE

1. Huxley, *The Doors of Perception,* 36.

2. Quoted in Marks, *The Search for the Manchurian Candidate,* 74.

3. Quoted in Marks, *The Search for the Manchurian Candidate,* 75.

4. Quoted in Klee, "Lysergic Acid Diethylamide and Ego Functions," 463.

5. Cambridge City, Massachusetts Policy Order 2021 #24 (February 3, 2021).

6. Horowitz and Palmer, *Moksha,* 149.

7. Letcher, *Shroom,* 157.

8. Bloom, *The Closing,* 314.

9. Hatsis, *The Witches' Ointment,* 139–51.

Bibliography

Aaronson, Bernard, and Humphry Osmond, eds. *Psychedelics: The Uses and Implications of Hallucinogenic Drugs*. New York: Anchor Books, 1970.

Abramson, Harold, ed. "Introductory Remarks." In *The Use of LSD in Psychotherapy: Transactions of the First Conference, April 22–24, 1959*. Josiah Macy Jr. Foundation, 1960.

———. "Lysergic acid diethylamide (LSD-25): III As An Adjunct to Psychotherapy with Elimination of Fear of Homosexuality," *Journal of Psychology*, no. 39 (1955): 127.

———, ed. *Neuropharmacology*. Madison, New Jersey: Madison Printing Company, 1956.

———, ed. *The Use of LSD in Psychotherapy and Alcoholism*. New York: The Bobbs-Merrill Company, 1967.

Adams, Joe K. "Psychosis: 'Experimental' and Real.'" In *The Psychedelic Reader*, edited by Timothy Leary, Ralph Metzner, and Gunther Weil, 65–88. Seacaucus, N.J.: Carol Publishing, 1965.

Alm, Torbjørn. "The Witch Trials of Finnmark, Northern Norway, During the 17th Century: Evidence for Ergotism as a Contributing Factor." *Economic Botany* 57, no. 3 (2003): 403–16.

American Medical Association, Judicial Council. "Supplementary Report of the Judicial Council." *Journal of the American Medical Association* (1946).

Atomic Energy Commission for Biology and Medicine, transcripts of meeting, 10 November 1950; accessed via the DOE Roadmap: Human Radiation Experiments Department of Energy Roadmap to the Story and Records website https://ehss.energy.gov/ohre/roadmap.

Bache, Chris. *LSD and the Mind of the Universe: Diamonds from Heaven*. Rochester, Vt.: Park Street Press, 2019.

Balaban, Judy, and Cari Beauchamp. "Cary in the Sky with Diamonds." *Vanity Fair*, August 2010, 142–48.

Ball, E.R. "The Nursing and Care of Mentally-Ill Patients Under d-Lysergic Acid Diethylamide." *Nursing Mirror* 100 (1955): 1531–32.

Barber, Chris. "Public Enemy Number One: A Pragmatic Approach to America's Drug Problem." June 29, 2016. Accessed via the Richard Nixon Foundation website.

Becker, A.M. "Psychopathologie der Lysergsäurediathylamidwirkung." *Wien. Z. Nervenhk. & Grenzgb* 2, 402 (1949).

Bedford, Sybille. *Aldous Huxley: A Biography*. New York: Carroll and Graf Publishers, 1985.

Belford Ulanov, Ann. "Jung and Prayer." In *Jung and Monotheisms: Judaism, Christianity, and Islam*, edited by Joel Ryce Menuhin, 91–110. Abingdon, United Kingdom: Routledge, 1994.

Bennett, Chris. *Liber 420: Cannabis, Magickal Herbs, and the Occult*. Oregon: Trine Day LLC, 2018.

Berg, James L., and Chris Freeman, eds. *Conversations with Christopher Isherwood*. Jackson, Miss.: University Press of Mississippi, 2001.

"Betsy Drake Was an Actress, LSD Advocate, Shipwreck Survivor, Novelist and Cary Grant's Third Wife." *National Post,* November 17, 2015. Accessible online.

Blewett, Duncan and N. Chwelos. *The Handbook for the Therapeutic Use of Lysergic Acid Diethylamide-25: Individual and Group Procedures*. 1959. Available on the MAPS website.

Bloom, Allan. *The Closing of the American Mind*. New York: Simon and Schuster, 1987.

Brinkley, Alan. *The Publisher: Henry Luce and His American Century*. New York: Vintage Books, 2011.

Busch, A.K., and W. C. Johnson. "LSD as an Aid in Psychotherapy." *Diseases of the Nervous System* 11, no. 241 (1950): 241–43.

Caldwell, W.V. *LSD Psychotherapy: An Exploration of Psychedelic and Psycholytic Therapy*. New York: Grove Press, 1969.

Callahan, Allen Dwight. *A Love Supreme: A History of Johnnie Tradition*. Minneapolis, Minn.: Augsburg Fortress, 2005.

Caporael, Linnda, "Ergotism: The Satan Loosed in Salem?" *Science* 192, no. 4234 (April 2, 1976): 21–26.

Chandler, Arthur, and Mortimer Hartman. "Lysergic Acid Diethylamide (LSD-25) as a Facilitating Agent in Psychotherapy." *Archives of General Psychiatry* 2 (March 1960): 286–99.

Cheever, Susan. *My Name Is Bill: Bill Wilson and the Creation of Alcoholics Anonymous*. New York: Simon and Schuster, 2004.

Cholden, Louis, Albert Kurland, and Charles Savage. "Clinical Reactions and Tolerance to LSD in Chronic Schizophrenia." *Journal of Nervous and Mental Disease* 122, no. 3 (September 1955): 211–21.

Chwelos, N., Duncan B. Blewett, C. M. Smith, and Abram Hoffer. "Use of d-Lysergic Acid Diethylamide in the Treatment of Alcoholism." *Quarterly Journal of the Study of Alcohol* 20 (1959): 577–90.

"Cinema: The New Pictures," *Time Magazine* 38, no. 9 (September 1, 1941).

Cohen, Sidney. *The Beyond Within: The L.S.D Story.* New York: Atheneum, 1972.

———. "Lysergic Acid Diethylamide: Side Effects and Complications." *Journal of Nervous and Mental Disease* 30, no. 1 (January, 1960): 30–39.

Cohen, Sidney, and Keith Ditman. "Prolonged Adverse Reactions to Lysergic Acid Diethylamide." *Archives of General Psychiatry* 8 (May 1963): 475–80.

Cohn, Norman. *Europe's Inner Demons: The Demonization of Christians in Medieval Europe.* Chicago: University of Chicago Press, 2000.

Colby, William. *Honorable Men: My Life in the CIA.* New York: Simon and Shuster, 1978.

Collins, Anne. *In the Sleep Room: The Story of the CIA Brain Washing Experiments in Canada.* Toronto: Key Porter Books, 1989.

Condrau, Gion. "Klinische Erfahrungen an Geisteskranken mit Lyserg-saure-diathylamid." *Digest Neurology & Psychiatry* 18, no. 149: 9–32.

"Control Law Set on LSD." *Desert Sun* 39, no. 256 (May 31, 1966).

Courtwright, David T. *Dark Paradise: A History of Opiate Addiction in America.* Cambridge, Mass.: Harvard University Press, 2001.

Croce, Paul Jerome. "Physiology as the Antechamber: The Young William James's Hope for a Philosophical Psychology." *History of Psychology* 2, no. 4 (November 1999): 302–23.

Cutner, Margot. "Analytic Work with LSD 25." *Psychiatric Quarterly* 33, no. 4 (December 1959): 715–57.

Davenport-Hines, Richard. *The Pursuit of Oblivion: A Global History of Narcotics.* New York: W. W. Norton and Co., 2002.

Day, Juliana. "The Role and Reaction of the Psychiatrist in LSD Therapy." *Journal of Nervous and Mental Diseases* 125, no. 1 (Jan–March 1957): 437–38.

"Deep Creek Memo." November 18, 1953. Accessible at frankolsonproject.org.

De Quincey, Thomas. *Confessions of an English Opium Eater and Other Writings.* Ontario: Broadview Editions, 2009. Edited by Joe Faflak. First published in 1821.

Dilley, Frank B. *Philosophical Interactions with Parapsychology: The Major Writings of H. H. Price on Parapsychology and Survival.* New York: St. Martin's Press, 1995.

di Prima, Diane. "The Holidays at Millbrook—1966." In *The Portable Sixties Reader,* edited by Ann Charters. New York: Penguin Putnam, 2003.

Ditman, Keith, Max Hayman, and John Whittlesey. "Nature and Frequency of Claims Following LSD." *Journal of Nervous and Mental Disease* 134, no. 4 (1962): 346–52.

Dobkin de Rios, Marlene, and Oscar Janiger. *LSD: Spirituality and the Creative Process.* Rochester, Vt: Park Street Press, 2003.

Doblin, Rick. "Dr. Leary's Concord Prison Experiment: A 34-Year Follow-Up Study." *Bulletin of the Multidisciplinary Association of Psychedelic Studies* 9 (1999–2000): 10–18.

———. "Pahnke's 'Good Friday Experiment': A Long-Term Follow-up and Methodological Critique." *Journal of Transpersonal Psychology* 23, no. 1 (1991): 1–28.

Dunaway, David K. *Aldous Huxley Recollected: An Oral History.* Lanham, Md.: AltaMira Press, 1998.

Dyck, Erika. "Flashback: Psychiatric Experimentation with LSD in Historical Perspective." *Canadian Journal of Psychiatry* 50, no. 7 (June 2005): 381–87.

Ebin, David, ed. *The Drug Experience.* NY: Grove Press, 1965.

Edwards, Michael. "The Sphinx and the Spy: The Clandestine World of John Mulholland." *Genii, The Conjuror's Magazine,* April 2001. Accessible on the Frank Olson Project website.

Eisner, Betty. "The Birth and Death of Psychedelic Therapy." In *Higher Wisdom: Eminent Elders Explore the Continuing Impact of Psychedelics,* edited by Roger Walsh and Charles Grob. Albany: State University of New York Press, 2005.

———. "The Influence of LSD on Unconscious Activity." In *Hallucinogenic Drugs and Their Psychotherapeutic Use,* edited by Richard Wilfred Crocket, Ronald Sandison, and Alexander Walk, 141–44. London: H. K. Lewis eds. 1963.

———. "Observations on Possible Order within the Unconscious." In *Neuro-Psychopharmacology,* edited by P. B. Bradley, P. Deniker, and C. Radouco-Thomas. Amsterdam: Elsevier, 1958.

———. *Remembrances of LSD Therapy Past.* Unpublished manuscript (2002). Available on the MAPS website.

Eisner, Betty, and Sidney Cohen. "Psychotherapy with Lysergic Acid Diethylamide." *Journal of Nervous and Mental Diseases* 127, no. 6 (December 1958): 528–39.

Eliot, Marc. *Cary Grant: A Biography.* New York: Three Rivers Press, 2004.

Ellens, J. Harold, and Thomas B. Roberts. *The Psychedelic Policy Quagmire: Heath, Law, Freedom, and Society.* Santa Barbara, Calif.: Praeger, 2015.

Ellis, Havelock. *The Art of Life: From the Works of Havelock Ellis.* Boston: Houghton Mifflin Co, 1929.

———. "Mescaline: A New Artificial Paradise." In Smithsonian Institute Board of Regents, *Annual Report of the Board of Regents of the Smithsonian Institution, Part 1.* Washington, D.C.: Washington Printing Office, 1898.

Estrada, Álvaro. *María Sabina: Her Life and Chants.* Translated by Henry Munn. Santa Barbara, Calif.: Ross-Erikson, 1981.

FDA Food, Drug, and Cosmetic Act of 1938. Pub. L. No. 215 (amended Oct 26, 1951).

———. Pub. L. 89–74 (amended July 15, 1965).

Federal Bureau of Investigation/Privacy Acts Release, "Subject: 'Michael' M. Hubbard," Washington D.C. 20535 (January 20, 1975). Accessed via archive .org.

Fleming, Anne Taylor. "Christopher Isherwood: He is a Camera." In *Conversations with Christopher Isherwood,* edited by James L. Berg and Chris Freeman. Jackson, Miss.: University Press of Mississippi, 2001.

Foreign and Military Intelligence: Book 1, Final Report of the Select Committee to Study Governmental Operation with Respect to Intelligence Activities, 94th Congress, 2nd Session Senate Report No. 94–755 (1975–1976) (Church Committee Drug Testing Report).

Forrer, Gordon, and Richard Goldner. "Experimental Physiological Studies with Lysergic Acid Diethylamide (LSD-25)." *Archives of Neurology and Psychiatry* 65, no. 581 (1951): 581–88.

Freidan, Betty. *The Feminine Mystique.* New York: W. W. Norton and Co., 2001.

Furst, Peter T. *Hallucinogens and Culture.* Novato, Calif.: Chandler and Sharp, 2000.

Geis, Gilbert. "In Scopolamine Veritas: The Early History of Drug-Induced Statements." *The Journal of Criminal Law, Criminology, and Police Science* 50, no. 4 (November–December 1959): 350.

Gelber, Steven M. "Sequoia Seminar: The Sources of Religious Sectarianism." *California History* 69, no. 1 (Spring 1990): 36–51.

Geronimus, L. H., Harold Abramson, L. Ingraham, and B. Sklarofsky. "Effects of LSD-25." *Annual Report of the Biological Laboratory, Cold Spring Harbor* (1954–1955): 39.

Gilliam, Bret. "Zale Parry: First Lady of Diving." Accessed via tdisdi.com.

Ginzburg, Carlo. *Ecstasies: Deciphering the Witches' Sabbath.* Chicago: University of Chicago Press, 1989.

Goodwin, Karin. "Drug Took Stevenson Face to Face with Hyde." *The Sunday Times* (London), March 20, 2005.

Graham, J. D. P., and Alaa ideen Khalidi. "The Actions of d-Lysergic Acid Diethylamide (L.S.D. 25) Part II." *Journal of the Faculty of Medicine* 18, no. 35 (1954).

Greenspoon, Lester. *Psychedelic Drugs Reconsidered, 3rd Edition.* New York: The Lindesmith Center, 1997.

Grob, Charles. "A Conversation with Albert Hofmann." In *Hallucinogens: A Reader,* edited by Charles Grob. New York: Tarcher/Putnam, 1992.

Grof, Stanislav. *LSD Psychotherapy.* Alameda, Calif.: Hunter House Publishers, 1980.

Hackman, William. *The Los Angeles Art Scene of the Sixties.* New York: Other Press, 2015.

Halifax, Joan. *Shamanic Voices: A Survey of Visionary Narratives.* New York: Penguin Press, 1991.

Hatsis, Thomas. *Psychedelic Mystery Traditions: Spirit Plants, Magical Practices, Ecstatic States.* Rochester, Vt.: Park Street Press, 2018.

———. *The Witches' Ointment: The Secret History of Psychedelic Magic.* Rochester, Vt.: Park Street Press, 2015.

Hays, John, ed. *The Selected Writings of Maurice O'Connor Drury: On Wittgenstein, Philosophy, Religion, and Psychiatry.* London: Estate of Maurice O'Connor Drury, 2019.

Heard, Gerald. "Can This Drug Enlarge Man's Mind?" In *The Psychedelic Reader: The Best from the Psychedelic Review,* edited by Timothy Leary, Ralph Metzner, and Gunther M. Weil, 1–11. Seacaucus, N.J.: Citadel Press, 1973.

———. *The Five Ages of Man.* New York: The Julian Press, 1963.

Hearings Before a Special Subcommittee of the Committee on the Judiciary, United States Senate, 89th Congress Second Session Pursuant to S. Res. 199 on LSD and Marihuana Use on College Campuses (statement of Timothy Leary).

Hearings Before the Subcommittee on Health and Scientific Research of the Committee on Human Resources, United States Senate, 95th Congress (1977) ("Human Drug Testing by the CIA").

Hearings Before the Subcommittee on Health and Scientific Research of the Committee on Human Resources United States Senate, 95th Congress, 207 (1977) (statement of Sidney Gottlieb).

Henderson, Harry. "Salvage: A New Hope for the Insane." *Congressional Record: Proceedings and Debates of the 81st Congress Second Session* 96, no. 15, part 6, May 17–June 13, 1950.

Herb Museum website. "History of Sandoz Pharmaceuticals." October 2009.

Herzstein, Robert E. *Henry R. Luce, Time, and the American Crusade in Asia.* Cambridge, United Kingdom: Cambridge University Press, 2005.

Heywood, Rosalind. *ESP: A Personal Memoir.* New York: E.P. Dutton and Co., 1964.

Higham, Charles. "Isherwood on Hollywood." In *Conversations with Christopher Isherwood,* edited by James L. Berg and Chris Freeman. Jackson, Miss.: University Press of Mississippi, 2001.

High Times. "Interview with Albert Hofmann: The Man who First Synthesized LSD." *High Times Magazine* (July 1976). Published online January 10, 2020.

Hill, Amelia. "LSD Could Help Alcoholics Stop Drinking, AA Founder Believed." *The Guardian,* August 23, 2012.

Hoch, Paul. "Experimental Psychiatry." *The American Journal of Psychiatry* 3, no. 787 (1955): 787–90.

———. "The Production and Alleviation of Mental Abnormalities by Drugs." Read at the Twentieth International Physiologica Congress, Brussels (July 30–August 4, 1956). *Abstracts of Reviews,* 429–42.

Hoch, Paul, James Cattell, and Harry Pennes. "Effects of Mescaline and Lysergic Acid (d-LSD-25)." Speech presented at the 107th Meeting of the American Psychiatric Association (May 7–11, 1951). Printed in *The American Journal of Psychiatry* 108, no. 8 (February 1952): 579–89.

Hoffer, Abram. "Nicotinic Acid Modified Lysergic Acid Diethylamide Psychosis." *Journal of Mental Science, London* 101, no. 12 (1955): 1–16.

———. "Studies with Niacin and LSD." In *Lysergic Acid Diethylamide and Mescaline in Experimental Psychiatry.* New York: Grune and Stratton, 1956.

Hofmann, Albert. "How LSD Originated." *Journal of Psychedelic Drugs* 11, no. 1–2 (January–June 1979): 53–60.

———. "LSD: Completely Personal." Speech Presented to the Worlds Consciousness Conference (1996). Available on the MAPS website.

———. *LSD and the Divine Scientist: The Final Thoughts and Reflections of Albert Hofmann,* translated by Annabel Moynihan. Rochester, Vt.: Park Street Press, 2013.

———. *LSD: My Problem Child,* translated by Jonathan Ott. Los Angeles: J. P. Tarcher, 1983.

———. "Stan Grof Interviews Dr. Albert Hofmann, Esalen Institute, Big Sur California, 1984." Interview by Stan Grof, MAPS bulletin 11 no. 2 (2001): 3.

hooks, bell. *Feminist Theory: From Margin to Center.* London: Pluto Press, 2000.

Horowitz, Michael, and Cynthia Palmer. *Moksha: Aldous Huxley's Classic Writings on Psychedelics and the Visionary Experience.* Rochester, Vt.: Park Street Press, 1999.

Huxley, Aldous. *The Devils of Loudun.* London: Chatto and Windus, 1952; New York: Harper Perennial Modern Classics, 2009. Page references are to the 2009 edition.

———. *The Doors of Perception* and *Heaven and Hell.* London: Chatto and Windus, 1954; New York: Perennial Library, 1990. Page references are to the 1990 edition.

———. *Island.* London: Chatto and Windus, 1962; New York: Perennial Classic, 1972. Page references are to the 1972 edition.

———. "Mescaline and the 'Other World.'" In *Proceedings of the Round Table on Lysergic Acid Diethylamide and Mescaline in Experimental Psychiatry,* edited by Louis Cholden (May 12, 1955).

Huxley, Thomas. *On the Physical Basis of Life.* New Haven, Conn.: The College Courant, 1869.

Hyde, Robert, Otto von Mering, and Kiyo Morimoto. "Hostility in the Lysergic Psychosis." *Journal of Nervous and Mental Disease* 118, no. 266 (1953).

Isbell, Harris. "Comparison of the Reactions induced by Psilocybin and LSD-25 in Man." *National Institute of Mental Health, Addiction Research Center, U.S. Public Health Services, Lexington , Kentucky* (May 5, 1959), 7–8.

Isbell, Harris, C. Logan, J. Miner, R. Belleville, and Abraham Wikler. "Studies in Lysergic Acid Diethylamide (LSD-25): Effects of Former Morphine Addicts and the Development of Tolerance During Chronic Intoxication." *American Medical Association Archives of Neurology and Psychiatry* 76, no. 5 (1956): 468–78.

Jacobson, Annie. *Phenomena: The Secret History of the U.S. Government's Investigations into Extrasensory Perception and Telekinesis.* New York: Little Brown and Co., 2017.

James, Henry, ed. *The Letters of William James Vol. I.* Boston: The Atlantic Monthly Press, 1920.

———. *The Letters of William James Vol. II.* Boston: The Atlantic Monthly Press, 1920.

James, William. "Subjective Effects of Nitrous Oxide." In *Altered States of Consciousness: A Book of Readings,* edited by Charles Tart. New York: John Wiley and Sons, 1969.

———. *The Varieties of Religious Experience.* New York: Signet Classic, 2003. First published in 1902.

Janiger, Oscar. "Personal Statement by Oscar Janiger." *Bulletin of the Multidisciplinary Association for Psychedelic Studies* 9, no. 1 (Spring 1999): 5–6.

———. "Psychiatric Alchemy: An Interview with Oscar Janiger." Interview by David Jay Brown, 2011. Accessed via Reality Sandwich website.

———. "The Use of Hallucinogenic Agents in Psychiatry." *The California Clinician* 55, no. 7 (1959): 251–59.

Jay, Mike. *Emperors of Dreams: Drugs in the Nineteenth Century.* Sawtry, United Kingdom: Dedalus Books, 2011.

———. *Mescaline: A Global History of the First Psychedelic.* New Haven, Conn.: Yale University Press, 2019.

Joint Hearing before the Select Committee on Intelligence and the Subcommittee on Health and Scientific Research of the Committee on Human Resources, 95th Congress 32 (August 3, 1977) ("Truth Drugs in Interrogation, Project MKULTRA, The CIA's Program of Research in Behavior Modification").

Kavaler, Lucy. *Mushrooms, Mold, and Miracles.* New York: John Day Co., 1965.

Katz, Sidney. "Dr. Osmond's New Deal for the Insane." *Maclean's Magazine,* August 31, 1957, 9–11, 41–43.

———. "My Twelve Hours as a Madman." *Maclean's Magazine,* October 1, 1953, 69–70. Reprinted in *Maclean's* December 25, 1995–January 1, 1996.

Ketchum, James. *Chemical Warfare: Secrets Almost Forgotten.* Santa Rosa, Calif.: ChemBooks, 2006.

Kilbourne Matossian, Mary. *Poisons of the Past: Molds, Epidemics, and History.* New Haven, Conn.: Yale University Press, 1989.

Kinzer, Stephen. *Poisoner in Chief: Sidney Gottlieb and the CIA Search for Mind Control.* New York: Henry Holt and Co., 2019.

Klee, Gerald, "Lysergic Acid Diethylamide and Ego Functions." *Archives of General Psychiatry* 8, no. 5 (1963): 463.

Kleps, Arthur. *Millbrook: The True Story of the Early Years of the Psychedelic Revolution.* Oakland, Calif.: The Bench Press, 1975.

Kobler, John. "The Dangerous Magic of LSD." *Saturday Evening Post* 236, no. 30 (November 1963): 30–39.

Kosten, Thomas R, and David A. Gorelick. "The Lexington Narcotic Farm." *Journal of American Psychiatry* 159, no. 1 (January 2002): 22.

Kurtz, Ernest. *Not-God: A History of Alcoholics Anonymous.* Center City, Minn.: Hazelden Publishing, 1991.

Lachman, Gary. *Turn Off Your Mind: The Mystic Sixties and the Dark Side of the Age of Aquarius.* New York: The Disinformation Company, 2001.

Lapinskas, Vincas. "A Brief History of Ergotism: From St. Anthony's Fire and St. Vitus' Dance Until Today." *Medicinos Teorija ir Praktika* 13, no. 2 (2007): 202–6.

Lawson, Deodat. *A Brief and True Narrative of Some Remarkable Passages Relating to Sundry Persons Afflicted by Witchcraft, in Salem Village: Which Happened from the Nineteenth of March, to the Fifth of April, 1692.* Boston: Benjamin Harris, 1692 (received by Duke University in 1936).

Leary, Timothy. *Flashbacks.* Los Angeles: JP Tarcher, 1983.

———. *High Priest.* Los Angeles: JP Tarcher, 1983.

———. *The Politics of Ecstasy.* Berkeley, Calif.: Ronin Publishing, 1968.

———. *The Politics of Psychopharmacology.* Berkeley, Calif.: Ronin Publishing, 1988.

Lee, Martin, and Bruce Shlain. *Acid Dreams: The Complete Social History of LSD, the CIA, the Sixties, and Beyond.* New York: Grove Press, 1985.

Lerner, Stephen D. "Leary Gets 30 Years on Marijuana Charge." *The Harvard Crimson,* March 12, 1966.

Letcher, Andy. *Shroom: A Cultural History of the Magic Mushroom.* New York: HarperCollins, 2007.

Levine, Carol. "Former Soldier Denied Compensation for Damages in Army LSD Tests." In *IRB: Ethics and Human Research* 4, no. 3, The Hastings Center (March 1982).

Lewin, Louis. *Phantastica: A Classic Survey on the Use and Abuse of Mind-Altering Plants.* Rochester, Vt.: Park Street Press, 1998.

Lightner, David A. *Bilirubin: Jekyll and Hyde Pigment of Life: Pursuit of Its Structure Through Two World Wars to the New Millennium.* New York: Springer, 2013.

Littlefield, Connie, dir. *Hofmann's Potion.* National Film Board of Canada, 2002.

"Living History Project: William J. C. McCurdy." Interview of Gilbert J. C. McCurdy by Jack A. End, c. 1971. University of Rochester Living History Project website.

Logan, William Bryant. *Air: The Relentless Shaper of the World.* New York: W. W. Norton and Co., 2012.

Lubasch, Arnold H. "$700,000 Is Made in '53 Secret Test Death," *New York Times,* May 6, 1987, Section B, 3.

Luce, Henry. "LSD: The Exploding Threat of the Mind Drug That Got Out of Control." *Life,* March 25, 1966. Accessible on the Erowid vaults website.

MacDougal, Dennis. *Five Easy Decades: How Jack Nicholson Became the Biggest Movie Star in Modern Times.* Hoboken, New Jersey: John Wiley and Sons, 2008.

McGilligan, Patrick. *Jack's Life: A Biography of Jack Nicholson.* New York: W. W. Norton and Co., 1996.

MacLean, J. Ross, D. C. MacDonald, Ultan Byrne, and Alfred Hubbard. "The Use of LSD-25 in the Treatment of Alcoholism and Other Psychiatric Problems." *Quarterly Journal of Studies on Alcohol* 22 (1961): 34–45.

Malmgren, Jeanne. "Other Marsh Chapel Survivors." *St. Petersburg Times,* 1994.

Mann, Thomas. *Letters of Thomas Mann 1889–1955.* Translated by Richard Winston and Clara Winston. Berkeley, Calif.: University of California Press, 1990.

Mannes, Marya. "The Raid on Castalia." *The Reporter* 34, no. 9 (May 19, 1966): 27–28, 30, 35. Available on the MAPS website.

Markel, Howard. "An Alcoholic's Savior: God, Belladonna or Both?" *New York Times,* April 19, 2010.

Marks, John. *The Search for the Manchurian Candidate: The CIA and Mind Control.* New York: W. W. Norton and Company, 1991.

Martin, Joyce. "A Case of Psychopathic Personality with Homosexuality Treated by LSD." In *Hallucinogenic Drugs and their Psychotherapeutic Use: Proceedings of the Quarterly Meeting of the Royal Medico-Psychological Association,* edited by Richard Crocket and Ronald Sandison. London: H. K. Lewis and Co., 1963. The conference took place in 1961.

———. "L.S.D. Treatment of Chronic Psychoneurotic Patients Under Day-Hospital Conditions." *The International Journal of Social Psychiatry* 3, no. 3 (Winter 1957): 188–95.

———. "Schizophreniform Reactions Under Day Hospital L.S.D. Therapy." In *Congress Report Volume II.* Zurich: Orell Füssli, 1959.

———. "The Treatment of Twelve Male Homosexuals with 'L.S.D.'" *Acta Psychotherapy* (1962): 394–402.

McCann, Graham. *Cary Grant: A Class Apart.* New York: Columbia University Press, 1996.

McGlothlin, William H. "Social and Para-Medical Aspects of Hallucinogenic Drugs." In *The Use of LSD in Psychotherapy and Alcoholism,* edited by Harold Abramson. New York: The Bobbs Merrill Company, 1967.

"Medicine: Happiness Pills." *Time Magazine* 50, no. 4 (July 28, 1947).

Melechi, Antonio. "Drugs of Liberation: From Psychiatry to Psychedelia." In *Psychedelia Britannica: Hallucinogenic Drugs in Britain,* edited by Antonio Melechi, 21–52. London: Turnaround, 1997.

Metzner, Ralph. "Initial Experiences from the Harvard Psilocybin Project." In *Sacred Mushrooms of Visions: Teonanacatl*, edited by Ralph Metzner, 179–91. Rochester, VT: Park Street Press: 2004.

Mitchell, Silas Weir. *Characteristics: Works of Silas Weir Mitchell.* New York: The Century Co., 1910.

———. "Remarks on the Effects of Anhelonium Lewinii (the Mescal Button)." In *The British Medical Journal* no. 2 (December 5, 1875): 1625–29.

Mooney, James. *The Ghost Dance Religion and the Sioux Outbreak of 1890.* Washington D.C.: Government Printing Office, 1896.

———. "The Mescal Plant and Ceremony." *The Therapeutic Gazette* 20, no. 12 (1896).

Moore, Jay D. *Alcoholics Anonymous and the Rockefeller Connection: How John D. Rockefeller and his Associates Saved AA.* Morrisville, N.C.: Lulu, 2015.

Morris, Sylvia. *Price of Fame: The Honorable Clare Booth Luce.* New York: Random House, 2014.

———. *Rage for Fame: The Ascent of Clare Booth Luce.* New York: Random House, 1997.

Muehlberger, C. W. "Criminal Confessions Under Narcosis." *Journal of Criminal Law, Criminology, and Police Science* 26, no. 3 (September 1935): 449–51.

———. "Interrogation Under Drug Influence: The So-Called 'Truth Serum' Technique." *The Journal of Criminal Law, Criminology, and Police Science* 42, no. 4 (November–December 1951): 513–28.

Nin, Anaïs. *The Diary of Anaïs Nin, Vol. 5: 1947–1955,* edited by Gunther Stuhlmann. Boston: Mariner Books, 1975.

———. *The Diary of Anaïs Nin, Vol. 6: 1955–1966,* edited by Gunther Stuhlmann. New York: Harcourt Brace Jovanovich, 1976.

Novak, Steven J. "LSD before Leary: Sidney Cohen's Critique of 1950s Drug Research." *Isis* 88, no. 1 (1997): 87–110.

"On and Off," *Newsweek* (May 2, 1966). Available on the MAPS website.

Osborne, Catherine R. *American Catholics and the Church of Tomorrow: Building Churches for the Future 1925–1975.* Chicago: University of Chicago Press, 2018.

Osmond, Humphry. "On Being Mad" and "Peyote Night." In *Psychedelics: The Uses and Implications of Hallucinogenic Drugs,* edited by Bernard Aaronson and Humphry Osmond, 21–28, 67–86. New York: Anchor Books, Doubleday and Company, 1970.

———. "Research on Schizophrenia." In *Neuropharmacology,* edited by Harold Abramson, 183–230. New York: Josiah Macy Jr. Foundation, 1956.

———. "A Review of the Clinical Effects of Psychotomimetic Agents." *Annals of the New York Academy of Science* 66 no. 3 (March 14, 1957): 418–34.

Otis, Laura. *Membranes: Metaphors of Invasion in Nineteenth Century Literature, Science, and Politics.* Baltimore: Johns Hopkins University Press, 1999.

Ott, Jonathan. *The Age of Entheogens and the Devil's Dictionary.* Kennewick, Wash.: Natural Products Co., 1995.

Packer, Sharon. "Jewish Mystical Movements and the European Ergot Epidemics." *The Israel Journal of Psychiatry and Related Sciences* 35 no. 3 (December 1997): 227–39.

Palmer, Cynthia, and Michael Horowitz. *Sisters of the Extreme: Women Writing on the Drug Experience.* Rochester, Vt.: Park Street Press, 2000.

Partridge, Christopher. *High Culture: Drugs, Mysticism, and the Pursuit of Transcendence in the Modern World.* Oxford: Oxford University Press, 2018.

Pass It On: The Story of Bill Wilson and How the A.A. Message Reached the World. New York: Alcoholics Anonymous World Services, 1984.

Perrine, Daniel M. "Visions of the Night: Western Medicine Meets Peyote 1887–1899." *The Heffter Review of Psychedelic Research* 2 (2001): 6–52.

Pittman, Bill. *The Roots of Alcoholics Anonymous.* Center City, Minn.: Hazelden, 1998.

Plutarch, *Moralia Volume 5.* Edited and translated by William W. Goodwin. Boston: Little Brown and Co., 1874.

Pollan, Michael. *How to Change Your Mind.* New York: Penguin: 2018.

Poller, Jake. *Aldous Huxley and Alternative Spirituality.* Boston: Brill, 2019.

Prentiss, D. W., and Francis Morgan. "Therapeutic Uses of Mescal Buttons (*Anhalonium lewinii*)." *The Therapeutic Gazette* 20, no. 12 (1896): 4–7.

Proceedings of the American Psychiatric Association, "The 106th Annual Meeting, Detroit." *The American Journal of Psychiatry* 107, no. 4 (October 1950): 283–305. Accessible in the *AJP* online archive.

Puharich, Andrija. *The Sacred Mushroom: Key to the Door of Eternity.* New York: Doubleday, 1959.

"Recruitment of Germans: Project Paperclip." *Memorandum of the Advisory Committee on Human Radiation Experiments*, April 5, 1995. Accessed via George Washington University National Security Archive website.

Reid, David. "The Possessed." In *Sex, Death, and God in L.A.* University of California Press, 1994.

Report on Alcohol, Drug Abuse, and Mental Health Administration Involvement in LSD Research, Kennedy Subcommittee Hearings (1975). Accessed via the New York Public Library.

Rhine, J. B., and Joseph G. Pratt. *Parapsychology: Frontier Science of the Mind.* Springfield, Ill.: Charles C. Thomas Publisher, 1962.

Richards, Bill. "Army Stockpiles BZ Drugs in Bombs." *The Washington Post,* August 3, 1975.

Ritchie v. Ira Feldman, in his individual and official capacities, Defendants-Appellees, United States Court of Appeals, No. 05-6401 (9th Circuit, June 26, 2006). Accessed via: caselaw.findlaw.com.

Rinkel, Max. "Discussion at Annual Meeting of the American Psychiatric Association in Detroit, May 1st, 1950." *Journal of Clinical and Experimental Psychopathology,* 12 (1951): 42.

———. "Experimentally Induced Psychosis in Man." In *Neuropharmacology: Transactions of the 2nd Conference* (May 25–27, 1955), edited by Harold Abramson.

Rinkel, Max, H. Jackson DeShon, Robert Hyde, and Harry C. Solomon. "Experimental Schizophrenia-Like Symptoms." *The American Journal of Psychiatry:* 108, no. 8 (February 1952).

Rinkel, Max, Robert Hyde, and Harry C. Solomon, "Experimental Psychiatry III: A Chemical Concept of Psychosis." *Diseases of the Nervous System* 15, no. 9 (1954): 259–64.

Roberts, Andy. "Reservoir Drugs: The Enduring Myth of LSD in the Water Supply." *Psychedelic Press U.K.,* March 12, 2014.

Roberts, Steven V. "Leary Goes to Prison on Coast to Start Term of 1 to 10 Years." *New York Times,* March 20, 1977.

Sandison, Ronald. *A Century of Psychiatry: Psychotherapy and Group Analysis.* London: Jessica Kingsley Publishers, 2000.

———. "The Clinical Uses of Lysergic Acid Diethylamide." In *Proceedings of the Round Table on Lysergic Acid Diethylamide and Mescaline in Experimental Psychiatry,* edited by Louis Cholden. New York: Grune and Stratton, 1956.

———. "Psychological Aspects of the LSD Treatment of the Neuroses." *Journal of Mental Science* 100, no. 508 (1954): 508–15.

Sandison, Ronald, Arthur Spencer, and John Whitelaw. "The Therapeutic Value of Lysergic Acid Diethylamide in Mental Illness." *Journal of Mental Science* 100, no. 491 (1954): 491–507.

Savage, Charles. "LSD, Alcoholism, and Transcendence." In *LSD: The Conscious Expanding Drug,* edited by David Soloman. New York: G. P. Putnam's Sons, 1966.

———. "LSD, Transcendence and the New Beginning." *Journal of Nervous and Mental Diseases* 135 (1962): 429–35.

———. "Lysergic Acid Diethylamide (LSD-25): A Clinical-Psychological Study." *American Journal of Psychiatry* 108 (February 1952): 896–900.

———. "The Resolution and Subsequent Remobilization of Resistance by LSD in Psychotherapy," from the Round Table "Psychodynamic and Therapeutic Aspects of Mescaline and Lysergic Acid Diethylamide," held at the annual meeting of the American Psychiatric Association, May 3, 1956. Transcripts reprinted in *Journal of Nervous and Mental Diseases* 125, no. 1 (January– March 1957).

———. "The Uses and Abuses of LSD in Psychotherapy." In *Third World Congress on Psychiatry, Montreal, Canada Part II* (1961).

———. "Variations in Ego Feeling Induced by d-Lysergic Acid Diethylamide (LSD-25)." *The Psychoanalytic Review* 42, no. 1 (January 1955): 1–16.

Savage, Charles, and Myron Stolaroff. "Clarifying the Confusion Regarding LSD-25." *Journal of Nervous and Mental Disease* 140, no. 3 (1965): 218–21.

Schiff, Jr., Paul. "Ergot and Its Alkaloids." *American Journal of Pharmaceutical Education* 70, no. 5, article 98 (2006): 1.

Scott, Austin. "Family Blames CIA for Father's Death." *The Washington Post* July 11, 1975, A1, A10.

Sexton, James. *Selected Letters of Aldous Huxley.* Chicago: Ivan R. Dee, 2007.

Shermer, Michael. *The Believing Brain: From Ghosts to Gods to Politics and Conspiracies.* New York: Times Books, 2011.

Shroder, Thomas. *Acid Test: LSD, Ecstasy, and the Power to Heal.* New York: Plume, 2015.

Siff, Stephen I. "Glory Visions: Coverage of LSD in Popular Magazines, 1954–1968." Unpublished Ph.D. dissertation, Ohio University, 2008.

Smith, C. M. "Some Reflections on the Possible Therapeutic Effects of the Hallucinogens: With Special Reference to Alcoholism." *Quarterly Journal for the Study of Alcohol* 20 (1959).

Smith, Grover, ed. *Letters of Aldous Huxley.* New York: Harper and Row, 1969.

Smith, Huston. *Cleansing the Doors of Perception.* New York: J. P. Tarcher/ Putnam, 2000.

Starkey, Marion L. *The Devil in Massachusetts: A Modern Enquiry into the Salem Witch Trials.* New York: Dolphin Books, 1961.

Starr, James, and Katherine Ramsland. *A Voice for the Dead: A Forensic Investigator's Pursuit of the Truth in the Grave.* New York: G. P. Putnam's Sons, 2005.

Stevens, Jay. *Storming Heaven: LSD and the American Dream.* New York: Grove Press, 1987.

Stolaroff, Myron J. "How Much Can People Change." In *Higher Wisdom:*

Eminent Elders Explore the Continuing Impact of Psychedelics, edited by Roger Walsh and Charles Grob. Albany: State University of New York Press, 2005.

——. *Thanatos to Eros: 35 Years of Psychedelic Exploration.* Berlin: VWB, 1994.

Stoll, Arthur. "The Impact of Studies of Natural Products on Chemical Industry." *Symposium on the Chemistry of Natural Products,* 357.

Stoll, Werner. "Ein neues in sehr kleinen Mengen wirksames Phantastikum." *Protocolo de la 108th assemblée les 22 et 23 novembre 1947 in Zurich*; reprinted in *Schweizer Archiv fur Neurologie und Psychiatrie,* 64, 483.

Stone, Trevor, and Gail Darlington. *Pills, Potions, and Poisons: How Drugs Work.* United Kingdom: Oxford University Press, 2004.

Strassman, Rick. *DMT: The Spirit Molecule: A Doctor's Revolutionary Research into the Biology of Near-Death and Mystical Experiences.* Rochester, Vt.: Park Street Press, 2000.

Stratton, Richard. "Altered States of America." *Spin Magazine,* March 1994. Accessed via frankolsonproject.org.

Tainter, Maurice, and G. Marcelli. "The Rise of Synthetic Drugs in the American Pharmaceutical Industry." *Bulletin of the New York Academy of Medicine* 35, no. 6 (June 1959): 387–405.

Testimony before the Presidential Advisory Committee on Human Radiation Experiments (March 15, 1995) (statement of Christine deNicola). Accessed via the George Washington University National Security Archive online.

Testimony before the Presidential Advisory Committee on Human Radiation Experiments (March 15, 1995) (statement of Claudia Mullen). Accessed via the George Washington University National Security Archive online.

Tonini, G., and C. Montanari. "Effects of Experimentally Induced Psychosis on Artistic Expression." *Confinia Neurologica* 15, no. 225 (1955): 225–39.

Toy, Eckard V. "The Conservative Connection: The Chairman of the Board Took LSD Before Leary." *American Studies* 21, no. 2 (1980).

Ulanov, Ann Belford. "Jung and Prayer." In *Jung and Monotheisms: Judaism, Christianity, and Islam,* edited by Joel Ryce. Abingdon, United Kingdom: Routledge, 1994.

Unger, Sanford M. "Mescaline, LSD, Psilocybin, and Personality Change." *Psychiatry: Journal for the Study of Interpersonal Processes* 26 no. 2 (May 1963). Accessed via the Psychedelic Library website.

United Press International. "$702, 044 Awarded in Drug-Research Death." In *The Arizona Republic,* May 6, 1987, A5. Accessed via: theshroomery .org. Posted by Learyfan on May 5, 2019, on the page "Today in Psychedelic History (05/05)."

United States Congress House Committee on Foreign Affairs. *Chemical-Biological Warfare: US Policies and International Effects*. Washington, D. C.: US Government Print Office, 1970.

U.S. Department of Justice. "Drug Scheduling." Drug Enforcement Administration website.

Von Bibra, Baron Ernst. *Plant Intoxicants: A Classic Text on the Use of Mind-Altering Plants*. Rochester, Vt.: Healing Arts Press, 1995.

Wall, William Henry. *From Healing to Hell*. Montgomery, Al.: New South Books, 2011.

Wasson, Robert Gordon. *The Road to Eleusis: Unveiling the Secret of the Mysteries*. Berkeley, Calif.: North Atlantic Books, 2008.

———. "Seeking the Magic Mushroom: A New York Banker Goes to Mexico's Mountains to Participate in the Age-old Rituals of Indians who Chew Strange Growths that Produce Visions." *Life*, May 13, 1957.

Wasson, Robert Gordon, and Valentina Wasson. *Mushrooms, Russia, and History, Vol II*. New York: Pantheon Books, 1957.

Wasson, Valentina P. "The Sacred Mushroom." *This Week* May 19, 1957.

Watt, Donald, ed. *Aldous Huxley: The Cultural Heritage*. New York: Rutledge, 1997.

Watts, Alan. *In My Own Way: An Autobiography*. Calif.: New World Library, 2001.

———. "Psychedelics and Religious Experience." *California Law Review* 56, no. 1 (1968).

Whitehall, John D. A. "A Case of Fetishism Treated with Lysergic Acid Diethylamide." *Journal of Nervous and Mental Diseases* 129 (December 1959).

Zaehner, R. C. *Mysticism: Sacred and Profane*. New York: Oxford University Press, 1980.

———. *Our Savage God: The Perverse Use of Eastern Thought*. London: Sheed and Ward, 1975.

———. *Zen, Drugs, and Mysticism*. New York: Vintage Books, 1974.

Index